B²
9.50

D1254190

13,589

HN
39
.U6
C35
1971

Carter
The decline and
revival of the
social Gospel

DATE DUE

OC 28 '76

The decline and revival of the social Go
HN39.U6C35 1971   13589

Carter, Paul Allen
VRJC/WRIGHT LIBRARY

The Decline and Revival of the Social Gospel

SOCIAL AND POLITICAL LIBERALISM IN AMERICAN

PROTESTANT CHURCHES, 1920-1940

The DECLINE AND REVIVAL OF THE SOCIAL GOSPEL

Social and Political Liberalism in American Protestant Churches,

1920-1940

*

By PAUL A. CARTER

Archon Books
1971

VERNON REGIONAL JUNIOR COLLEGE LIBRARY

©1954, 1971 BY PAUL A. CARTER
FIRST EDITION 1956

LIBRARY OF CONGRESS CATALOG CARD NUMBER: 70-122413
INTERNATIONAL STANDARD BOOK NUMBER: 0-208-01083-1
THE SHOE STRING PRESS, INC., HAMDEN, CONNECTICUT 06514

PRINTED IN THE UNITED STATES OF AMERICA

Preface: 1971

"After a period of years," Richard Hofstadter has written, "a book acquires an independent life, and the author may be so fortunate as to achieve a certain healthy detachment from it, which reconciles him to letting it stand on its own." [1] Theologically, this amounts to saying that in writing books we must not only (as Luther put it) "sin bravely," but must also not try to tamper with the historical fact of our sin after the book reviewers have called us to repentance. *The Decline and Revival of the Social Gospel*—begun twenty years ago, published in book form in 1956, and out of print this half decade—has presumably become by now just such an independent entity as Hofstadter described.

Nevertheless, upon rereading these pages closely for the first time in several years I am unable to let them stand quite untouched. For one thing, too much else bearing upon this general subject has since been published. [2] But an experimental attempt to revise the first chapter quickly convinced me that to rewrite the manuscript now would be, quite literally, impossible; my own political, historical, theological, and personal perspectives have sufficiently changed that the argument of a new version would soon diverge from the narrative line of the old so far as to make it a different book altogether. (In any case, that possibility is foreclosed by the technology of present-day book production.)

What I have done instead, therefore, is to add some afterthoughts in the form of *Postscripts* to the individual chapters. A few of these merely augment what was said in the pages that precede them, but most are intended as warnings to the reader that the views from a 1956 perspective that he has been reading would not necessarily be the opinions he would get from the writer now. For the concluding chapter, however, this brief treatment is not enough, because that portion baldly stated some *predictive* assumptions about the Social Gospel—assumptions which quite frankly have since been proved wrong.

Some of these appear in the book well before that closing chapter. In retrospect it scarcely seems possible, for example, that anyone writing in 1956 about American society in the 1930's could have stated that "secular social history . . . was moving inevitably in the direction of [racial] integration." [3] Martin Luther King's great stride toward freedom was under way by that time, of course, and had King's way been the end of the story it would now be possible to argue that where the white man's Social Gospel had lagged, a self-generated black Social Gospel had providentially saved the day. But waiting in history's wings were the Black Panthers! A gospel that had called for the full (and nonviolent) integration of the black man into the white man's world was now forced to share the stage with a gospel of revolutionary black separatism, and at this writing it is not yet clear which will prevail; perhaps neither way will prevail. The white Social Gospelers of the Fifties, or the Thirties, might have understood James Forman's dramatic appearance in Riverside Church in 1969 to demand that white Americans pay reparations to the descendants of

slaves; they would have been less likely to understand the pro-
liferation in most of their own denominations of Black cau-
cuses, [4] which from the standpoint of the integrationism they
had long been preaching would have seemed socially regressive.
And from their premise that "constant concrete interracial
contact" in the churches was necessary if their claim that all
men are brothers were to be taken seriously, [5] they would have
been disconcerted, to say the least, by the discovery toward
the end of the 1960's that, according to some spokesmen for the
black community such white activists sought to serve, sometimes
the most brotherly thing they could do was to withdraw.

Activist white Protestant churchmen of the Fifties might also
have been surprised by what would happen in a few years to
the massive influence of Reinhold Niebuhr and of neo-orthodoxy. In the concluding paragraph of this book I rashly predicted that "the ministerial generation of the 50's and 60's"
would be "the products of this Niebuhrian atmosphere" which
had become "a part of the natural climate in some of the theological seminaries of the United States in the 40's." [6] It would
be difficult indeed, from the overt behavior of the churches
into which that generation of clergy was ordained, to infer that
such had been the case. One of the avant-garde movements that
came on stage instead was the "radical," or "death-of-God,"
theology, whose spokesmen were wont to charge that neo-orthodoxy, which had begun as a movement of social criticism, was
all too prone to backslide into sheer conservatism; "old Niebuhrians," William Hamilton wrote (somewhat unfairly) in
1966, "tended to go to the back pages of the *National Review*
to die." [7]

Could a neo-orthodox Social Gospel, I wondered in 1956,
"be translated into a form which can be assimilated by the
casual churchgoer without simplifying it into Fundamentalism"? Sydney Ahlstrom, in a long and perceptive review of this
book one year later, countered by saying that I had not expressed what seemed to him "the equal or greater danger of its
being simplified into a pessimistic and empty Neo-Modern-
ism." [8] In this case neither author nor critic had it quite right.

vii

"Neo-Modernist" the "God-is-dead" movement was, with a vengeance; whether it was empty or profound has been a matter for considerable debate, but it was certainly not pessimistic. Hamilton's comment occurred in the course of a remarkable essay "The New Optimism—from Prufrock to Ringo," the point of which was that T. S. Eliot's bleak imagery of modern life in terms of "hollow men" in a "Waste Land" had given way to an imagery of play, of celebration, of affirmation and joy.

The "radical theology" of Hamilton and Thomas J. J. Altizer may perhaps have been the most transient of vogues; but by the end of the 60's Christians (and others) who were much less radical had also become a bit restive under neo-orthodoxy's homilies on Original Sin. They may have sensed that to claim categorically that man is evil, as against the liberal Protestant or sociological view that man individually considered is innocent (or blank), may lead to a stance equally as bland and self-justifying as liberalism's. When the central character in Arthur Miller's play *After The Fall* (1964) was made to claim on behalf of Everyman the responsibility for Auschwitz and Hiroshima, with the ulterior dramatic purpose of transferring away and excusing his own prior *personal* conduct, he seemed unconsciously to be saying that if all men are guilty of everything in general, then no one is guilty of anything in particular.

Moreover, the march of a science and a civilization that seemed each year to put individual human beings into increasingly insignificant pigeon-holes suggested that fallen man needed to be reminded not so much that he was fallen as that he was man. When Malcolm Muggeridge—from a perspective that was, of course, Tory rather than neo-orthodox—launched in 1969 one of his characteristic brilliant diatribes against the sinful pride of modern man, one reader retorted that the kind of self-assertiveness condemned by such writers was becoming extinct: "Postmodern man neither elevates himself nor humbles himself in any classic sense. He is automated electronically and chemically. Any essay aimed at redemption must translate the genetic insight that a God breathed into his nostrils, and that he is a living being." [9]

viii

In the meantime the historical context for any Social Gospel, be it liberal, radical, neo-orthodox, or Fundamentalist (for the evangelicals have of late appropriated a good deal of the old liberal social-action vocabulary), [10] had drastically changed. The Protestant social actionism of the New Deal and Second World War periods was treated in this book as a "successful" response, at least in terms of morale, to the challenge of an on-rushing secularism. In this judgment I was no doubt influenced by the post-World War II "religious revival," which by the mid-Fifties—measured either by church membership statistics or by intellectual fashionableness—had not quite reached its crest. Then, in the fall of 1960, theological seminary enrollments took a sharp drop; in response to a questionnaire which Martin Marty sent to the presidents or academic deans of twenty-five leading schools of theology, a majority expressed their feeling "that the religious revival of the 1950's is over and gone." [11]

As the postmortems rolled in, less was heard of the way organized religion in America had been revitalized and transformed after its decline into defensiveness in the 1920's, and instead more was heard of a present era variously dubbed post-Protestant, post-Christian, or post-modern. (Admittedly we sometimes overdramatize the uniqueness of the years *we* happen to be living through; was the era, perhaps, merely post-Eisenhower?) Typical of these newer voices—although of course the older ones, Niebuhr, Tillich, Barth, Schweitzer continued for most of the decade also to be heard from—was Harvey Cox, who in *The Secular City* (1965) at once celebrated and lamented the passing of traditional religious institutions:

We now stand at the end of the epoch of the church's dominance in Western culture. The church still lives on the interest of the accumulation it laid aside during the long Constantinian era. But the capital itself is shrinking, and the whole treasure will soon be gone. Shorn of its political might by two hundred years of revolutions, deprived of its cultural influence by the Enlightenment, and finally robbed of its psychological power by the casual this-worldliness of modern urban man, the church may very soon have to go back and start from scratch.[12]

But if judgments like that of Cox are correct, then the way Protestant social activism was reshaped between 1920 and 1940 was fraught with disaster. For the "revival" of the Social Gospel after its "decline," as set forth in the pages that follow, was in a form that was not only neo-orthodox but also "high church." Summing up part of the book's argument in that same concluding chapter I asserted that "the nineteenth-century doctrine of the continuity between the social order and the Kingdom of God was replaced by the Augustinian doctrine of the World and the Church as distinct entities." [13] But we cannot have them so, say advocates of Cox's "secular city," of Hamilton's "death of God," of Dietrich Bonhoeffer's "religionless Christianity." If the world is too much with us, we must turn and embrace it. And in doing so, if it and the Church are distinct (and, ultimately, hostile?) entities, then we must reject the Church—or, at best, regard it with the affection we feel for a phase of our existence we have outgrown. President Victor Butterfield once told a gathering of Wesleyan University alumni that if college had *really* been the best years of their lives, then their lives afterward had been wasted; in this sense, wrote James A. Pike shortly before his passing in 1969, members of the Church who had become conscious of its limitations should graduate from it and become, not sentimental "Old Grads," but mature and emancipated "church alumni". [14]

Those who elected to stay in—or, extending Bishop Pike's metaphor, those who returned to their alma mater after having taken an advanced degree elsewhere—might find that the Word they would preach, whether theological, devotional, or social, was all but nullified by the archaic patterns of corporate worship through which it had to be expressed in church. "The real ecumenical crisis today," argued Cox, "is not between Catholics and Protestants but between traditional and experimental forms of church life." Marshall McLuhan has had his vogue in the Church, as elsewhere; the demiurge of television, which had

x

been changing American political style and also conceivably its substance, presumably would not leave the traditional mode of American Protestant worship unmarked. Speaking for church-men over thirty, who were "too old to be fully receptive to the changed modes of perception; we grew up on radio, not on TV," James F. White wrote in 1968 on "Worship in an Age of Immediacy":

The question we have been accustomed to hear from someone who missed church was "What did he say?"—meaning "What was the sermon about?" But we are the minority, or soon will be. Those of the younger generation are more likely to ask "What happened?" For them the problem is that nothing, or very little, happened; the nearest thing to a happening was the congregation's standing, sing-ing some hymns and going home.[15]

Hence jazz masses—or rock, since jazz to some young people had come to seem fusty and traditional; hence flower children in liturgical procession, blowing bubbles and releasing balloons, on their way to hear a sermon comparing the situation in first-century Palestine with that in latter-day Viet Nam: "Galilee was the impregnable stronghold of a national liberation front. . . . The twelve apostles were born Vietcong." [16] For staid, tra-dition-bound parish churches of the kind that Harvey Cox and James Pike condemned, such happenings could be gloriously liberating therapy, and for the jaded worshipper in such churches the unfamiliar sound (in that setting) of drums and amplified guitars could be a means of real religious regenera-tion; it was a very long time since most "mainstream" white American Protestants had taken Psalm 150 at its emotional face value. "You have repeated the same old words Sunday after endless Sunday—until they become a meaningless mutter—the ghost of an echo from a dead and dusty past," wrote one local daily newspaper's feature editor in 1969. ". . . Then one Sunday, out of curiosity, you attend a 'jazz mass' in a church (not your own). . . . And something happens. You feel it. . . . You hear what you are saying. You believe what you are saying—and you feel someone is listening again." [17]

And yet, bearing in mind how contemporary and meaningful —and effective!—neo-orthodoxy and Faith and Order had seemed only yesterday, one becomes uncomfortably aware that this newer gospel of swinging with McLuhan in the secular city might be subject in turn to the same charge of being a cultural fad, and perhaps with more justice. Was the "medium" really so dominant over the "message" as to warrant Professor White's claim on behalf of A. B. Dick, the inventor of the mimeograph, that "Gutenberg made it possible to put prayer books in the hands of the people; Dick made them obsolete"? Could a "new optimism", banishing all gloomy theologians and timorous Pruf-rocks from the modern world, be made somehow to celebrate the miseries of Biafra and the massacre at My Lai? Did it really make Christ more "relevant" to modern man to portray Him as a scion of the Viet Cong than it had to imagine Him in First World War battle-dress going "over the top" at dawn?

From a Social Gospel point of view, churchmen (or "church alumni") who freed themselves from traditional religious forms should thereby be enabled to confront in an unencumbered way those social forms that needed abolition or change. Yet it was the (obsolete?) Book of Common Prayer to which a num-ber of activist New York churchmen had recourse "in a dark, urine-soaked cell in the Brooklyn jail" after their arrest for par-ticipation in a sit-in, Richard John Neuhaus reported in 1967; and "Bishop Kilmer Myers' celebration of the mass on a Mont-gomery street was a powerful symbol," continued the same writer, "precisely because it was not a new rite devised for the occasion; it carried the solemn weight of catholic tradition to the dusty lanes and dirty politics of Alabama." As if in response to Harvey Cox's prediction that the Church might "very soon have to go back and start from scratch," Neuhaus argued that this would be literally and logically impossible: "Because it is defined by history, the church does not begin from scratch with each generation but must carry on in lively faithfulness to its own bundle of parables, symbols and icons."

Radical, at times painful, reshaping of the Church's life there would have to be; but "the operation must be conducted in credible continuity with the past and in respect for the [religious] community's identity." Ralph Waldo Emerson in his Divinity School Address, which assailed the religious Establishment of his day in terms so radical as to make the "radical" American theology of our own century sound tame, took care to leave intact those structures—"the Sabbath" and "the institution of preaching"—which activist New England ministers had to have in 1838 if they were to function at all; [18] similarly Neuhaus, in his essay on "Liturgy and the Politics of the Kingdom," was careful to distinguish between saying that ours is "a post-*Christendom* era," a development he celebrated and accepted ("Formal mergers of throne and altar are a thing of the past, Billy Graham's ritual breakfasts with the President notwithstanding"), and saying that ours is a post-*Christian* era, in which case "the very possibility of Christian community is shut out."

The hope I had expressed in 1956 (admittedly in neo-orthodox terms) for a Church which could "change *with* the times without adapting itself *to* the times, in an age which makes a fetish of adjustment to a norm and powerfully facilitates that adjustment through the pressure of the mass media of communication," Pastor Neuhaus in 1967 carried down to the local parish level: "In a mass society, the parish community can bestow identity on, and sustain values for, people who make no meaningful associations between their private lives, on the one hand, and their sense of belonging to the nation-society on the other." It could moreover give "dignity to the individual beyond his immediate usefulness for a particular social goal." [19] (What, after all, were even the most active of activists expected to do *between* confrontations?) The "church alumnus" might retort that the mature graduate would no longer need to have institutions make that kind of associations for him—but alumni, be it remembered, are also expected to provide the oncoming generation with scholarships, libraries, and endowed chairs.

Cutting across the disjunction in American Protestant church life between traditionalism and experimentalism was an older and more basic division, between word and sacrament, between

xiii

freewheeling evangelism and churchly form, between prophecy and priestcraft, between Dionysos and Apollo, or, in a dialectic suggested in 1961 by H. Richard Niebuhr, between "Protestantism as movement" and "Protestantism as order." [20] Though *The Secular City* was an attempt to come to grips with religious and social reality in a manner that was unequivocally modern, its philippic against the Church's spiritually deadening formalism was consistent with an American piety that was, for this untraditional country, deeply traditional; as old as revivalism, as old as Puritanism. And although "Liturgy and the Politics of the Kingdom" was in its own way as experimentalist as anything concretely proposed by Cox, still it insisted that there had to *be* a historically conditioned liturgy; the whole point of Dom Gregory Dix's scholarly study *The Shape of the Liturgy,* for men like Neuhaus, was that liturgy does have a shape. (Even the radical, "death-of-God" theologians may have been more conditioned unconsciously by traditional Christian ways of doing theology than they were quite aware; for millions of Americans who lacked this conditioning, the apparent death of Yahweh seems to have led not to an optimistic secularized radicalism but to astrology.) [21]

To put a Protestant intramural debate into categories like these was to break out of certain historiographic biases inherent in the prior study of the Social Gospel. For in terms of Richard Niebuhr's dialectic of "Protestantism as movement and Protestantism as order," both this book and Henry F. May's *Protestant Churches and Industrial America,* which preceded it, were weighted heavily on the anti-formal and evangelical side. [22] (We also neglected anti-formal and evangelical denominations of a predominantly Southern cast, such as the Disciples of Christ and the Southern Baptists, even though in the Sixties the former would produce a landslide victor for the American presidency and the latter would outstrip the combined Methodist membership and become the largest branch of American Protestantism, but that neglect probably reflected biases of a kind other than theological.) This book, for example, used as a sample of Episcopalian opinion the "low-church," militantly modernist weekly

The Churchman, without counterbalancing it by reference to its Anglo-Catholic antithesis, *Living Church;* and although the first major coalescence of Lutheran synods in America took place during the period I described, *The Decline and Revival of the Social Gospel* on the whole treated the confessional tradition of Lutheranism as something that was happening far away in Germany.

Donald Meyer's *The Protestant Search for Political Realism 1919–1941,* informed by a spirit quite different from Henry May's or my own, has given us some hints as to how to transcend these categories, both for interpreting the vicissitudes of the Social Gospel during the Twenties and Thirties and for placing in its historical context the Cox–Neuhaus debate which was to follow. From a theology of politics, Meyer contends, socially-conscious Protestants had to make a transition to a theology of culture, a transition which in the New Deal years was very imperfectly accomplished; and, in a paradox that out-Niebuhred Niebuhr, Meyer declared: "The final upshot of the social gospel was that the gospel had to be more personal." [23] For Meyer (drawing on Paul Tillich) the final Christian political insight is into the danger that politics, by *identifying* individual with social ethics, may dehumanize man. It is an insight that the contemporary New Left and old Right, both grimly insistent that this identification be made, would do well to ponder.

De Kalb, Illinois

NOTES

1. Richard Hofstadter, Author's Note to the revised edition of *Social Darwinism in American Thought* (Boston, 1955).

2. There are cross-references to some of this newer material in the *Postscripts* to the chapters that follow. In addition, on the Social Gospel

prior to 1920, see Clyde C. Griffen, "Rich Laymen and Early Social Christianity," *Church History*, XXXVI (March, 1967), 45–65 (which has an
important bearing also on my fifth chapter), and John Lee Eighmy, "Religious Liberalism in the South During the Progressive Era," *ibid.*, XXXVIII
(September, 1969), 359–372. David Burner has written on the climate of
opinion described in my second chapter in his essay "1919: Prelude to
Normalcy," in John Braeman *et al.*, eds., *Change and Continuity in
Twentieth-Century America: the 1920's* (Columbus, 1968), 3–31. On
Prohibition, see in the same volume Joseph R. Gusfield, "Prohibition:
the Impact of Political Utopianism," *ibid.*, pp. 257–368, and the second-
ary works cited in that article's footnotes; but compare also my adverse
review of one such work in *The American Scholar*, XXXI (Spring, 1962),
328ff. On Fundamentalism, Ernest R. Sandeen, *The Origins of Fundamentalism: Toward a Historical Interpretation* (Philadelphia, 1968) is
important, but compare also LeRoy Moore, Jr., "Another Look at Fundamentalism: a Response to Ernest R. Sandeen," *Church History*, XXXVII
(June, 1968), 195–202. Robert T. Handy gives insight into the morale
of the churches during the Twenties in *The American Religious Depression 1925–1935* (Philadelphia, 1968); see also my monograph *The Twenties in America* (New York, 1968). A dissertation by John Franklin Piper,
"The Social Policy of the Federal Council of Churches during World War
I," done at Duke University in 1965 [abstracted in *Church History*, XXXV
(September, 1966),355f.], is a major revision of most historians' assumptions concerning the role of the churches in that war, and therefore of
what is said on pp. 91–94 of this book. On the New Deal, a brief but
very influential revisionist work is Paul Conkin, *The New Deal* (New
York, 1967). On Catholic social thought during that period, important for
context in any discussion of Protestantism, David J. O'Brien's *American
Catholics and Social Reform: the New Deal Years* (New York, 1968), is
excellent. On the U. S. reaction to the German crisis of the Thirties, see
Frederick K. Wentz, "American Protestant Journals and the Nazi Religious Assault," *Church History*, XXIII (December, 1954), 321–338, and,
for context, Franklin H. Littell, "The Importance of the Church Struggle
to the Ecumene," *Franz-Lieber-Hefte: Zeitschrift für Politische Wissen-
schaft*, III (Herbst 1959), 32–45. On religion and race, in counterpoint
to the Methodist case study described within (pp. 196–199), see David M.
Reimers, "The Race Problem and Presbyterian Union," *Church History*,
XXXI (June, 1962), 203–215; and, for broader revisionist perspective,
Joseph R. Washington, *Black Religion: the Negro and Christianity in
the United States* (Boston, 1964). Sydney E. Ahlstrom has discussed the
permeation of American theology by European concepts, in "Continental
Influence on American Christian Thought Since World War I," *Church
History*, XXVII (September, 1958), 256–272, and my article *The Idea of*

Progress in American Protestant Thought 1930–1960 (Philadelphia, 1969) approaches the same question from a slightly different perspective.

3. See the discussion of the Church and the Negro in Chapter X, esp. p. 132.

4. A special report on this subject entitled "Roundup: the Year of the Black Manifesto," by Michael Stone, appeared in the *Christian Century,* LXXXVII (Feb. 11, 1970), 185–188.

5. P. 132, below.

6. P. 231, below.

7. William Hamilton, "The New Optimism—from Prufock to Ringo," in Hamilton and Thomas J. J. Altizer, *Radical Theology and the Death of God* (Indianapolis, 1966), p. 158. (First published in *Theology Today,* January, 1966).

8. Pp. 230–1 below; Sydney E. Ahlstrom, reviewing *The Decline and Revival of the Social Gospel* for the *Review of Religion,* XXI (March, 1957), 208.

9. Elmo Pascale, letter to the editor of *The Christian Century,* LXXXVI (April 9, 1969), 486, commenting upon Muggeridge's essay "Men Like Gods" (Feb. 5). This Anglo-American shift from pessimism about the human condition back to optimism took place also in Germany; the theologian Jürgen Moltmann, who in the Forties had "read Kierkegaard and studied dialectical theology and admired the young Luther's theology of the cross," by the mid-Sixties was evolving a "theology of hope." Moltmann, "Politics and the Practice of Hope," in the series "How My Mind Has Changed in This Decade," *ibid.,* LXXXVII (March 11, 1970), 288–291. Compare also the vogue by the end of the Sixties, in both Catholic and Protestant circles, for the evolutionary optimism of Teilhard de Chardin.

10. An informative but somewhat condescending discussion of this phenomenon may be found in Roy E. Branson, "Time to Meet the Evangelicals?", *ibid.,* LXXXVI (Dec. 24, 1969), 1640–1643.

11. Martin E. Marty, "Seminary Enrollments 1962," *ibid.,* LXXIX (Nov. 7, 1962), p. 1362. See also Herbert J. Muller, "Second Thoughts on the Religious Revival," *Harper's,* CCXXVIII (February, 1964), 82–93.

12. Harvey Cox, *The Secular City: Secularization and Urbanization in Historical Perspective* (New York, 1965), 219f.

13. Below, p. 225.

14. James A. Pike, "Why I'm Leaving the Church," *Look*, April 29, 1969, 54–58, esp. p. 58. The statement by Victor L. Butterfield was made at the alumni luncheon at Commencement, June 10, 1950, and is paraphrased from my personal recollection.

15. Harvey Cox, *op. cit.*, p. 160; James F. White, "Worship in an Age of Immediacy," *The Christian Century*, LXXXV (Feb. 21, 1968), p. 228.

16. Elsie Thomas Culver, "The Hippies' Pastor is Ordained," *ibid.*, LXXXV (April 10, 1968), p. 467; and see also Robert A. McKenzie, "The 'Free' Church of Berkeley's Hippies," in *ibid.*, pp. 464–466.

17. Evelyn King, " 'Soul' Sits In During Sunday Services," *Daily Missoulian* (Missoula, Montana), Feb. 2, 1969, p. 19. The photographs which accompanied this article, taken with church officials' permission at a "rock mass" the preceding Sunday, in themselves made an informative comment.

18. Ralph Waldo Emerson, "Divinity School Address," as reprinted in Joseph L. Blau, ed., *American Philosophic Addresses 1700–1900* (New York, 1946), p. 604.

19. Richard John Neuhaus, "Liturgy and the Politics of the Kingdom," *The Christian Century*, LXXXIV (December 20, 1967), 1623–1627.

20. H. Richard Niebuhr, "The Protestant Movement and Democracy in the United States," in James Ward Smith and A. Leland Jamison, eds., *The Shaping of American Religion* (Princeton, 1961), p. 36.

21. The news media began to take account of the renascence of this ancient substitute for religion in the spring of 1969; for example, "Astrology: Fad and Phenomenon," *Time*, March 21, 1969, 47–56. Systematic study of this movement is needed; nobody to my knowledge has touched upon, for example, the subtle "generation gap" *within* the ranks of astrological believers. Younger persons who cast horoscopes seemed to be doing so in a mood of experimentation and rejection of conventional forms, cognate to much else they did in defiance of their elders; older persons, and especially professional seeresses and astrologers, often tied their astrological lore to a highly conventionalized evangelical Christian rhetoric, and to right-wing politics.

22. Professor May has intimated that the study of religion in America *must*, in the very nature of the case, be done in this way: "American Christianity should be treated not as a series of institutions but as a prophetic movement, never completely embodied in any institutional forms." Henry F. May, "The Recovery of American Religious History," *American Historical Review*, LXX (October, 1964), p. 85. For a discussion

of some of the differences between the way scholars with a church orientation and those without have tended respectively to conceive of the history of religion in the United States, see my essay "Recent Historiography
of the Protestant Churches in America," *Church History*, XXXVII (March,
1968), 95–107, and on the problem of the professional relationship between the church historian and his colleagues in secular history, Sidney E.
Mead, "Church History Explained," *ibid.*, XXXII (March, 1963), 17–31.

23. Donald B. Meyer, *The Protestant Search for Political Realism
1919–1941* (Berkeley and Los Angeles, 1960), p. 285; compare also my review of Meyer's book for *Church History*, XXX (March, 1961), 126f.

Acknowledgments

THE writing of a doctoral dissertation (which this was) is one of the loneliest intellectual endeavors known to man and, paradoxically, at the same time one of the most intensely cooperative. My debts to others in this work are many.

Richard Hofstadter, of Columbia University, who supervised the work, is known for the force and charm of his writing in American history. If he did not succeed in rescuing this work from my own tendency to point a moral and adorn a tale, he did direct my attention to areas and ideas indispensable to this study which otherwise would not have been included.

Robert T. Handy, of Union Theological Seminary, cosponsor of the work in its dissertation form, originally stimulated my interest in the history of the American churches. His detailed criticisms of early drafts of Chapters I through IV were of great help in getting the manuscript "off the ground," and his friendly encouragement at all stages of the work has been invaluable.

Harold C. Syrett, Henry Steele Commager, and Joseph Blau,

all of Columbia, served on the committee before which this manuscript was defended as a dissertation and made many valuable criticisms and suggestions.

Beyond these more formal acknowledgments, I cannot hope to give all the credit that is due, for one pilfers intellectual currency unconsciously. I owe much, I know, to the quiet but eminently quotable Dr. John C. Bennett of Union Seminary. Chapter I originated, in part, in the stimulating seminar in church-state relations conducted in the spring of 1952 by Noel Dowling of the Columbia Law School and Dean James A. Pike of St. John's Cathedral. Many friends have listened patiently to oral readings of these chapters, and I am particularly indebted to Miss Helen Braun for the disappearance from the manuscript of certain of the barbarities of graduate-school literary style. For the great number that remain I plead sole responsibility. More recently, the editorial staff of the Cornell University Press, in particular Mrs. Elsie Myers, has been most helpful in this direction.

I am indebted to innumerable students and several faculty members of Union Theological Seminary, whose table talk in the Seminary refectory has served this mere historian in lieu of a theological education. They also, of course, are absolved of any heathen misinterpretation of the Queen of Sciences on my part. No work of this kind would be possible in our day without libraries, and those of Union Theological Seminary, the Harvard Divinity School, the General Theological Seminary, Columbia University, and Harvard College, with the public library in Bangor, Maine, were all helpful. The staffs of Union and of Harvard Divinity in particular spent long hours at my behest in search of obscure books and periodicals, and I am deeply appreciative.

An author's obligations to others continue to grow in number even as the work moves into its final stages. For their cheerful and careful reading of galley proofs with me, I am indebted to my colleagues in the University of Maryland, Earl S. Beard, William B. Catton, Michael S. McGiffert, H. S. Merrill, Patrick W. Riddleberger, and David Sparks; and, for providing

ACKNOWLEDGMENTS

the food and drink which went far to convert proofreading from a chore to a pleasure, to their charming wives.

Finally there is a special debt of gratitude to my father. Minister, writer, and artist, he has been more responsible for my intellectual growth than he can ever know. This study is dedicated to him with deep affection.

PAUL A. CARTER

Boston, Massachusetts
August 10, 1955

Contents

CONTENTS

PART ONE

THE BACKGROUND OF THE

SOCIAL GOSPEL IN AMERICA

CHAPTER I

The Rise of American

Social Christianity

WHEN the President of the United States declared on March 4, 1933, that "the money changers have fled from their high seats in the temple of our civilization," he was speaking to a country in the grip of an unprecedented political and economic emergency. But, although the situation was new, the mood and the imagery and the words themselves came from roots as deep as any in our culture. Franklin Roosevelt was not the first political leader to invoke the ethical imperatives of the New Testament. Such use of a religious reference for social criticism and action —such a "Social Gospel"—is, in fact, as old as the Gospel itself. Indeed, it is older, for the symbolic act of cleansing the Temple at Jerusalem was in a tradition of earnest nonconformist itinerants of a far earlier time, prophesying doom on kings of Israel who "beat my people to pieces, and grind the faces of the poor."

Since antiquity, religion has moved men to work for the betterment of their common lot. To be sure, "betterment" has been variously interpreted, as men have combined their religion with other beliefs springing from caste and class and social function. Sometimes their faith has seemed to them to require charity toward the poor, and no more, or it has prompted them to seek to keep their brother's conscience and led them into crusades and inquisitions and prohibitions. But at other times it has involved them in a sharply critical view of political and economic powers-that-be and on occasion has called them to the support of sweeping utopias and violent revolutions.

Paradoxically, the Christian Church has been throughout its history both a conservative and a radical force. Its teachings have been, for Western society, both social cement and social solvent. Authoritarian state churches have ranged themselves against religious revolutionaries. It is the radical tradition, of protest and reform, which will concern us in this study.

As recently as the second half of the nineteenth century, this tradition of social reform, which recurs throughout the history of the Hebrew-Christian religious quest, underwent an important change of emphasis. This new current appears on the European continent as Social Catholicism; in the Church of England as Christian Socialism; among Jews in certain of the doctrines of Reform Judaism. Congruent with secular social-reform movements of the same period, it yet had a motivation and rationale of its own. I have chosen to focus upon the American and Protestant phase of this movement, which is what is historically meant by the "rise of the Social Gospel."

In what did this change of emphasis consist?

Intellectually, the first premise of the Social Gospel was that man in society stands under religious judgment. This idea, while it differs sharply from some other modes of Christian thought, was of course not new. But the rationale of the Social Gospel went on at once to another declaration, namely, that this religious judgment is to be passed, not upon individual men only, but also upon the collective institutions which men have made. Foreshadowings of such an approach appear in medieval and early modern Christian social thought, but the idea had long been neglected in Protestantism [1]—and nowhere had the neglect

4

been greater than in the United States of America. Therefore, this notion came upon the scene as a new and far more radical critique of existing society than Americans were accustomed to hear. For only upon such a premise can the Church go beyond an individualistic ethic and pass moral judgment upon (for example) capitalism, the labor movement, and the state in terms of their intrinsic value as institutions rather than in terms of the souls of individual businessmen, trade unionists, or government officials.

If it is in any sense true that social good and evil is collective in nature, as the proponents of the Social Gospel argued, not simply a sum total of the good and evil of individuals, then men are obliged to act directly upon the social order and work for its reconstruction, as a part of their religious responsibility to their fellow men. Here, it seems to me, is the crux of the Social Gospel. Such a doctrine in the hands of men who take seriously the traditional antithesis between the City of God and the City of Man implies, at the very least, drastic criticism and, at the most, social revolution. When American churchmen reached this point in their thinking, they repeated an act which had distinguished precedents. Like St. Francis, John Hus, and George Fox, they undercut the Church's support of the social *status quo* by a fresh reading of that subversive tract, the Bible.

In order fully to appreciate how new a departure the Social Gospel was, one must examine the older social Christianity in America out of which it sprang. Our understanding of American religious history has sometimes been distorted by putting too much emphasis upon colonial New England. It would be all too easy to find the basis for the kind of Christian social action I have been talking about in the Puritan Bible commonwealth, but we must take certain other facts into account.

In the first place, the social action of Christians in that epoch was not often directed against the social *status quo*, since the social and religious elites were identical. It is, of course, true that the famous "election sermons" of the Congregationalist divines, when directed against the British just prior to the American Revolution, constituted action against the *status quo*

5

in a sense. But on the other hand, in five of the British colonies the Church of England was formally established, and a very large number of the pastors of that church cast their lot with king and country. Then, too, in Pennsylvania and elsewhere there were many Christians, among the German-speaking immigrants in particular, whose theology forbade them to resist the state, or in some cases to participate in politics at all, or even (as the Mennonites) to take part in the common life of the secular community. So, if the roots of the American Social Gospel lie in the soil of American Puritanism, this is not enough by any means to explain what made the plant grow.

Furthermore, the penetration of any kind of gospel into the colonies, let alone a social gospel, was far from general. Indeed, the impression one gets from contemporary discussions, such as those that surrounded the formation of the Society for the Propagation of the Gospel, is that the religious life of the American colonies was so much more "this-worldly" in tone than that of England as to be viewed with great alarm by churchmen. Even in Massachusetts Bay, and in the other, non-Puritan religious experiments of Pennsylvania and Georgia, one finds a strong secularist current running under the theocratic surface and diluting the intensity of religious life. Despite men's concern for the state of their own and one another's souls, the criminal statistics of the Bay Colony show that the World, the Flesh, and the Devil had their innings also—all of which should occasion no surprise. A society composed of beachheads at the edge of a primeval wilderness could not afford to be too cavalier toward the things of this world. This fact should be borne in mind also when weighing the social significance of colonial Christianity.

Instead of assigning the characteristic era for American religious faith to the time of the Mathers, Roger Williams, and Edwards, I should place it in the often-misunderstood Middle or National Period of American history, between the turn of the nineteenth century and the outbreak of the Civil War. And the great divide between the Christianity of the British colonies and the Christianity of the new republic I should place in the emotional crises of the First and Second Great Awakenings, which burned their way across English-speaking North America in the middle and latter part of the eighteenth century.

Perry Miller and others have concerned themselves with these religious revivals chiefly as "democratizing" and "leveling" influences; here, they say in effect, the life of the Church passed from the exclusive enjoyment of a covenanted elect and became the possession of all sorts and conditions of men. The First Awakening thereby became a harbinger of the Revolution, a mass action which transformed American society. This is to a large extent probably true, although the Second Awakening canceled part of the political effect of the First by promoting a reaction against the "godlessness" associated with Jeffersonian democracy. But in any event, the long-run consequences of both Awakenings were something rather different. They imposed upon religion in America the pattern of revivalism, that is to say, the pattern of the decisive, once-for-all individual experience of conversion, an experience which remained individual, paradoxically, even though usually undergone en masse.

The effect of this kind of religious conversion had important political as well as religious consequences. It reinforced the individualism which was to be a dominant theme in the American political tradition throughout most of our history. Coupled with the American version of the doctrine of the separation of church and state, which came to flower during the Revolution, it created a curious dialectic between the Church and secular society which was once summed up as follows: "The connection between Church and State in America is intimate and vital. It is not legal . . . yet neither can do without the other, . . . the State giving freedom to the Church, and the Church giving to the State moral character." [2]

The impact of this kind of church upon this kind of state was greater in the area of a priori ideals than in that of pragmatic democratic politics. Professor Gabriel may overstate the case somewhat in declaring that "the foundation of [American] democratic faith was a frank supernaturalism derived from Christianity." [3] This ignores, for example, the contribution of the

7

anticlerical French Enlightenment. But a convincing case can nevertheless be made to support his assertion that the working out of the democratic dogma in America had about it a great deal of the temper of evangelical Protestantism.

In the realm of practical social politics, also, this kind of religion had its contribution to make, as Theodore Parker and Charles G. Finney and Theodore Weld attest. Characteristically, American expression of the impulse to social reform took the form of rather loosely organized voluntary societies, and the American churches were admirably suited institutionally for this species of social action. As religious revivalism reached its peak in the middle of the ante-bellum (National) period,[4] so also did associations for the promotion of temperance, women's rights, world peace, prison reform, and above all the abolition of slavery come into their heyday, and the connection between the revivals and the societies was direct.[5] The leading evangelical figure of the day, Charles G. Finney, exhorted his converts to throw themselves into one or another of the social reform causes, under the slogan "Saved for Service."

The amount of effective work done in this fashion was no doubt considerable, but the mood was far from that of the Social Gospel as I have essayed to define it. American social religion remained fundamentally individualistic; churchmen and statesmen alike had a long road to travel before they would come to treat society institutionally and as a whole. Only a few religious "heretics" like Theodore Parker and Orestes Brownson went beyond the casual, associationist analysis of social needs which was characteristic of secular and religious thought alike.

But, it should be noted, this does not imply that such an approach to social reform was inadequate or reactionary in terms of what the spirit of the age made socially possible. On the contrary, the reformers were frequently in advance of their time; abolitionism in particular was damned as destructive of the established order, and if the peace and women's rights movements received somewhat less vilification, it was only because these did not strike as deeply and as effectively at an entrenched social interest. If churchmen of the 1830's and 40's did not see beyond

8

economic laissez faire, neither did Andrew Jackson, and it would be a mistake to evaluate the political folkways of the National Period by our own.[6]

But if the churches cannot be damned for lagging behind the social thought of the 1830's and 40's, neither can they be praised for running ahead of their times. Adequate as it seemed in the more or less open society of that time, their conception of social reform would not serve in the disenchanted age which was on its way. The easy optimistic trust that political ills were to be cured by mere "good government" and economic ills by mere "better business" was to be shattered; consequently, programs of reform through the moral suasion of individuals by voluntary societies were doomed. The first and severest blow to the old optimism was dealt at Fort Sumter.

The Civil War was and remains a great watershed of American history. It was our most destructive war; there were, for example, more military casualties than the United States sustained in all the theaters of the Second World War. And the experience was too numbing even to produce a literature of protest, as happened after the First World War. Hardened but not matured, the postwar generation responded to its traumas with a cynical reaffirmation of the prewar social individualism in its narrowest and most brutal form.

America's age of innocence was over; Americans, particularly in the South, had experienced the horrible genuineness of evil as never before, and the moral steam went out of the reform movements of the previous epoch. A few abolitionists followed through on their previous work by assisting the freedmen, but most rested on the accomplishment of freeing the slaves and sought no new laurels. As for rejuvenating the radical tradition by espousing new causes, Wendell Phillips stood almost alone. The rest of America hardly noticed. Men were too busy scrambling for a share in what Parrington calls "the Great Barbecue" of uninhibited capitalism.

As for the churches, their response to this situation did them little credit. Henry F. May in his study, *Protestant Churches and Industrial America,* describes the period of 1861–1876 as "the

9

summit of complacency" in American Protestantism. It was not simply that the churches failed to protest the looting of the federal treasury and of the continent by the spoilsmen; rather, they rationalized the code of the unrestrained businessman in theological terms and enthusiastically preached it. Perhaps the characteristic churchman of the era was Henry Ward Beecher, whose well-turned sermons expressed the very best thought of his upper-middle-class Brooklyn congregation and hardly ever anything more.

The genesis and growth of such a movement as the Social Gospel out of this dismal setting calls for some explanation. Many have argued that the Social Gospel appeared through a process of "challenge-and-response" (to use Mr. Toynbee's sometimes serviceable phrase), the "challenge" consisting of the series of economic disasters which darkened gilded America from 1877 through the Age of Bryan. The great railroad strike in the Hayes administration; the activities of the "Molly Maguires" of the Pennsylvania coal mines; the rise, and fall, of the Knights of Labor; the Haymarket bombing; the growth of the city, and of the slum; and the events of the unaccountably named "Gay" Nineties (which decade included a major depression, the bloody Homestead and Pullman strikes, the Populist and Bryanite protests, and finally a war!)—this series of crises of poverty and violence forced the American churches to reconsider their untroubled acceptance of things as they were. Confronted by an increasingly angry and articulate labor movement which had little use for the Church, the churchmen's "optimistic theory had to be reconsidered in the light of burning freight cars." [7]

This thesis assumes that the Social Gospel was generated by forces wholly external to the churches. More recently, this has been challenged by church historians. The American churches, these men contend, *found* the Social Gospel, in the course of working out the logic of their evangelistic quest "for a Christian America." [8] They point out that changes in the content of American religious belief, nonsocial in character, had to take place before the Social Gospel became possible, and that these changes were not simply the product of social and economic

forces. For example, a key figure in this development was Horace
Bushnell, who was socially a conservative, but his theology had
important liberal social consequences. Moved by distaste for a
religious culture which placed young children in morbid terror
of hellfire until they had been "saved," Bushnell argued for a
gradualistic concept of salvation. Training in and practice of
Christian ethics and worship, he said in his important work,
Christian Nurture (1861), can lead by insensible degrees toward
a state of grace. He was not thinking of the secular social order.
Yet it is not a very long step from a belief in Christian nurture
to the discovery in society of elements making for un-Christian
nurture and from there to an attack on these elements through
social and political action.

But, whether economics or theology was the major force back
of the Social Gospel—a decision which I leave to the reader's own
philosophy of history—in due course the Social Gospel was born.
It appeared first here and there in the pulpits of individual dissenters, ranging across the spectrum of church organization and
theology from Anglicans to Congregationalists. These men were,
very often, men whose bourgeois complacency had been eroded
away by firsthand experience with the poverty of an urban parish
(Walter Rauschenbusch) or with labor unrest (Washington
Gladden).

The Social Gospel continued throughout its history to be
a preaching movement. But it also entered into the denominational press and adopted the strategy of the committee. Unofficial
groups appeared, representing their point of view to what was
at first an indifferent or hostile majority within the Church.
Later came a more general denominational concern in what was
then called "the social question," a concern which was embodied
in official church agencies. The climax in this drift toward official recognition came in 1908 with the founding of the Federal
Council of the Churches of Christ in America. It is an indication of how far the Social Gospel had permeated the Church
that in those days it was the one issue upon which groups as
diverse as the Episcopalians and the Quakers could agree sufficiently to permit it to be used as a basis for ecumenical union.[9]

Almost at the outset, this quickening of social consciousness among American Christians differentiated itself into a left, a right, and a center—what Henry F. May calls respectively "radical social Christianity," "conservative social Christianity," and "progressive social Christianity." I shall accept these definitions for the purposes of this present study, but with two words of caution. In the first place, they are latter-day distinctions drawn for purposes of historical analysis and do not occur in the literature of the Social Gospel. And in the second place, they are social and political, not religious, distinctions; one should not assume that political and religious "liberalism" and "conservatism" are necessarily parallel. Some of the most vigorous preachment of social reconstruction, as embodied, for example, in the Church League for Industrial Democracy, came out of the deeply traditionalist Protestant Episcopal Church. On the other hand, many Unitarian leaders in this period, whose theology would have to be classified as liberal, seemed satisfied that the environs of Boston approximated the conditions of the Kingdom of Heaven and remained among the economic and political stand-patters for another generation.

Of these three branches of the Social Gospel, "conservative social Christianity" most closely approximated the individualistic, voluntaristic social reform movements of the National Period. But it was considerably subtler than the simple Christian stewardship of wealth—Wesley's old formula "gain all you can, save all you can, give all you can"—which Rockefeller and others offered as the Gilded Age's conscience money. It assumed, for one thing, that society was in actual need of reform; it asked businessmen not to found philanthropies but to raise wages. When it took the form of social settlement work, it accepted the challenge of urban social politics with the full understanding that more was involved here than a more systematic almsgiving. This branch of American social Christianity showed the strong impress of the Tory-Socialist sentiment which was then helping to shape Christian and secular thought and action in contemporary England, but it followed the humbler pattern of the

Salvation Army as well as the *noblesse oblige* of London's Toynbee Hall.

"Radical social Christianity," the opposite wing of the Social Gospel, argued that this kind of social uplift was worse than useless, because its advocates received the emotional satisfaction of reform without achieving reform in actuality. Society was out of joint more than individual morality—so much so that the only way a Christian could transcend the moral ambiguity of his position was to renounce his stake in existing society and work for a totally different kind of social order. The mood, although not usually the rhetoric, of Marxist social determinism entered readily into this kind of Christian thinking. But Christian radicalism seems at that moment in history not to have been viable in American soil, perhaps because prior to the calamities of 1914 and 1929 few Americans were ready to abandon to this degree their belief in the openness of society. Christian social radicals were prone either to leave the Church altogether (George D. Herron) or ultimately to abandon the whole social sphere in favor of mysticism (J. O. S. Huntington). The left wing of the Social Gospel seemed practically to have run its course during the two decades 1900–1920.[10]

With the coming of the twentieth century and the Progressive Era, the center of the social Christian movement gained at the expense of the right and left. In "progressive social Christianity," there was acceptance of the radicals' contention that the salvation of society would require institutional as well as personal moral changes, but these social gospelers of the center rejected the claim of many religious and secular socialists that the institutional changes would of themselves bring the millennium. Indeed, as a counterweight to the radical—perhaps one may say prophetic—condemnation of society as such, there was a decided balk at any wholesale scrapping of that society's institutions for others which might prove no better.

If this sounds like middle-class ambiguity, it only tends to validate May's use of the term "progressive social Christianity" as a synonym for the Social Gospel. For the Social Gospel, much to its advocates' disappointment, made little headway either with the conservative wielders of secular power or with the urban workingman. Insofar as it was successful, its appeal was to the middle class. Its historical genesis was in the pattern of labor strife, urban social transformation, native political radicalism, and corporate consolidation which was simultaneously promoting the rise of middle-class uneasiness and political progressivism. Both its strength and its weakness—its positiveness that something ought to be done and could be done about the ills of society and its tendency to "neglect completely the complicated problem of ends and means in a surge of revivalistic confidence" [11]—remind one irresistibly of the progressive psychology of the Age of Theodore Roosevelt.

As the Social Gospel matured as a shaper of opinion, so also matured its underlying ideology, which is to say, its theology. Walter Rauschenbusch summed up this process at the end of the prewar period in his *A Theology for the Social Gospel* (1917). His major contribution was to socialize and institutionalize the concepts of spiritual regeneration and of the Kingdom of God. "Social ills," he asserted, "are bred in the unChristianized areas of modern life." The prime example of such an area was the capitalistic system, "an unregenerate part of the social order." Therefore, man's salvation was impossible as long as that system remained structurally untouched. Social gospelers differed as to how much change there would have to be for the regeneration of the social order, but most agreed that, as it stood, capitalism constituted a formidable obstacle to the advent of the Kingdom of God on earth. "The hope of the Kingdom contains the revolutionary force of Christianity," and that force must be brought to bear upon the *status quo* if mankind is to be saved.[12]

Of equal importance with this more immanent concept of the Kingdom of God, for the theology of the Social Gospel, was new emphasis upon the personality of Jesus. This emphasis had been formulated independently of social progressivism, partly as an outgrowth of the "higher criticism" of the Bible by nineteenth-century German scholars. These men had assaulted the historicity of the Gospel narratives with an appalling thoroughness, and their conclusions drove many out of the Christian faith entirely. Others, however, such as Harnack, found this ruthlessness bracing and clarifying, and were led to a fresh examination of the ethical implications of "the historical Jesus," stripped of the accretions of belief added during the course of Christian history. When this inquiry passed from the professionals to a more popular level, it took the form of increasing the immediacy of the ethical imperatives of Jesus, as distinguished from the abstractions drawn therefrom by the Church.

Here, if one may speak dialectically, is the thesis to which Rauschenbusch's idea of the immanent Kingdom of God is the antithesis: the Kingdom-theology institutionalizes and socializes the judgment of the Christian upon society, and the emphasis upon the ethic of Jesus deepens the personal, anti-"world" basis for this judgment. Emphasis upon the personal-ethical side found expression in the Social Gospel of the right, in its promotion of social solutions of the settlement-house, "social work," stewardship type. Emphasis upon the social or "Kingdom" side bore fruit in the Social Gospel of the left, in its call for complete reconstruction of society in the name of Christian Socialism. The dialectical tension between these two emphases gave shape to the Social Gospel of the center, where the main strength of the movement lay.

There remains the question of just how far the Social Gospel penetrated among, and was accepted by, the American people and, in particular, the rank and file in the churches where that gospel had been born. Certainly the advocates of the Social Gospel gained great leverage from the fact that they often controlled the denominational machinery, and politicians were not always aware that churchmen making liberal pronouncements did not necessarily speak for their full constituency of church members (which is to say, voters). The Federal Council of Churches, through its Washington bureau, very quickly became an important lobby, with a "Social Creed of the Churches," adopted in 1912 to provide a reasonably official minimum frame of reference for a Protestant Christian approach to social and political issues.

But both May and C. H. Hopkins, in their histories of the movement, are careful to point out that the Social Gospel probably never won over a majority of the lay leadership in the American churches. Therefore, the question of the larger influence of the Social Gospel in American life remains open.

To answer it, one must go beyond the history of the Progressive Era. Our study begins, then, at the close of the First World War.

Postscript: 1971. May's "Right-Left-Center," "conservative-radical-progressive" categories were premised upon the commonly held historical assumption that Progressivism—the political movement which was the Social Gospel's nearest secular analogue—was in fact middle-class in makeup and outlook. More recently the work of historians like Samuel P. Hays and Gabriel Kolko has suggested that "Progressivism," rather than having been an expression of middle-class protest *against* the established order, may have been a process of social change imposed *by* the conservative ruling class itself, in its own interest. Little thought has been given, as yet, to what this historiographic insight might mean for our understanding of the Social Gospel, although a beginning has been made in one revisionist article which argues that Walter Rauschenbusch himself, the prime theologian of the Social Gospel, was rather more elitist than we had assumed. See John R. Aiken, "Walter Rauschenbusch and Education for Reform," *Church History,* XXXVI (December, 1967, 456–469.

CHAPTER II

The Social Gospel and
the Spirit of the Times—1920

POLITICAL liberals look back on the year 1920 as an uncommonly bad one. It was a year that saw hundreds of alien radicals deported from these shores, by the sheer fiat of the Attorney General of the United States; a year that saw trade union membership sliding away while businessmen promoted the open shop as an "American Plan" to save the country from Red Russia; a year that saw the League of Nations receive its death blow at the hands of the United States Senate and saw the blow confirmed and approved by millions of voters as they made Warren Harding their President. It was, then, a year of events and tendencies and personalities peculiarly hostile to the creed which thousands of churchmen had espoused and preached under the name of the Social Gospel. For this very reason I choose the year 1920 as our starting point.

The historians of the Social Gospel's younger days have concluded the story as of 1915. But 1915 was a transitional year, when the liberal politics of Woodrow Wilson and the western Progressives and even William Jennings Bryan had not lost their hold upon American life. By 1920 the picture of the kind of world in which Americans—and American churchmen—would have to live for the next decade was much clearer. Thus we can come at once to the point: between the high aspiration of Wilson's crusade "to end war" and the gray reality of Armistice Day, Progressive politics had been virtually swept from the stage. What, then, of progressive Christianity? Would a social gospel born "in the light of burning freight cars" in America turn out to have perished in the light of burning cities in Europe?

The question is probably unanswerable in quantitative terms. Public opinion, never easy to assess, becomes particularly elusive when one deals with the notorious inexactness of religious statistics. Qualitatively, however, one can seek for a meaningful answer in the pages of the Protestant church press. The weekly denominational magazine, which for many years was a major influence not only in the Church but in American journalism generally, has been used as a historical source before; Henry F. May studied such periodicals for the years 1865–1895 and found that the Social Gospel appeared and was developed in their pages in full accord with the other landmarks in its rise. Therefore, it would seem reasonable that a survey of the journals of the same denominations for the year 1920 would throw some light upon how that Social Gospel had changed.[1]

Of course one must allow for social inertia. Many of the consequences of World War I and its aftermath took several years to unfold, if indeed they have run their course even today. As we consider the state of the Social Gospel in 1920 this factor of inertia must be kept in mind, for the conclusion to be drawn from reading this material is hardly the one which might logically have been expected. The spokesmen for the Social Gospel, like all the rest of the Protestant clergy, came from the same middle-class walks of life as had the secular progressives of the previous two decades, and they were certainly subject to the same series of disillusioning blows which affected the country and the middle class at large and drove men into political "normalcy." And yet the most striking single fact which comes out of intensive reading in the denominational weeklies for the year 1920 is that their pages were filled with articulate and vigorous social criticism.

The church editors discussed a wide variety of issues, ranging from pre-Social Gospel standbys, such as prison reform, to questions which before the war had not even existed. Moreover, the new social challenges—the Non-Partisan League among the Dakota farmers, the new urban Negro in the North, the closing down of the immigration frontier—were handled in a way that evidenced both a rootage in the older Social Gospel tradition and a capacity to apply that tradition to the living issues of the postwar world.[2]

There were dissenting, *status quo,* and reactionary voices also; but so had there been in the religious press of the Social Gospel's flood tide before the war. On the other hand, Social Gospel views were consistently a part of the editorial policy of the *Baptist* and the *Christian Advocate,* whose staffs were periodically elected by their churches' respective governing bodies— which would seem to mean that the Social Gospel was still reasonably "official" in those denominations. Theology was no absolute bar; the ultraliberal *Continent,* which was campaigning to abolish Presbyterian creedal requirements, advocated the Social Gospel, but so also did the *Watchman-Examiner,* the journal which coined and first used the term "Fundamentalist." The *Churchman,* one hundred and sixteen years old, was for the Social Gospel; and so also was the *Baptist,* which was in its first year of publication. So widespread a witness, in the face of so hostile a *zeitgeist,* is a remarkable tribute to the emotional hold which this blend of religious ethics with political liberalism had achieved among American Protestants during the formative years before the First World War.

Consider, for example, the pronouncements by these journals on organized labor. The labor movement in the United States in 1920 was under a barrage of condemnation from the secular press, which at times seemed to equate trade unionism with

19

VERNON REGIONAL
JUNIOR COLLEGE LIBRARY

Bolshevism. And yet the *Churchman* found kind words even for the frankly revolutionary Industrial Workers of the World. An article titled "Why the Timber-Beast Rebels, a Story of How the Lumberjack Lives," written by a former West Coast lumberjack, described the living conditions of these men who had been attracted into "Wobbly" violence. "The lumberjack," he asserted, "is the finished product of modern capitalism. He is the perfect proletarian type—possessionless, homeless, rebellious." And therefore, the *Churchman* editorialized a few issues later, "even so drastic an organization as the I.W.W. may have its esoteric uses in the fostering of some kind of a spirit of unity among the labor outlaws of the world." [3]

Even in avowedly Social Gospel journals, enthusiasm for the labor movement did not usually go quite this far. The Methodist bishops, in their pastoral letter to the Methodist General Conference of 1920, confined themselves to denouncing the more obvious injustices: "all murderous child labor, all foul sweat shops, all unsafe mines, all deadly tenements, all starvation wages, all excessive hours"—and then took some of the sting out of their words by rapping the knuckles of labor as well as of management ("all brutal exactions, whether of employer or of union, all overlordships, whether of capital or of labor").[4] This was hardly adequate; organized labor in the United States in 1920 had its back to the wall and was in no position to exercise overlordship over anyone. But others in the Church did realize this, and in its annual Labor Sunday message for 1920 the Federal Council of Churches sounded a solemn warning to its middle-class hearers:

If . . . labor organization itself is fought to a finish, . . . we shall have an autocratic management of industry on the one side, and either a kind of serfdom on the other or a militant, bitter, and class-conscious organization of labor growing yearly more revolutionary. . . . The Church must stand for the right of organization and collective action . . . not only for prudential reasons, and because it is right, but because the manhood and freedom of the workers are at stake. . . . The Church cannot allow itself to be stopped from this course either by pressure from reactionary employers on the one hand, or by the manifest evils of the labor movement on the other.[5]

This was bold language for any period of American history, not to mention such a union-breaking year as 1920. But social talk is usually less indicative of the stand a group has taken than social action. Consequently, the most important labor news of the year, for our purposes, was the release on July 28, 1920, of the most directly effective social document ever to originate in the American churches: the Interchurch Report on the great steel strike of 1919.

Practically the entire secular daily press had treated this strike almost exclusively in terms of the radicalism ("Bolshevism," in the language of the day) of the strike leaders. There were indeed radicals among the workers' leaders, including the now notorious William Z. Foster, but this fact did not deter the churchmen's Commission of Inquiry from the real business at hand: a painstaking analysis of the conditions under which the strike had taken place.

This involved a study of how the iron and steel industry in America was being run in those days, and consequently Judge Gary and several state Manufacturers' Associations denounced the Commission as Communist-inspired. For the commissioners had put everything on the record: the consistency of Big Steel's anticollective bargaining policy, including the methods used to control the workers and forestall their organization, the pyramid of labor with the immigrants at the bottom, the casual inhumanities which resulted from a divorce of control from production, the long hours and low wages, the lack of any machinery for the expression and redress of workers' grievances, and, not least of all, the reasons for the strike's failure.

None of this had been reported to the general public. The Report, therefore, came to millions as new information, even though it appeared months after the strike had been broken, and it created an unprecedented sensation. "More newspaper attention [has] been given to this report than to any similar findings of the past fifty years," observed the New York *Tribune,* which atoned on behalf of its fellow newspapers for the previous conspiracy of silence by giving the Commission's findings maximum publicity.[6] In the denominational journals, there was widespread endorsement of the Report, frequent reprinting of summaries, and no little moral indignation, directed not only at the United States Steel Corporation but also at the secular press for having failed to carry out its function of enlightenment.

As for the Communist label, it did not stick. "The conclusions of this report, signed by men whose intelligence and reputation . . . are beyond question, cannot be ignored," the *Christian Advocate* declared. "If the corporation cannot clear itself, it will have to clean house"—an opinion which proved to be prophecy.[7]

For, although the strike had been crushed, sentiment against the twelve-hour day eventually prevailed, a sentiment generated in large measure by the impact of this report. Protestant groups such as the Federal Council of Churches were joined in their pressure for reform in the steel industry by the National Catholic Welfare Council and the National Council of Rabbis. The chorus of appeal swelled until even President Harding joined in, and in 1923 the twelve-hour day in steel was duly abolished. Middle-class as the social gospelers may have been in their outlook, they had unquestionably played a role in transforming the conditions of American labor. We must conclude that the forthright labor gospel of Rauschenbusch and Gladden continued in 1920 to be a factor in American Protestantism.

But in a sense this was only to be expected. Labor was, after all, the area of the Social Gospel's earliest concern, and persistence of this concern in men long habituated to thinking in prolabor terms might have been expected. Perhaps a better index to the postwar Social Gospel, therefore, is its application to an issue of comparative insignificance in the Progressive Era: the entering of international affairs directly into American domestic politics.

And as the denominational weeklies resisted the antilabor sweep that was under way in 1920, so also they stood against isolationism, turning aside thereby from some secular liberals like Borah and LaFollette. Church opinion had been prepared for internationalism by the enormous expansion of foreign missions during the nineteenth century. Many a congregation had had its mental horizons widened by the vivid accounts of returned missionaries. The Student Volunteer Movement, founded to recruit missionaries, was still operating in 1920 under the slogan: "The Evangelization of the World in This Generation," and the sentiment behind such a slogan was readily transferable to a Wilsonian secular internationalism.

Moreover, for people conditioned to making personal financial sacrifices for missionary activity, the cruder varieties of America-Firstism could have little appeal. Indeed, at times a self-critical note was sounded that was completely out of harmony with international "normalcy":

For an American to be in Europe at this time is humiliating and sometimes almost disheartening. . . . "America first" sounds to thoughtful Europeans just a little like the words which used to come from across the Rhine—"Deutschland über Alles"—not with the same sense of aggressiveness but with something of the same selfishness.[8]

The most elementary level of internationalist action was direct economic relief, and this so obviously followed from the Christian fundamentals that the point need not be dwelt upon. Even the *Presbyterian,* a paper which opposed practically all the rest of the Social Gospel, responded to the dreadful news from Central Europe and Siberia and the East with a call for "the relief of this world-wide cry of misery."[9] More significant for our purpose were the reactions of the churches to the less transient aspect of United States foreign policy, which for the year 1920 means their views of the League of Nations debate.

Both before and after the final failure of the Senate to ratify the Treaty of Versailles, various individuals and groups representative of churches urged acceptance of the League of Nations. Northern and Southern members of the Joint Commission on the Unification of Methodism took time out from their labor over the reunion of their long-divided church to pass a resolution urging ratification of the treaty, and at the Northern church's

General Conference of 1920 the bishops demanded "a real and effective League of Nations" in which the United States would "have a proper and honorable place . . . in preserving the peace and bearing the burdens of the world." The Presbyterian General Assembly adopted two strong resolutions favoring the League. The Northern Baptist Convention unanimously urged ratification of the treaty, although protecting its unanimity by adding "with suitable reservations." [10] When, after all the clamor, the treaty was not ratified, widespread disappointment was reflected in the denominational press. "Don't Abandon the Peace Ideal," the *Continent* editorialized:

The Church . . . must fight the disgusts of impatient men who peevishly conclude, when progress in right lines is stopped by various stupidities and stubbornness, that idealism is all a fraud. . . . It is hard, indeed, to see the League of Nations ruined . . . but the chagrin of that frustration does not subtract one iota from the grandeur of the original proposal. . . . If the ideal was ever worth a strong man's allegiance, it demands such allegiance more imperatively . . . in its hour of discredit than in its heyday of popularity.[11]

The *Congregationalist,* also, conceded that "public interest with regard to a League has reached low-water mark" and predicted "a long, hard fight" for ratification. Most atypically for an official denominational newspaper—and particularly for one edited in Cabot Lodge's Boston!—this journal took sides as between the President and the Senate and unequivocally placed the major share of blame upon the latter. Moreover, it followed the logic of this partisanship into the political campaign which was getting under way. As far as foreign policy was concerned, the most it could say for the Republican National Convention of 1920 was that it "does not leave us in utter despair":

We deplore its lack of vision, its lack of courage, its lack of statesmanship and its lack of Christian leadership for the world. . . . "Hoch der party" is still a considerable slogan . . . a disillusioning and disheartening spectacle . . . utterly reactionary, pusillanimous, cowardly, selfish.[12]

24

But if many American Protestants in the year 1920 carried into the international scene the constructive idealism of the pre-war Social Gospel, they also carried over that movement's too-easy optimism. With the exception of the *Congregationalist,* just cited, there was surprisingly little understanding of the fact that the national political campaign of 1920 all too faithfully reflected the feelings of the American people on foreign policy at that time. There was, instead, a great deal of wishful thinking on the part of church editors that, in spite of the rejection of the League Covenant in the 1920 Republican platform, and in spite of the nomination of Warren Harding, the international question would work out and we would somehow get a League of Nations.

The *Churchman,* for example, predicted on October 23 that "the party which appeals most loudly and fatuously to a narrow and selfish nationalism in America, will lose the election." When the party and candidate which at the time most closely fitted this description won in a landslide, the same paper nevertheless reasoned that "people are generally persuaded . . . that the United States should go into a league of nations" and called for "such a pressure of public opinion as will compel Mr. Harding to turn for counsel to Mr. Taft and Mr. Root," the leaders of pro-League sentiment in the Republican party. Again, the *Continent,* lulled by Harding's insubstantial internationalist words, managed to editorialize in spite of everything that "the nation has grown amazingly in unselfishness." But the high-water mark in this kind of prophecy was reached by the *Baptist.* Beguiled by the fact that the President-elect was a Baptist layman, the editors noted that "Baptist principles and tenets have bulked large with the Hardings," and predicted that "the 'Baptist conscience,' should Senator Harding become President, is expected to stand the United States in good stead." [13]

What is astonishing about these statements is not so much their fatuity as their authorship, for they were made by men capable of penetrating insights into the sickness of the body politic, as we have seen. Here we find something in the social Christianity of the year 1920 that appears outdated. In an era of the degree of impersonal international malevolence which was to follow, such whistling in the dark would be fatal. If the Social Gospel were to survive as its practitioners gradually became aware of the profound difference between the pre- and postwar worlds, something a good deal less facile would have to enter into it.

There was nothing facile, however, in the Church's response to another challenge of the year 1920, more serious than the swing to antiunionism and of more immediate danger than the failure of the League, namely, the threat to freedom of opinion occasioned by conservative fright at the birth of Soviet Russia.

Free speech is usually the most vulnerable point for attack upon republican institutions, and in the "Red Scare" of 1919–1921 it was in worse repute in America than at any time since the French Revolution. The mantles of Mr. Tenney and Mr. McCarthy were then worn by Mr. Lusk and Mr. Palmer, and worthy ancestors they were. Yet in that first Red Scare, as in the one which has followed the Second World War, there were leaders in the Church who stood against the hysteria of their time and demanded a fair hearing for unpopular ideas.

As an example, consider the response of the clergy of New York City to the ejection from the state legislature of five properly elected Socialist members. On the eleventh of January, 1920, the Sunday following the incident, there appeared in the New York daily newspapers a letter of protest signed by a list of Protestant ministers who amounted to a Who's Who of the metropolitan clergy—such men as the President of Union Theological Seminary, A. C. McGiffert; the Dean of the Cathedral of St. John the Divine, Howard C. Robbins; and such prominent pastors as Henry Sloane Coffin, Ralph W. Sockman, and Harry Emerson Fosdick.[14] It should be noted, however, that the impressive prestige and quality of this group failed to move the legislature, which did not seat the Socialists even after three of them had been re-elected—a fact whose implications I shall discuss in the seventh and final chapters.

Nevertheless, the record of witnesses to free speech is impressive. The Methodist New York East Conference went literally to the rescue of immigrants seized for deportation without trial in Attorney General Palmer's famous raids, and a speaker at the Northern Baptist Convention's 1920 session accused Palmer of "violation of the laws and the constitution of the United States." [15] The *Churchman* blasted a New York State antisubversive law, fathered by the infamous Lusk Committee, as "a type of legislation which has not been tolerated in England or America for more than two hundred years." [16] The *Congregationalist* published a series of sympathetic sketches of individual radicals titled " 'Reds' I Have Known," concluding that "the world is not so perfect that noble spirits should not be attracted to revolutionary camps." Poised enough to observe that some of the fears of the middle class were not only groundless but funny, this journal printed a letter which one of its readers had written on that reddest of all red-letter days, May Day: "I hope to live the day out and even to have a little golf this afternoon. . . . I don't know a better place for the capitalistic system to make its last stand and as long as the golf balls hold out we will not be without ammunition." [17]

Thus in the area of civil liberties, as in those of labor and of international relations, Protestant Christians in postwar America were devoting a vigorous and detailed attention to specific social and political issues, bearing up surprisingly well in comparison with the Social Gospel of the Progressive Era. Nor was this criticism all fragmentary and unrelated; from time to time, in editorials with titles like "The Recrudescence of Selfishness," writers showed awareness of the temper of their times and consciously set themselves against it. The *Churchman* wondered "how any one can feel great hope for . . . a civilization, the surface of which, scratched at almost any point, discloses hard and sordid mammon worship." The *Congregationalist* saw postwar America "plunging again into an orgy of business." And the *Baptist* worried that "we are even questioning our own enthusiasms" and warned against "going back to the old ideas that made a hell of the world." [18]

But none of these writers anticipated what rough going lay ahead for the doctrine they preached. Already, long before

1920, social trends antithetical to every article of their creed, religious as well as social, had been in the making, and other challenges whose existence was hardly suspected lay beyond the horizon. Nor had the full consequences of the First World War penetrated very far into the consciousness of society and of the Church.

Advocates of the Social Gospel did recognize that "idealism [was] on the wane," but their prescription for this situation consisted simply of "courage, reasonable optimism, and a resolute defence of Christian ideals." [19] One wonders if the editor who wrote these words realized how unreasonably his optimism was going to be tried. His statement was published the week after the election of Mr. Harding.

Postscript: 1971. Since the opening of the Harding Papers to scholars (1964), Mr. Harding has not looked quite so bad. Indeed, one biographer—Robert K. Murray, in *The Harding Era: Warren G. Harding and His Administration* (1969) —has written what would have seemed preposterous only a few years ago: a comprehensive *defense* of that régime, by comparison both with Coolidge's and with the waning months of Wilson's. The dismal events of 1920 chronicled in this chapter did after all take place during what technically was still the presidency of Woodrow Wilson, and can not properly be blamed on the president-elect—except to the extent that coming events do sometimes cast their shadows before them. But that judgment applies also to what was about to happen to the Social Gospel.

PART TWO

THE SOCIAL GOSPEL UNDER FIRE,

1920-1929

CHAPTER III

Prohibition, Left and Right

THE Social Gospel, as we have just seen, continued to live
and flourish in America after the First World War. But between the generation of the muckrakers and the generation of
the Red-baiters a great gulf lies in American history, and no
movement which linked two such disparate generations could
have carried over that gulf unchanged. For while the older
Social Gospel had been in harmony with its secular milieu, Progressivism, the newer Social Gospel was in the deepest dis-
harmony with its setting, "normalcy." And it is a stubborn fact
that even the most wholehearted opposition to a social environment necessitates some adaptation to it. Crusading slogans can
be amended out of all meaning, as witness Orwell's "All animals
are equal, but some animals are more equal than others." One
of the most remarkable instances of such a change in social
meaning can be found in the impact upon the Social Gospel of
that unique American phenomenon, Prohibition.

The history of the Eighteenth Amendment presents a special

problem in hindsight. Our mental image of Prohibition comes down to us from the Roaring Twenties, and is colored by the notion that Prohibition was exclusively the work of moralizing Puritans compensating for the repressions of their own harsh code in a spurious indignation at the pleasure of their neighbors. We tend to lose sight of the thousands of sincere and not particularly ascetic folk who believed that they "fought liquor, not because it has made men happy, but because it has made men unhappy." [1] Therefore we have forgotten that, prior to the passage of the Volstead Act, the dry crusade spoke the language of social and humanitarian reform—and had the profoundest kinship with the Social Gospel. That image from the 1920's is a vivid one; it is hard, indeed, intellectually or emotionally, to accept the idea that prohibitionism ever was, or ever thought it was, liberal in the social and political meaning of that word. Yet I submit that to assume some degree of genuinely humane social-welfare temper in the Prohibition movement helps to explain much in American church history which otherwise would make very little historical or psychological sense.

An affinity between social reform and the antiliquor campaign is evident as early as the Age of Jackson. It will be remembered from our discussion in the first chapter that one of the early impulses to the improvement of American society, along with abolitionism, prison reform, and so on, had been a temperance movement. After the Civil War, Gerrit Smith, a former abolitionist leader, and others continued the tradition by founding the Prohibition Party. The interesting fact about this third party is that the platforms upon which it contested every Presidential election from 1872 on did not confine themselves to the liquor question. And the other, nonprohibitionist causes which these men supported were usually as far in advance of the regular Republican and Democratic platforms as those of any other third party. Thus in 1872 the Prohibition Party came out for the direct election of Senators, the abolition of the electoral college, and woman suffrage; in 1876 it called for "the separation of the money of Government from all banking institutions," thirty-seven years before the Federal Reserve Act was passed; and in the Roosevelt-Wilson era its platforms endorsed a variety of other social changes, including employers' liability legislation and the abolition of child labor, which specifically identified this as a party of the native American left.[2]

"Fighting liquor," for men of this sort, meant fighting not merely the rhetorical abstraction "the demon Rum," but an entrenched, well-organized, wealthy industrial enterprise, which engaged in political corruption often enough to enable its enemies to cast it in the role of a "vested interest" of the sort dear to the hearts of Populist and Progressive crusaders. Therefore, attacks on the liquor business could employ the language of attacks on the trusts:

In a time when the social conscience of America was aroused as never before to condemn grafters who stole from the people profits for which they rendered no tangible return, the distilling and brewing businesses loomed up as the grossest of all such offenders. For they were fleecing the poorest classes of millions on millions of hard-earned cash without ever returning to them a pennyworth of any kind of value, economic, physical, or social.[3]

Viewed from this rationale (or rationalization; there were elements of both), the issue of Prohibition was not the propriety of a personal act, but rather the legitimacy of a business. And it is from this point of view that one must consider the relationship between Prohibition and the Social Gospel. For, with the exception of the Protestant Episcopal, all the churches which had been permeated by the Social Gospel *were also officially committed to Prohibition.*[4] Thus if one does not posit an element of left-wing, populistic, social-reform feeling in their prohibitionism, one would have considerable difficulty in explaining how the Social Gospel could have arisen in these churches at all.

The Methodist Episcopal Church, South, says the perceptive Virginius Dabney, "was the most militantly aggressive of all the large American churches in its hostility to the saloon"; and yet their "vigorous excoriation of lynching, and their exhortations to employers to grant their employees a living wage, stamped them as the Southern denomination that . . . probably

33

did most to further social well-being" in that period.[5] The denominational weeklies which were examined in our last chapter, with the obvious exception of the Episcopal *Churchman,* all hailed the advent of the Noble Experiment with enthusiasm. The Social Creed of the Churches was amended in 1912 to include "protection of the individual and society from the social, economic and moral waste of the liquor traffic." [6] And the Federal Council itself, founded in large measure to implement the Social Gospel, spent $150,000 in the years 1916–1920 to help put Prohibition across. Not only did Prohibition and the Social Gospel arise in the same churches at the same time, but evidently political liberals in those churches were as often as not political "drys" as well; and some of them regarded the one reform movement as part and parcel of the other.[7]

But Prohibition as simply a field for exhortation was unfortunately not the same thing as Prohibition emergent in law. There continued to be echoes of the older liberalism throughout the Volstead Era—no less a radical than Upton Sinclair wrote a slashing antiliquor novel as late as 1932, titled *The Wet Parade,* but on the whole the achievement and enforcement of Prohibition as a concrete political program worked a striking change in its ideology.

The social idealists of the Prohibition Party had prepared the way, but they were not the kind of people who brought Prohibition into existence. Even before the Eighteenth Amendment removed its *raison d'être,* the party had begun to decline, and the leaders of the Anti-Saloon League and of the Methodist Board of Temperance, Morals and Public Instruction (*sic*) were of a different stamp from Gerrit Smith and John P. St. John. Frances Willard, President of the Woman's Christian Temperance Union in the 80's, had been an honorary member of the Knights of Labor; her successor as President of the same organization from 1925 to 1933, Mrs. Ella Boole, was a member of the Daughters of the American Revolution.

The temperance movement had taken shape in churches— Methodist and Baptist—which had made their first great conquests along the trans-Appalachian frontier, and whose constituencies traditionally had been small-town or rural. Prohibition came into being at a time when "the political center of gravity in this country" (as Dabney puts it) was still "in Junction City and Smith's Store and Brown's Hollow," rather than in the metropolitan areas "with their armies of foreign-born and their vociferous anti-prohibitionist newspapers." [8] Those of the cities which were dry before Prohibition were located for the most part in areas which then could hardly have been said to be dominated by the urban mind—Birmingham, Salt Lake, Atlanta, Denver, Richmond, Des Moines. If, then, the temper of the Prohibition movement had changed from the days of Frances Willard and John P. St. John, it was in part because the politics of rural America had changed. Other political ideas had, for the time at least, displaced those usually associated with agrarian reform. The sons of the Populists wore the white nightshirts of the Klan. The struggle for Prohibition was between town and country, and in that sense a last Bryanite rally of the West and South against the urban East; its essential tragedy was that the symbolism of an agrarian political crusade had long since lost its meaning.

In the final showdown vote in Congress to override President Wilson's veto of the Volstead Act, the urban East was the only section of the country to give a majority for sustaining the veto. Thus the rural-versus-urban aspect of this conflict was sufficiently clear to draw appropriate comment from dry leaders. "What we commonly hear," said the Methodist bishops in 1932 (arguing against local option as a substitute for national prohibition), "is, 'leave it to the communities that want the traffic back again to solve the problem for all of us. Leave it to the sidewalks of New York and the slums of Chicago.' " [9] At times, men like this defended Prohibition by exalting rural over urban folkways per se, in accents strikingly reminiscent of Mr. Bryan:

Great city domination has been the rock upon which past civilizations have been wrecked. . . . When the great cities of America actually come to dominate the states and dictate the policies of the nation, the process of decay in our boasted American civilization will have begun.[10]

But the great political dilemma of the drys was that the agitation leading to the enactment of the Eighteenth Amendment took place in the same decade which saw the rural-urban population balance tip irreversibly in the direction of the city. In 1910, rural Americans—defined for census purposes as that part of the population living in communities with fewer than twenty-five hundred inhabitants—constituted 54.2 per cent, or a majority, of the American people. Ten years later, their percentage of the total was down to 48.6, and it was evident that, insofar as historical predictions are ever valid, this trend must continue downward. Assuming considerable correlation between the dry vote and the wheatfields of Kansas, on the one hand, and the wet vote and the sidewalks of New York, on the other, one must then conclude that the Volstead Act was passed at a singularly unpropitious moment in American history. The prohibitionist tide had turned even before it reached its highest surge.

Couple this statistical fact with the hardheaded pragmatism of the pressure group which did the most to bring Prohibition in, and the shift in the dry psychology from reform to reaction becomes easier to understand. For the Anti-Saloon League, unlike the churches which supported it and unlike the idealistic Prohibition Party with which it was in a perpetual state of feud, was devoted not to an evangelistic ideology but to an immediate practical objective: the enactment of Prohibition as law. Its politicking was of a straightforward reward-and-punish character, irrespective of party; indeed it did not ask that the candidates it supported for office be by conviction or practice dry, so long as they voted dry. And in order to avoid losing votes over other issues it refused to become involved in social and political causes other than its own. (The single exception was woman suffrage, which the A.S.L. supported in several states in the expectation that women would tend to "vote dry.") For men of this stamp, committed to a particular task without ideological or moral complications, the fact that the democratic process would shortly cease to work for Prohibition because of the movement into the cities of the mass of voters suggested one easy and obvious solution—short-circuit the democratic process.

Wayne Wheeler, Legislative Superintendent (i.e., chief Congressional lobbyist) of the Anti-Saloon League, saw this very clearly when he observed in December, 1917, that the Eighteenth Amendment would have to pass in the current session of Congress: "We have got to win it now because when 1920 comes and reapportionment is here, forty new wet Congressmen will come from the great wet centers with their rapidly increasing population." [11] Later, when the drift toward repeal was unmistakable, the editor of the Anti-Saloon League *Yearbook* opposed the ratification of a repeal amendment by state conventions, frankly admitting that he did so in order to protect the *status quo* in "wet states with dry legislatures." [12]

But for the mass membership of the American churches, with somewhat tenderer feelings toward the democratic process, and for those leaders of the churches who remained, as of 1920, committed to a total program which included the Social Gospel and Prohibition, such arguments were obviously out of place. Many, indeed, contended that Prohibition did represent a settled conviction of the American people. And a plausible case could have been made for this thesis if one overlooked the country-to-town trend, for, after all, in due course forty-six states ratified the Eighteenth Amendment through their legislatures. But the denominational leaders did not rest their major argument on the shaky ground of pro-Volstead public opinion. The key slogan during the years of the Noble Experiment was "Obey the Law."

Quite apart from the merits or otherwise of Prohibition, this phrase had considerable appeal. Modern students of Prohibition should not overlook the moral leverage that any group enjoys which has the law on its side. There were those in public life, like William Howard Taft, who fought Prohibition coming in but chose to abide by the rules of the game afterward, and it was this cue which was most frequently picked up by the denominational press. And, verbally at least, in this they had the support of three Presidents of the United States. Mr. Hoover complained that "a surprising number of our people . . . have drifted into the extraordinary notion that laws are made for

37

those who choose to obey them"; Mr. Coolidge more bluntly declared that "enforcement of law and obedience to law . . . are not matters of choice in this republic." The American people were even confronted on one occasion with the happy spectacle of Warren Harding devoting an entire speech to celebrating the majesty of the law.[13]

Of course conversely it could be argued, and was, as Walter Lippmann did, that the nullification of an undesired law was "a normal and traditional American method of circumventing the inflexibility of the Constitution." [14] The general public, meantime, drank or did not drink in accordance with the dictates of law, conscience, or social pressure.

But in any case, the stress upon the law-enforcement issue had one patently undesirable consequence: it focused public attention upon the bootlegger and the speakeasy, and by implication upon their customers, rather than, as in the movement's early days, upon the liquor industry and the reform of society. *The humanitarian concern for the drunkard as victim was replaced by righteous indignation at the drinker as criminal.* The fact of being in authority and armed with the law did more, in my opinion, to divorce prohibitionism from its own humane, reformist, Populist-Progressive roots than any other single cause.

Furthermore, the stress upon constitutionalism and law enforcement had the effect of strengthening the Anti-Saloon League's strategy of the politics of the single idea—with disastrous results. Prohibitionism had been relatively nonpartisan; the denominational weeklies could and did urge their readers to support dry candidates for office without seeming to endorse a particular point of view just as long as the two major political parties were able to duck the whole wet-dry issue. And then came a day in July, 1928, when Alfred Emanuel Smith dramatically forced the issue by repudiating the Prohibition enforcement plank of the Democratic party platform.

A presidential election is not the same as the canvass of a Congressional district. The drys who took up this challenge by Smith inevitably involved themselves and their cause in every other issue of the campaign. On May 17, the Methodist General

Conference adopted a report declaring that that church would "not support uncertain candidates," nor "willingly tolerate in positions of responsibility those who do not sustain the law"; and the die was cast. A Louisiana delegate to the conference warned the Democrats what to expect: "Tell Al Smith and everybody else that the Church stands for holding up [the] principles of morality and right and Christianity." [15] The political campaign began, and the Methodists and the Baptists and the W.C.T.U. and the Anti-Saloon League went to work with a will.

Throughout the South in particular the Church's role in the Hoover campaign was unprecedentedly direct. Virginius Dabney writes that

at virtually every anti-Smith meeting there were ministers on the platform; generally the program opened and closed with prayer; and not infrequently the prayer was for a Hoover victory. Throughout the principal address ejaculations of "Amen" or "Amen, brother," were to be heard from the clergy on the platform or from the faithful in the audience. Often a hymn or two was sung.[16]

The last hymns were sung; the last prayers were said; Election Day came, and the Solid South was smashed for the first time since Reconstruction. The Anti-Saloon League, in its annual survey of "Progress Toward Prohibition in the Several States," claimed every Hoover victory as an advancement of the dry cause. And so it was, up to a point. Beyond that point, the League's politics of the single idea broke down. Prohibition, as a reason for crossing party lines in 1928, merged with an uglier one: Alfred E. Smith was a Roman Catholic.

To be sure, there were drys who fought fairly, according to their lights, and took care to dissociate themselves from religious bigotry. ("When I find a long line of lousy kluxers agreeing with me," wrote the liberal Kansas dry, William Allen White, "I want to go out and be a repeater above seven times for Smith." [17]) And there were, also, Catholics—and Democrats—who were willing to charge that any opposition to Smith, on any grounds, constituted "anti-Catholicism." They were wrong, of course, rationally. Yet, in another way, they were quite right.

39

To appeal to voters as church members, through their church organizations, on a religious basis, was a legitimate conclusion from the premises of the Social Gospel. But in the case of this man and this issue and this election year it was to play with fire. Even under ordinary circumstances the very name "Protestant" connotes certain habitual attitudes toward the Church of Rome —including a lively distrust of it as a political entity. Such attitudes can be expressed and implemented in a way that does not implicate one in religious bigotry or persecution, but this was 1928. The lurid glow of the Klan's fiery crosses was cast across Smith's political pathway. The South and Middle West were dry; the South and Middle West were also infected by the Ku Klux Klan. To appeal for votes against a Catholic candidate, even if one did so purely in wet-dry terms, was inevitably to stir a traditionally, bitterly anti-Catholic constituency, which was more than usually inflamed already.

Furthermore, the distinction between these two different premises for an anti-Smith campaign was blurred by some in the churches who opposed Smith, as a Roman Catholic, because the Catholic Church was itself "wet." [18] To be sure, this is a legitimately distinct argument from those employed by bigots who opposed Smith, as a Roman Catholic, on the assumption that any Catholic's confessor is an agent of a sinister foreign power. But legitimate distinctions of a merely logical sort are not enough during an election year in America. In the heat of a presidential campaign, these distinctions between the several forms of anti-Smith sentiment could not and did not hold.

"Nobody objects to the distinguished gentleman who is running on the Democratic ticket . . . because of his religion," the *Baptist* hopefully editorialized. And after the election, putting the best possible construction upon the motives of the citizenry, this journal declared that the American people as a whole had clearly decided "one thing and only one thing," namely, Prohibition.[19] Alas for liberal Protestantism's sanguine view of human nature! The American people had not by any means "decided" Prohibition; five years later they were to repeal it. For all the good will of social-gospeling drys, such as the editors of the *Baptist*, the order of the day for rural America in this election was not reformist Populism but Know-Nothingism; and Governor Smith paid the price. What remains to be added is that for their involvement in his defeat, to which they came by way of Prohibition, the Protestant churches paid a price also. Well might a prophetic churchman have exclaimed: "Another such victory and I am undone."

It was not merely the association which came to be made in the minds of many Americans between the Protestant churches and extreme political reaction that was damaging—although these churches certainly did not benefit from the fact that the mystique of the Ku Klux Klan was couched in Protestant Christian phraseology. But also, beyond their involvement in this nativist side of the campaign of 1928, the churches were put in the position of having stood up to be counted for Herbert Hoover. Four years later this fact would carry a different meaning for American voters. Organized labor, one should remember, fought Prohibition from the pre-Volstead era onward.[20] And one of the sweeping social changes which came after March 4, 1933, was the repeal of the Eighteenth Amendment.

In its march from the political left to the political right, Prohibition carried many Social Gospel spokesmen with it; in the Hoover-Smith campaign in particular their social witness therefore became almost hopelessly confused. But the experience of Prohibition had more indirect and at the same time more serious consequences for the Social Gospel. In the first place, the emotional heat generated by the wet-dry controversy destroyed, in the minds of many supporters of Prohibition, any sense of the proportionate importance of social issues other than the Demon Rum. In the second place, the general prestige and moral influence of the churches suffered unprecedented damage, so that all of their teaching—religious as well as social—was rendered less effective. Let us consider these consequences of Prohibition in more detail.

In the first year of the Noble Experiment (which Hoover actually called the "experiment noble in purpose," a distinction with a difference), a correspondent who signed himself "an

41

old-fashioned parson" wrote for the *Churchman* an article titled, "Bringing In the Millennium: Reflections on Blue Laws," which sourly entered an exception to the hallelujahs still ringing in other quarters of the denominational press. In particular he took issue with the Social Gospel interpretation of Prohibition which had helped to give the movement its strength:

It seemed to require small courage to rampage about strong drink, when the captains of industry financed the campaign because big business suffered through the bad habits of the proletariat. One wondered whether there were not other and greater evils against which a valiant Christian knight could tilt his word.[21]

This criticism is essentially one which has continued to be leveled at evangelical Protestantism ever since. Liquor is something about which a minister can be forthright and still be safe. His congregation may not be dry; indeed, statistically, outside of certain parts of the South and Midwest it is probably not dry. But temperance sermons have so long been a part of American religious folkways that they are tolerated, perhaps even expected of him, just as a Bible-based pacifism is sometimes accepted from a minister where it would not be tolerated in a layman.

The movement toward national Prohibition, as we have seen, had originally shown some of the characteristics of pre–World War I political reformism. And once it was in being as the law of the land, its advocates took the credit for as many contemporary advancements of the general welfare as they could. Prohibition was claimed as a cause of the lower death rate, the higher standard of living, the improvement in general public health during the 20's; it had "relieved distress of poverty, . . . opened new lines of commercial opportunity [!], . . . given to labor greater efficiency." [22] But the other side of this coin is that a clergyman thus prone to overstress the benefits of Prohibition was prone to understress other social issues, or subordinate them to the dry cause—in other words, *to make Prohibition a surrogate for the Social Gospel.*

This is a statement easier to make than to document. There are, nevertheless, indications. One of the most revealing occurs in the minutes of the Methodist General Conference of 1936.

The previous session of this church legislature had met in 1932, while Prohibition was still in force but confronted with the prospect of repeal, or in the words of the bishops with "a serious crisis in our work for a sober world." The crisis had come and passed, and the world had presumably gone out and got drunk. So necessary a conclusion was this from the logic of Prohibition that it forced an incredible inversion of these men's values. Back in 1924, the year of the Teapot Dome scandals, they had adopted a resolution rejoicing in "the good that is found in the public life of today," and declaring that "in quantity it far exceeds the evil." But in 1936—when, by all odds, a modicum of social and civic responsibility had returned to American public life—they found that "the moral and social decline of the past quadrennium has startled the socially minded people of the world. The long, hard ascent up the heights of Christian idealism has been countered with a demoralizing avalanche." Such was the transvaluation of values that Prohibition disastrously forced upon the Social Gospel.[23]

While the Northern Methodists were adopting the curious resolution just quoted, a leader of the sister Methodism of the South was complaining that his church "used to have a Board of Temperance and Social Service. It paid mighty little attention to social service." [24] The official weekly magazine of the Anti-Saloon League was called *The American Issue;* and its use of the definite article in that title says a great deal about what was done to the Social Gospel by Prohibition.

Beyond the damage done within the churches, there was the damage done to their standing vis-à-vis the secular world. I have suggested that the Anti-Saloon League's politics of the single idea promoted a singular moral obtuseness among many dry leaders in relation to The Cause. William E. ("Pussyfoot") Johnson, one such leader, acknowledged in the May, 1926, *Cosmopolitan* that he "had to lie, bribe, and drink to put over Prohibition in America," that he would have done it over again if necessary, and that he was proud to have lied for The Cause in a way "to make Ananias ashamed of himself." [25] Such declarations did irrepara-

43

ble injury to the effectiveness of the churches' counsels in the realm of ethics, social and otherwise. Rev. H. D. Russell, founder of the Anti-Saloon League, once declared that the League "was begun by Almighty God"; [26] if God truly worked in the mysterious ways of Wayne Wheeler and Pussyfoot Johnson and Bishop James M. Cannon His wonders to perform, it is not surprising that the era of Prohibition was also an era suffused by a righteously indignant secularism.

It was not only the personal ethical failings of the professional dry politicians that damaged the Church's moral prestige. That same "old-fashioned parson" who had complained in the *Churchman* of Prohibition's status as a substitute Social Gospel went on to ask

Are we to be content with a merely negative religion? . . . These glad young folk do not like the thing which they know as religion . . . from what they see of the reforming army of the Lord, and they say . . . "We don't want to be like them." . . . They think that the sort of life demanded of them is neither beautiful nor happy.[27]

Only rarely did the dry leaders understand how much they were advancing the secularist bias of the rising generation by causing it to associate the Church simultaneously with a joyless legalistic morality and with dubious ethical practices in its achievement—in short, with hypocrisy. Once, Bishop Edwin Holt Hughes sensed it. "When I went in the last ten years . . . to the temperance gatherings in our land," he said in 1936, "the thing that frightened me beyond measure was that nearly always those who attended them were beyond middle life. We need to get back to our childhood." [28]

His remedy for the situation? An exhortation for the signing of temperance pledges by the youth of his church. Yet this same bishop had at one time suggested that his church abolish a certain paragraph of blue laws in its own book of *Doctrines and Discipline,* on the ground that such petty legalism was contrary to the Protestant spirit. Moreover, he had pointed out at the time that many people knew little of that church save its blue

44

laws, which hid "our hospitals, our orphan homes, our immigrant hostelries, our academies, our colleges"—in short, their social services—"from the view of multitudes." [29] That the same great bishop (and Hughes was great, in many ways) could see so clearly inside his church and so dimly outside of it is one more illustration of the fact that man is only intermittently a rational animal.

Postscript: 1971. To the foregoing judgment I would now add that issues of the kind symbolized in the Eighteenth Amendment were not foreclosed by its repeal. Since the discovery of LSD, we have found again that people can become excited about the connection between morality and chemistry. More generally, Henry David Thoreau's observation (as grimly quoted by Eric Hoffer) that the man who would be his brother's keeper ends by becoming his brother's jail-keeper—together with the anguished rejoinder "Should I, then, stand by and let my brother perish?"—has become relevant again in an America torn by the conflicting claims of personal freedom, social responsibility, and "law and order."

On the other hand, my inference that Al Smith was defeated by an "unwritten law" against the nomination or election of Catholics, a "law" with which Prohibitionists and Social Gospelers unwittingly or knowingly conspired, seems now to have been premature. I have argued this question out at length with my colleagues in "The Campaign of 1928 Re-examined: a Study in Political Folklore" (*Wisconsin Magazine of History*, 1963) and in "The Other Catholic Candidate: The 1928 Presidential Bid of Thomas J. Walsh" (*Pacific Northwest Quarterly*, 1964).

CHAPTER IV

The Social Meaning

of Fundamentalism

OF THE many scenes which rise in one's imagination on hearing the phrase, "The Roaring Twenties," none is more dramatic than the packed courtroom in rural Tennessee where, on a hot July day in 1925, William Jennings Bryan and Clarence Darrow nearly came to physical blows over the paternity of mankind.[1] That a judge and jury could solemnly have put the Darwinian theory of evolution on trial, and two of the leading public figures of the day have argued the case, with passages from the Book of Genesis admitted as evidence—in the time of Einstein and Freud, of aerodynamics and quantum theory —is one of the many paradoxes of that incredible era.

The Scopes "monkey trial" was a good deal more than simply a sign of cultural lag, however. It was the high-water mark of a strong surge of feeling and opinion in the American churches, which went under the name of Fundamentalism. Like Prohibition, it came into the national consciousness at the end of the First World War, after a period of incubation, and its indirect effects upon the churches and upon the Social Gospel were equally profound.

Politically, Fundamentalism in America has generally been taken to be of the far right. Yet the belief that the Biblical narratives are literal history does not, on the face of it, compel its believer to any given political or social point of view. On the one hand, a person who believes that the first chapters of Genesis are a factual account of the appearance of man on earth may argue that any compromise with this account is to dethrone God and exalt man, and it is easy to reason from this premise to a politically reactionary conclusion. Or, on the other hand, a literal belief in the judgment of God upon all of man's enterprises can lead into a social critique that is thoroughly radical. The Seventh-Day Adventists to this day assail capitalism in language which is often quite as harsh as that used by the Marxists, and Bryan himself sometimes saw the controvery over evolution in Social Gospel terms.[2] Logically, then, Fundamentalism could lie either to the right or to the left, politically speaking. That, as it developed, it is definitely classifiable as right-wing therefore requires a digression by way of explanation.

In our last chapter we saw that Prohibition, also, contained elements of right and left. But, although prohibitionism and Fundamentalism rose out of the same general historical situation in the same country, there was at least one crucially important psychological difference in the way they took shape. Before its legal enactment in 1920, Prohibition was a program yet to be achieved, which is to say that it was oriented toward the future. Fundamentalism, from the moment of its inception, was a system-in-being, oriented toward the past. Moreover, it was a system under sharp criticism, and thus not to be equated with the Protestant orthodoxy which had been America's ruling faith during most of the nineteenth century. Prohibition was a crusade striving to become an orthodoxy; Fundamentalism was *orthodoxy challenged*.

Prohibition reminds one of the legislation of Massachusetts Bay; Fundamentalism reminds one of the legislation of the

Council of Trent. The one, however much looking back to Mosaic law and the primitive Church, was existentially a new beginning; the other, however much looking forward to church reform and missionary outreach, was existentially the stiffening of a vested interest under attack. The Catholic response to the challenge of Luther and Calvin took, among other forms, that of a hardening of dogma and discipline; so in America did the orthodox Protestant response to the challenge of science and scholarship. And the analogy can be carried a step further. The rejuvenated Catholic Church of the seventeenth century checked the inroads of Protestantism only to find that its new ideological solidity was to be a handicap in its conflicts with eighteenth-century skeptics and anticlericals. Similarly with modern American Protestant orthodoxy, in an age of popular acceptance of the scientists' probings into areas formerly the prerogative of the theologian, a creed based on Biblical literalism was of necessity on the defensive.

If a term like reactionary is still semantically useful in this era of imprecision, it means just such a psychological state as those Protestant Americans were in—a state in which, instead of resolving the conflict dialectically by intellectual give-and-take between the old and new, the old declares total war on the new. And a theological defensive aggressiveness of this kind is so closely akin, psychologically, to the economic and political defensive aggressiveness that we associate with reaction, that in spite of occasional examples of socially liberal Fundamentalism one finds that the general trend of the movement was toward a strong dissent from the Social Gospel.

Furthermore, if the psychological conditions of Fundamentalism tended to lead it away from the Social Gospel, its financial support was not of a kind conducive to leading it back again.

The Fundamentalist movement had adopted a doctrinaire, proof-text method of teaching the Bible to make it a simple formula for evangelism—in a world that refused to stay simple. Consequently, its greatest appeal was to the people who had been the least touched by the findings of modern science, folk who were likely to be economically and educationally at a low

48

level of subsistence. But the message had to be carried to them through the apparatus of revivalism, which during the 80's and 90's had been professionalized to make full use of modern mass communication. In addition to the evangelists and the books and the publicity, there were the new schools to be founded for the training of a more orthodox ministry. All of this cost a great deal of money.

Fundamentalism, therefore, was from the outset dependent for its social impact upon the contributions of wealthy laymen to the cause. I am here implying, if you will, a semi-Marxist interpretation of the rise of Fundamentalism. It should not be pressed too far; other wealthy laymen, such as the younger Rockefeller, were spending some of their millions on the propagation of a more liberal theology. But neither should it be regarded entirely as a matter of religious zeal that certain well-heeled self-made men [3] found congenial a theology which relegated social criticism to a negligible place in the drama of salvation. Nor is it a mere polemical quirk that an advertisement in 1920 for a fund drive by the Moody Bible Institute was entitled, "The Answer to Labor Unrest." [4]

The socially reactionary character of Fundamentalism appears more clearly as one sees the way it moved into militant action in the 1920's. The history of the conflict in the American churches between Fundamentalism and what came to be called Modernism is an intricate chronicle, detailed study of which would take us far in digression; I propose therefore to focus upon one denomination as a case study, choosing for this purpose the Baptist Church because in no other religious body is the shape of the controversy quite so clear.[5]

The Fundamentalists in the Baptist Church first became aware that there was a liberal and/or secularist enemy within the fold in connection with foreign missions. During 1917, the president-emeritus of Rochester Theological Seminary, A. H. Strong, made an extensive overseas journey through some long-time strongholds of Baptist missionary activity and discovered that the Gospel being preached to non-Christians in those lands was not the literal gospel of orthodoxy. Christian apologetic inevitably

49

tends to adapt itself to the culture milieu of non-Christian civilizations in which it finds itself, but this seemed an alarming concession in the direction of religious relativism. The blame was placed upon the institutions where these missionaries had been trained. In 1918, the *Watchman-Examiner,* an independent Baptist weekly, took up this criticism and turned it into a journalistic crusade against the Baptist theological seminaries. Two years later, it coined and first used the word "Fundamentalist." [6]

By that time, the movement was ready for a test of strength. Prior to the 1920 annual meeting of the Northern Baptist Convention, one hundred fifty leaders in the church issued a call to a pre-convention "Conference on the Fundamentals." This unofficial gathering was keynoted by an address on "The menace of modernism in our schools," [7] and when the Convention itself came formally into session, a motion was presented for an official investigation of the religious opinions taught in Baptist schools, colleges, and seminaries (a motion which, we are told, "created the wildest disorder"). [8] After unusually bitter debate, a commission was set up to investigate the loyalty of teachers in the Baptist schools.

This was not, yet, a clear-cut mandate for Fundamentalism; while the resolution insisted upon the teaching of "the gospel in all its simplicity, purity, and power," it also stated flatly that "we will not seek to have dominion over one another's faith." [9] Still, it challenged the Baptist democratic tradition; it raised the age-old question with which religious authority has so often confronted believing democrats: "Does error have any rights that truth is bound to respect?" The Fundamentalists proposed, for example, that the denomination's official paper, the *Baptist,* refrain from publishing letters from its readers on the matter—on the ground that in giving equal space to both sides of the debate it was unfair to "the truth," or Fundamentalism. This, unhappily, sounds more faithful to the mood of 1920 than does the vigorous Social Gospel which some of the same Baptists were preaching in the same year.

The investigating commission escaped a showdown in its report to the 1921 Convention by invoking the Baptist principle of local autonomy: "The real power of control over our schools is in the Baptist constituency in the general locality where the school stands. . . . We must leave the matter . . . to the local body of Baptists." [10] Nothing daunted, the Fundamentalists shifted their strategy. At the 1922 session of the Northern Baptist Convention, the same choice between the conflicting traditions of liberty and zeal was offered again, this time in the form of a proposed doctrinal test for Baptist church membership.

The situation was tense; Harry Emerson Fosdick had only recently preached his famous sermon, "Shall the Fundamentalists Win?" which had roused the latent ill temper of the orthodox in such diatribes as John R. Straton's "Shall the Funnymonkeyists Win?" [11] Nevertheless, this time the Fundamentalists were beaten disastrously. Not only was the proposed doctrinal test voted down; in addition the Convention went on record to affirm that "the New Testament is the all-sufficient ground of our faith and practice, and we need no other statement." [12] The Baptist democratic tradition had triumphed; the church had decided that "epithets and excommunications are very illogical and awkward in Baptist hands." [13]

The opponents of Fundamentalism—both the theological liberals and those conservatives who opposed the breaking of their church's inclusive fellowship—continued to win the parliamentary battles in later conventions. The Fundamentalist leaders were thus faced with the clear choice: surrender or secede. Compromise, for most such men, was surrender if they assumed, as some of them did, that they were Christians and their opponents were not. Yet J. B. Massee, who had dominated the floor debates of 1920 and had invited his modernist opponents to leave the Church, made his peace with his denomination and in 1927 preached its Convention sermon; he was a Baptist before he was a Fundamentalist. On the other hand W. B. Riley, leading light in the World Christian Fundamentals Association, took a course which carried him increasingly far from his church, until eventually he left the denomination; he was a Fundamentalist before he was a Baptist. The fellowship of the Church being what it is (with all its faults), more of the leaders took Massee's way than Riley's.

The pattern of the conflict in the other churches during the 1920's is a variation on the Baptist story: attempts to curb heterodoxy in the mission field, investigations of church-controlled colleges and schools, a war of belles-lettres in the denominational press, and attempts to impose doctrinal tests upon ministers and church members. The eventual defeat of Fundamentalism along all these fronts was repeated for Methodism and Congregationalism and Presbyterianism. The death of William Jennings Bryan immediately following the Scopes Trial was a particularly severe blow to Fundamentalists of all denominations, for although there followed much scrambling for the Peerless Leader's mantle, no one man emerged who proved capable of wearing it. And for the next generation of the Protestant leadership, the battle was already lost; a survey of the beliefs of seven hundred ministers and theological students at the end of this period disclosed that less than half the ministers and only one-twentieth of the students accepted the account of the creation of man given in the Book of Genesis "in any form." [14]

But if a historical movement dies, it often leaves progeny. What was the meaning of Fundamentalism for the later development of the Social Gospel? Our answer must take into account both its legacy to the denominations wherein it had flowered and its effect through the activities of those who in its name withdrew from their churches. Let us first consider the latter —the longer-range influence of the "Ministry of Schism." [15]

In our own day, the most conspicuous outgrowth of this nonconformism of the right has been the American Council of Christian Churches. Founded in 1941 and thus falling somewhat outside the scope of this study, it yet has its roots in the controversy we have just been considering, and its leading figure, Carl McIntire, was one of the men who followed J. Gresham Machen out of Princeton Theological Seminary in 1929 to found a more conservative institution. The American Council carries on the Fundamentalist crusade against its larger rival, the National (formerly Federal) Council of Churches, accusing it of "modernism," "liberalism," and—oddly enough—fellow-traveling with the Pope.

What is this modernism, in social rather than in theological terms? Briefly, it seems to be socialism, in the rather broad construction which the far right in America puts upon that word —and, to some extent, pacifism. John T. Flynn praised the American Council for information which he used in his famous right-wing tract, *The Road Ahead,* to attack the Federal Council's usually mild social pronouncements as "socialistic." American Council leaders are given to such statements as, "The capitalistic system, in its ideal and essential ingredients, comes from no other person than the Lord Jesus Christ," and their antipacifism has taken the form of veiled advocacy of preventive war.[16]

It hardly needs to be said that if this kind of thing is characteristic of Fundamentalism at its farthest pitch of development, then that development did not bode well for the Social Gospel. But even this is not the ultimate in Fundamentalist social thought; at times it has passed far beyond mere lock-step reaction into something more sinister. There was always a thread of conspiratorial argument in Fundamentalist propaganda, and it was but a step, psychologically, from attributing the entire Modernist movement to a conscious plot emanating from the theological seminaries of Germany to attributing it to the plot of "international Jewish bolshevism," if I may resurrect a hideous phrase. The backwash of Fundamentalism mingled in the 30's with the dark currents of American Fascism.

Anti-Semitism is an answer which Christians bent on simplifying their Gospel have all too often given to the question "Why did Jesus die?" It remained latent while the Fundamentalist-Modernist struggle went on at the top level of nationally responsible Protestant bodies, but when the battle had been fought and lost, it moved dramatically to the fore among the schismatic ministry.

W. B. Riley, for example, who had spent most of the 20's trying to save the Baptist Church from evolution, spent the 30's writing pamphlets on *The Protocols and Communism*—referring to the infamous and fictitious "Protocols of the Learned Elders of Zion," which was put to such horrible use by the Russian and then by the Nazi secret police—and contributing to the *Defender,* edited by Gerald B. Winrod. Winrod himself had won his spurs in the antievolution campaign, but in the 1930's he was called by the gentle William Allen White "a Fascist, raw and unashamed" when he sought to run for the Senate from Kansas, "as good a Nazi as Hitler" [17] (after Pearl Harbor, the courts concurred). Add Gerald L. K. Smith to this group and it is clear what the "Ministry of Schism" meant for social Christianity in America.

But these were, for the most part, ministers who had cast loose from their denominational moorings. Within the older churches, the Fundamentalist witness against the Social Gospel was rarely this extreme. But by virtue of avoiding the extreme it was so much the more important an influence.

For one thing, the Fundamentalist quarrel left a deepened gulf between the clergy and the laity. This was to have momentous consequences, as we shall see. We have already observed that the Fundamentalists had in effect lost their war before they started because the sources of men and ammunition —the theological seminaries—were already in the hands of the enemy. The orthodox strategy, consequently, had perforce to be the enlistment of those who had not felt the corrupting touch of the "higher criticism" of the Bible at all, that is, the laity. "The laymen constitute the overwhelming majority in God's army," the *Fundamentalist* declared in 1922. "We have now a generation of preachers who have been turned out of the sceptical schools and seminaries of today." But skepticism, this editor continued, was not prevalent among laymen "to any such extent," and therefore the time had come "when the laymen ought to organize thoroughly for the defense of the faith." [18]

Unfortunately for Fundamentalism, the *educated* laity were already lost for such a purpose, for if the seminaries were becoming liberal, the secular colleges and universities were becoming explicitly naturalistic. But it was nevertheless true that Fundamentalism had one attraction for the kind of layman who was commonly called a "pillar of the church": because of the fact that it swung the pendulum back toward religious individualism, it was a more reliable support than Modernism for the economic system in which such a layman lived and moved and had his being. A layman of the sort who was interested in maintaining the *status quo* need not require that the Church lend its sanction to, let us say, the open shop; it would suffice if the Church declined to pass judgment upon social questions and returned to "the old-time religion"—that is, to the saving of individual souls. Theologically, the outcome of all this was a controversy between the "social" and the "individual" gospel; this, in its relationship to the rising power of the church layman, will be the subject of our next chapter.

Fundamentalism also helped to diminish the influence of the Social Gospel upon the American layman in a more indirect fashion. Incidents such as the Scopes trial undercut the intellectual and moral prestige of religion in general, hence, that of representatives of the Church whenever speaking in their capacity as churchmen, and, hence, that of secular movements claiming religious sanction, such as the Social Gospel.

We have observed this same phenomenon in connection with Prohibition, and the fact that prohibitionism and Fundamentalism in the 20's found strong mass support in the same geographic regions and among the same kind of people greatly reinforced the discrediting effect. The Fundamentalist controversy, coupled with the election of 1928, focused national attention upon the "Bible Belt"; and Mr. Mencken's part-for-whole brand of anticlericalism was highly convincing for many who observed that the most conspicuously Bible-based culture in the land was at the same time the most conspicuously ignorant.

Indeed, it was even suggested that the Fundamentalists were themselves paying unwilling tribute to secularism. "In religion," the liberal German theologian Adolf Harnack had said perceptively in a lecture in 1900, "rigorism always forms the obverse side of secularity," [19] and in 1927 Reinhold Niebuhr declared, "Extreme orthodoxy betrays by its very frenzy that the poison of scepticism has entered the soul of the church; for men insist most vehemently upon their certainties when their hold upon them has been shaken. Frantic orthodoxy is a method for obscuring doubt." [20]

There was nevertheless an intrinsic power in the Fundamentalist critique of the Social Gospel, which one did not need to be a political conservative to find attractive. It appealed to many plain people for whom the Social Gospel and the liberal theology which went with it, far from being too radical, were insufficiently critical of the existing order. Even the wildest millennialist apocalypses, after the horrors of the First World War, seemed more plausible to some than the liberal faith in automatic and inevitable progress. The religious attack upon Darwin was in a sense eschatological; the ascent of man was confounded and set at naught by the judgment of God. And the Social Gospel, with its coolly melioristic solution of all the world's ills, simply did not seem to do justice to the tragedy of living.

Fundamentalism's naïve but genuine warmth and individuality, also, carried a nostalgia that transcended the merely political. The impersonalism of modern mass society had penetrated the churches too; they were, after all, organizations of hundreds of thousands of people. Love of one's fellows can dissipate in the machinery set up to put it into practice, and a social liberalism designed to bring men to the fulfillment of personality can, in operation, be thoroughly impersonal. People whose protests were of this deeper sort were in the 1920's rapidly filling new small sects whose spontaneity and individualism, however indecorous from the standpoint of the intelligentsia, satisfied needs which the rational conservative church and the rational liberal church both overlooked. Between 1926 and 1952 the major Protestant denominations were to show an average membership increase of 60 per cent; but new Fundamentalist sects—Pentecostals, Churches of God, Holiness Churches —were to gain *between 400 and 900 per cent*.[21] Much of what they were striving for is reflected in a passage written in 1923 by perhaps the most perceptive and "intellectual" of all the Fundamentalist leaders, J. Gresham Machen:

At the present time, there is one deep longing of the human heart which is often forgotten—it is the deep, pathetic longing of the Christian for fellowship with his brethren. One hears much, it is true, about Christian union. . . . But the union that is meant is often at best . . . a forced union of machinery and tyrannical committees. . . . Sometimes, it is true, the longing for Christian fellowship is satisfied. There are congregations, even in the present age of conflict, that are really gathered around the table of the crucified Lord; there are pastors that are pastors indeed. But such congregations, in many cities, are difficult to find. Weary with the conflicts of the world, one goes into the Church to seek refreshment for the soul. . . . Alas, too often, one finds only the turmoil of the world. The preacher comes forward, not out of a secret place of meditation and power, not with the authority of God's Word permeating his message . . . but with human opinions about the social problems of the hour or easy solutions of the vast problem of sin.

Is there no refuge from strife? . . . Is there no place where two or three can gather in Jesus' name, to forget for the moment all those things that divide nation from nation and race from race, to forget human pride, to forget the passions of war, to forget the puzzling problems of industrial strife, and to unite in overflowing gratitude at the foot of the Cross? If there be such a place, then that is the house of God.[22]

Much more was at stake in the protest against Modernism than monkeys in Tennessee or Fascism in Kansas. Men could assent to this kind of criticism of liberal religion who would have found Bryan only pathetic.

It is a paradox that Fundamentalism, which as a movement in the history of the American churches was theologically and socially reactionary, was at the same time, as Herbert Schneider points out, "a twentieth-century movement of protest and unrest . . . apocalyptic, prophetic, critical . . . reflecting sensitivity to contemporary moral problems" in its very disillusionment with all secular solutions—including those given a Christian aura by the Social Gospel.[23] This aspect of its appeal reached far beyond the limitations of men capable of a literal Biblicism. Indeed, to formulate a world view which would answer this challenge and at the same time retain the Social Gospel has become a major task for American theology.

Postscript: 1971. No chapter in the 1956 version of the book drew more critical fire than this one. Although Fundamentalism, "like all other phenomena in human history," could "be correlated with material, mundane factors," Sydney Ahlstrom wrote (in the *Review of Religion* for March, 1957), still "the fact remains that the effort to find simple 'social sources' of Fundamentalism has never been satisfactory, whether it be a rural-urban, a sectional, or a social-class diagnosis that is attempted." And in a review of this book for *Religion in Life* (Spring, 1957), C. Howard Hopkins sharply commented: "The tacit assumption that Fundamentalism is a closed issue would appear to be somewhat unrealistic."

Mindful of observations like these, I have published more recently, under the title "The Fundamentalist Defense of the Faith," an essay which substantially revises the judgments of this chapter (see John Braeman *et al.*, *Change and Continuity in Twentieth-Century America: The 1920's*, Ohio State University Press, 1968, pp. 179–214). By an irony of history, "semi-Marxist" interpretations are now far more in vogue among American historians than they were when I was writing the book, and perhaps as a result some who have read both the 1956 and the 1968 treatments of Fundamentalism have told me they found the earlier version more persuasive.

CHAPTER V

The Churches' Business

in a Business Society

THE Social Gospel, as was seen in our first chapter, represented a sharp break with the past in American churches, not only politically but theologically as well. Walter Rauschenbusch, in writing his definitive formulation of that theology in 1917, contended that the Social Gospel compelled a re-thinking of the very nature of the religious experience itself:

The terms and definition of salvation get more realistic significance and ethical reach when we see the internal crises of the individual in connection with the social forces that play upon him or go out from him. . . . Any religious experience in which our fellow-men have no part or thought, does not seem to be a distinctively Christian experience. . . . When we submit to God we submit to the supremacy of the common good. Salvation is the voluntary socializing of the soul.[1]

Was this true? Was the Gospel social, or was it individual? Part of the sharp rejoinder of Fundamentalism to Modernism was a condemnation of this social understanding of man's religious situation. To believe and be saved, according to their way of looking at the matter, did not require such sophistication. But other voices, by no means Fundamentalist in temper, were raised to make the same objection: that the social liberals were neglecting what they considered the primary task of the Church, namely the winning of individual souls to the faith.

In 1911 there was established in the Federal Council of Churches a Commission on Evangelism to counterbalance the work of the Social Service Commission. From its inception, this body sometimes criticized the advocates of the Social Gospel for losing sight of that gospel's religious roots: "If anywhere social service has become solely a matter of humanitarian interest, and social betterments have anchored themselves only in a philosophy of vague good-will," the Commission declared in 1928, "it is time to repeat the words of Bushnell, 'The soul of reform is the reform of the soul.'" [2]

Nor were the terms of traditional evangelism the only way in which an "individual" gospel was affirmed. The "Oxford Groups" (not to be confused with the Oxford Movement), which arose in the 20's, challenged the Social Gospel in a more novel way. Based upon a curious marriage between Christian doctrine and the psychoanalytic concept of healing through self-revelation, these groups conducted mutual confessionals and searched for religious guidance in the secular surroundings of the English-type "house party." For them, the Social Gospel was not so much erroneous as irrelevant. When one of their leaders felt called upon in 1929 to answer some of the objections raised against the Oxford Groups—obscurantism, emotionalism, preoccupation with sex—he did not mention, even by implication, the feature which most disturbed liberals, the limitation of the Groups' appeal for practical purposes to the psychology and leisure-time arrangements peculiar to the well-to-do. He called the movement "a first-century Christian fellowship"; one wonders how much at home the slaves, lepers, and other outcasts among the first-century Christians would have felt in the atmosphere of a house party on Park Avenue. [3]

Still another individual challenge to the Social Gospel was developing among Protestant theologians in Europe. The "crisis-theology" of Karl Barth could be taken, if one chose, as a rebuttal to Walter Rauschenbusch. American churchmen, the Europeans seemed to feel, were cluttering modern man's search for his soul with an array of committees and programs designed to save a society which was by theological definition beyond redemption. I shall defer further comment upon this European critique until a later chapter; of more immediate relevance to our discussion is the affinity between the objections raised to the concept of social salvation—Fundamentalist, evangelical, psycho-religious, and theological—and the successful businessman's conviction that the workings of the society which nourished him were none of the Church's business.

There were two ways in which one of the "Christian men to whom God in His infinite wisdom has given the control of the property interests of this country" could express this conviction.[4] One was to dismiss the Social Gospel from its function of Christianizing the social order on the ground that the social order was already Christian; the other was to declare bluntly that Christian ethics had nothing to do with social policy.

Of the former view, the most startling statement was by Bruce Barton in *The Man Nobody Knows,* which is an exegesis of sorts from Luke 2:49, "Wist ye not that I must be about my Father's business?" Defining "business" in the strictly economic sense, Mr. Barton's biography extols Jesus Christ as the founder of salesmanship and advertising, in a fashion verging on blasphemy. (The Revised Standard Version translates the line "Did you not know that I must be in my Father's *house,*" which makes Mr. Barton's thesis singularly irrelevant.) The book was, in its day, a best seller.

Of the latter view, the weekly journal *Industry* furnishes us with an example. At the conclusion of a series of articles attacking the churches for their role in the 1919 steel strike, its editors charged that the Social Gospel leaders "intimated that the teachings of Jesus Christ should be brought into the in-

61

dustrial field"—presumably meaning that such an intimation was preposterous.[5]

A variation on this theme was the "leave-the-field-to-experts" argument: "Suppose the United States Chamber of Commerce or the National Association of Manufacturers," argued C. F. Adams, "should take a vigorous stand on such matters as infant baptism, papal infallibility, the literal inspiration of the scriptures, vicarious atonement, and the immaculate conception. Would the clergy accept these views as 'competent, material, or relevant'?"[6]

This was one of the most telling arguments against the Social Gospel, as many a minister could testify who had plunged into the struggle for secular power and been broken by sheer lack of knowledge and experience. Churchmen were in due course to work out a satisfactory intellectual solution to the dilemma here posed,[7] but meantime the force of the argument doubtless silenced many.

Nor were churchmen lacking to endorse wholeheartedly Mr. Adams's proposal that men's affairs be divided between experts speculating in two distinct species of futures. The social function of the churches, the *Presbyterian* editorialized, was "character-building": "to produce good men and so make good citizens." The Federal Council of Churches was "only a means of cooperation in religious and spiritual activities"; when it criticized imperialistic gestures toward Mexico, it became "meddlesome and presumptuous."[8] There was enough of such acquiescence in a "division of labor" between ministers and businessmen even in the midst of the vigorous Social Gospel of 1920 to prompt a charge by a writer in the *Christian Century* that "Religion Stagnates While Society Changes."[9]

But this setting of individual evangelism over against social reconstruction, as being, not merely distinct, but conflicting methods of saving mankind, tended to become a laymen's rather than a parsons' cause. In the first place, many more of the former were involved in the economic process as a primary vocation; and in the second, the churches declined officially to write a promissory note on the American business community for an ethical holiday. Rather, the characteristic official position of the Church came to be that the terms of the individual versus social gospel debate were spurious.

Torn as it was by Fundamentalism's first bid for control of the denomination, the 1920 Northern Baptist Convention took time out to bear witness to the Social Gospel. "No such antithesis exists between social service and evangelism as some have fancied," the *Baptist* declared; and, significantly, the *Watchman-Examiner,* champion of Baptist Fundamentalism, criticized the "heresy" of some of its comrades-in-orthodoxy who "sneer at the term 'social service' and deprecate all attempts to make the world a better place to live." [10] Similarly with the Methodists, "the Church . . . is not compelled . . . to follow where others lead," their bishops asserted. "Our authority is authority over every form of evil." [11]

Since the churches refused to come out for the individual as against the social interpretation of Christian ethics, those who stood to "profit most from the existing arrangement of society" had to meet the problem of preserving that arrangement from religious subversion at another level: that of the local church.[12] If it was impracticable—and undesirable, considering the churches' prestige as a stabilizing social force—to censor, for example, the pronouncements of a House of Bishops or a General Conference or a National Council, it was eminently practicable and desirable to censor some of the sermons preached in thousands of parish churches every Sunday. Laymen paid the piper; they were often in a position to call the tune. As one Fundamentalist leader put it, "They outnumber the preachers a hundred to one, and they are the ones who have to pay the bills." [13]

As for the ministers, in the words of a contemporary liberal, "It is less important that they create a new earth than that they raise the benevolence moneys which support the boards which ask them to create a new earth." [14] Complaints that "more and more men who are preaching the social implications of the Gospel are finding that their way is being made hard for them" were being heard even in 1920, as an undertow accompanying the Social Gospel's high tide. And nine years later, when a Federal Council of Churches commission recommended that "each local church should address itself to industrial conditions in its own community," a minister who had himself been a casualty of this struggle retorted: "No doubt it should. But the ministers who attempt to lead their churches in such a program will do well to save some of their energy with which to look for another job." [15]

Conservative businessmen who were members of local churches were immensely aided in their quest for a more congenial pulpit by the class structure of the American churches. The consensus of all surveys and estimates that have been made to my knowledge is that Protestantism in the United States has been overwhelmingly a movement of the middle and upper classes and the nonurban lower classes. "The number of church members in a population increases with both the economic and educational status of the members of the population," Hadley Cantril wrote in 1943; "or, conversely, the number of those without church membership increases as the income or educational levels are descended." [16]

That Protestantism is middle-class in membership is not by any means a recent discovery; this notion is the mainspring, after all, of Max Weber's *Protestant Ethic and the Spirit of Capitalism* and all the scholarly controversy generated thereby. But it becomes sharply significant when we consider a crucial power-area in American Christendom, namely that body of laymen—vestry, session, or official board—which is responsible for the financing and organization of the local church and in many denominations for the summoning and dismissing of ministers. A study of 387 church boards of the major denominations made in 1932 convinced its author that "there is a class control of the Protestant churches":

Fifty-five per cent of [the board members] are either proprietors, managers, or in some professional service. Omitting towns under 5,000, the merchants are by far the most numerous class on the boards, with the clerks and bankers ranking on the average next.

On all church boards, including those in towns under 5,000, in proportion to their numbers the bankers are most often elected chairmen, while manufacturers follow.[17]

In short, the clergyman was financially dependent upon "those men in his community who are least likely to approve . . . criticism of the existing economic order." [18] Nor should it be assumed that most, or even many, of the clergy differed enough in ideology from these men who paid their way that they needed to be silenced. Some clergymen saw in any proposed reconstruction of society a threat to the Church itself as an accepted element in the old order; the experience of the Church in Russia and Mexico was before them as a painful example. Moreover, the minister of more liberal views was confronted with a special dilemma: a consistent antagonism to the middle-class and upper-class majority of his congregation would injure his pastoral relationship to them.

Nevertheless, there were men who fought and were punished. One could fill out the remainder of this chapter with examples of the conservative squeeze upon the Social Gospel: letters, mostly anonymous, from the columns of the denominational papers, written by men who had been forced out of their pulpits for preaching social liberalism; accounts of such suppressions of the free pulpit as occurred during the A. F. of L. Convention of 1926, when the Detroit Board of Commerce succeeded in inducing the YMCA and most of the churches of that city to withdraw invitations to labor leaders to speak under their auspices; or descriptions of the "company churches" which Southern textile mill operators built and supported as adjuncts to their company towns in order to protect "their" people from college-trained ministers with "crazy socialistic ideas." [19]

But such a catalogue of small tyrannies would leave a basic question unanswered. The class membership and financial control of the Protestant churches seemed in the 20's to be having an effect on the fortunes of liberal ideas in those churches which it had not had to nearly the same extent during the decades before the First World War. The Social Gospel preached in the year 1920 could not have reached its pitch of vigor unless it had successfully overcome similar opposition directed against it in 1900 or 1910. Had not American capitalism been riding high between 1895 and 1915? And had there not, nevertheless, arisen a Social Gospel? Why was there a difference in the relationship between the Church and business before and after the war?

Part of the answer may lie in the fact that Big Business was even bigger in the third decade of this century than it had been in the first. If the banks of 1895 had been able to bail out a bankrupt federal treasury, the banks of 1925 were creditors to all the world. What the apotheosis of the dollar, which went with America's expansion, meant to the national consciousness is an oft-told story. This was an age when the United States could be described as "a mill which turns everything into business" —and its millwrights were the men who sat on the Church's boards of control.[20]

But it is not so much the pressure of these men on the Church, as in the Church, that is a measure of the difference between the pre- and postwar periods; for the visible Church is a creature as well as a maker of its times. "Our religious fellowship has not escaped the influence of big business tactics," the *Christian Advocate* asserted in 1929. "Highly accomplished exponents of 'pep' and 'push' sit in all our councils." [21] All sorts and conditions of men were caught up in the worship of their own prosperity in greater degree than ever before, and the Church itself was far from immune to this spirit.

In 1920, for example, under the auspices of the Interchurch World Movement (which, ironically, had also produced the report on the 1919 steel strike, discussed in Chapter II), some thirty American denominations for the first time in their history co-ordinated their individual budget plans into one united fund drive. They anticipated the raising over a period of five years of the staggering sum of $1,300,000,000. The primary motives for the campaign—their national and world responsibilities, including the vast challenge of postwar overseas relief in an era with no Marshall Plan—were unexceptionable. But into their implementation, as this drive's promotional literature clearly shows, there frequently crept the clamor of the high-pressure salesman and the jangle of the cash register.

If there is conflict between the ethic of Jesus and the ethic of the fast buck, then in such instances the Church, out of which the Social Gospel had come, was being undermined in its turn by the very economic order which the advocates of the Social Gospel were working to transform. The "prophet"—the socially critical minister—was set at odds with the "priesthood"—the ecclesiastical bureaucracy of which he was a part. The task of those who wished to silence him was made easier by the fact that the Church had already succumbed in large measure to their own standard of value.

Moreover, in any "church-type" denomination, there is always a good deal of accommodation to the reality of secular social power.[22] That reality, in the postwar period, differed from the prewar *status quo* not only quantitatively—in dollar volume, so to speak—but psychologically as well. From around 1902 until the outbreak of war, social reform had been respectable in a sense in which from around 1918 to 1929 it was not.

Progressivism, as a number of historians have reminded us, had been a movement of the middle class; its mass support came from the same elements of the population who made up the great bulk of the Protestant church membership. But this group, in the era of "normalcy," had for the most part bidden farewell to reform; such men did not turn out for the LaFollette-Wheeler ticket in 1924 in numbers even remotely comparable to the Roosevelt-Wilson-Debs reform landslide of 1912. The point to be drawn from this change is that the kind of man who in 1925 might have driven a minister from the pulpit for criticism of local employment practices would in 1910 have been almost as likely to be agitating for workmen's-compensation laws. Small wonder, then, that there had arisen a flourishing Social Gospel; and small wonder that when that gospel burst in all its vigor upon the brave new world of 1920, such citizens of that world as vestrymen and trustees, who in the earlier period had helped the social prophets to find a calling, now afforded them the opportunity for Christian martyrdom.

But there remains yet more to be said in explanation of this darkening atmosphere for the Social Gospel. A major change in the standing of the clergy in society had taken place during that intervening generation. It may be illustrated in the experience of the early Social Gospel leader W. S. Rainsford, rector of the fashionable St. George's Church in New York during the 1880's and 90's. His senior warden happened to be the elder J. Pierpont Morgan. It is not to be supposed that their social and economic views dwelt together in amity. Yet Morgan never, as wealthy vestrymen were to do in similar situations in the 20's, sought to silence Rainsford. They disagreed, violently; but Morgan was a devout Episcopalian and deferred even to Rainsford's desire to include wage earners as members of the vestry, because this man was an ordained priest and furthermore was Morgan's pastor.[23]

The point of this story is that the Social Gospel's pioneers had the advantage of the traditional deference accorded by believers to clergymen as custodians of the Word of God. But the Social Gospel's advocates of the 20's had this advantage in far less measure, because in the meantime America had become far more permeated with the spirit of secularism. Some of the reasons for this we have discussed already, notably the reflections of civilized men upon the moral and intellectual implications of Prohibition and Fundamentalism; others will be considered in a later chapter. In the meantime it should be observed that the spirit of secularism was abetted by any force which, like material prosperity and capital expansion, tended to displace religion as the *summum bonum*. I do not mean to imply that reaction and secularism are natural political allies (far from it, they are usually at swords' points), but, rather, that in this historical situation each possessed certain qualities which made for the strengthening of the other.

The claim of religion upon men's loyalty is, if not absolute, at any rate central; hence, as H. E. Luccock has suggested, "A pious 'spirituality' which accepts the exclusion of its religion from the political and economic realm worships a God who does not really count in this world." [24] But the individual gospel which I suggested earlier was the characteristic ethical rationale

68

of the uninhibited businessman came down to just such a "pious spirituality." In other words, the relationship between political reaction and the secularist spirit in the 20's was reciprocal. If the former gave the latter room to grow by exalting the profit motive at the expense of the religious ethic, the latter facilitated the former's incursions into and control of pulpit opinion by reducing the special psychological aura which had sometimes in the past preserved the minister from rough handling by his fellow men. The nature of the churches' business in a business society was determined not only by the degree to which they were permitted to make effective in that society the faith for which they stood, but by the effectiveness, in and out of the churches, of that faith as an active motivation for the reasoning and behavior of men.

Postscript: 1971. Bruce Barton's *The Man Nobody Knows* has long been held up to scorn as an example of Babbitt at his vacuous best. But Donald Meyer, in his stimulating study of *The Positive Thinkers* (1965) , has reminded us that Barton's version of Christ—not as "a man of sorrows and acquainted with grief," but as a man of "supreme heedlessness . . . spontaneous laughter . . . inner abundance"—carried also a message that America's repressed Victorian–Protestant 'culture badly needed to hear. By 1970 the Protestant avant-garde, as evidenced in the book reviews the *Christian Century* published in its number for All Fools' Day (Vol. LXXXVII, April 1, 1970, pp. 389ff.) , had responded to this need by evolving a "theology of play."

CHAPTER VI

The Changing Ministry:

A Study in Clerical Self-Respect

A HIGHLY successful Presbyterian minister, in excellent standing with his church, declared in 1930 that it was "a fairly safe generalization to say that no profession of men is so thoroughly empty of dignity and grace as that of the Protestant ministry today." [1]

The clergyman whose gospel continued to be social rather than individual in the Harding-Coolidge-Hoover era lay in no bed of roses. But this quotation suggests that some of his troubles did not stem from the Social Gospel alone. These are harsh words for any man to say about his own professional class; were they true?

Evidently, to judge from the denominational press of those years, they were acknowledged as true in the Church. We are told that "relatively few of the keenest-minded, most highly-endowed of the young men in our colleges are going into the ministry today [1929]," because the "man of affairs," who was the culture-hero of the age, seldom "says or does anything to indicate that he regards the Christian ministry as a real challenge to a man who wants to do big, worth-while things with his life." Other "red-blooded" young men avoided the ministry to keep from being placed on the far side of a "great gulf . . . between the clergy and the rest of the human family," some of whom "positively refuse to treat the minister as a real man." Those who did go into the ministry were recruited "haphazardly" and were often "mediocre men . . . who have failed in other kinds of work." They were accused of preaching "dull and uninteresting" sermons which were "not related to life." Such social deference as they did receive was a "sham"—"a device for limiting the activity of a troublesome character who makes most people feel uncomfortable." And at the last, disillusioned and exhausted in this "hazardous calling," which one of them called "a trapeze performance without any net," many of the abler ones voluntarily left the ministry.[2]

There were, of course, pastors in plenty during the decade 1920–1930 to write and speak of the ministry as "the most satisfying calling in the world"; but throughout the period this darker theme persists.[3] Of course, the clergy had been under fire before; "no institution and no established order really likes prophets," as Bishop Parsons put it.[4] But at other times in American history when the ministry had been attacked, as, for example, during the disestablishment controversy in New England, in which the power of the Puritan state-churches was broken, the criticism had been of a somewhat different kind. The ministry had then been a vocation of high social prestige which drew into its ranks many of the ablest men of the time; the opposition to it had been a popular protest against an elite. What we have in these complaints of the 1920's, on the other hand, is the assertion that the ministry was no longer an elite at all.

The actual objective status of the clergy in the 1920's is somewhat difficult to assess. The utterances of H. L. Mencken and his imitators, and the favorable reviews of such books as Sinclair Lewis's *Elmer Gantry,* give the impression that all reasonable men in the 20's went out bagging preachers for breakfast.

71

VERNON REGIONAL
JUNIOR COLLEGE LIBRARY

The utterances of the Presidents of the United States, who do, after all, reflect one facet of public opinion (even Mr. Harding), give the impression that America's Protestant Christian faith expressed itself through the churches and their pastors with traditional power. To see the actual social status of the clergy in the 20's more clearly, we must examine something more crassly tangible: the financial relationship between these ministers and their constituencies.

If the epigram that "America has no honors list except the tax list" was true of America in the 1920's, then the honors of the ministry were few indeed.[5] In 1918, a *Literary Digest* survey had indicated that a scant 1,671 out of 170,000 ministers in the United States paid taxes on incomes of over three thousand dollars. Two years later, the Interchurch World Movement survey of the material state of the Church disclosed an average annual pastoral income of $937.[6] The revelation of this state of affairs seems to have aroused churchgoers' consciences and led to a general rise in ministerial salaries, but not enough to bring them abreast of the cost of living. Will H. Hays—one of the last persons who might have been expected to view an aspect of the economic *status quo* with alarm—told the 1923 Presbyterian General Assembly that together a minister and his wife in that church received, "to keep them and their family clothed and fed, about $30 a week—scarcely more than the wage of the garbage collector. . . . The complaint is made that there is a dearth of promising young men in the ministry. How could it be otherwise?"[7]

The *Homiletic Review,* a monthly journal edited specifically for preachers and having considerable standing among them, led off one discussion of ministerial salaries by saying: "When a clergyman was offered a professorship the other day he declined it, as his present occupation yields him five hundred dollars a month. He is a plasterer." This article, titled "Honest Pay for the Preacher," continued with a comparison between the average weekly salary paid to the ministers of seven major denominations and the average weekly wage paid to a comparable variety of workers in industry and the building trades. Dis-

72

VERNON REGIONAL
JUNIOR COLLEGE LIBRARY

counting parsonage rent for the one, and bonuses and overtime for the other, a Baptist minister made a few cents less per week than did a boot and shoe worker; a Methodist minister made a dollar a week more than did a furniture maker; and a Congregational minister's wages compared very favorably with those of an electrical worker or hod carrier and were only $3.62 a week short of those of an iron and steel worker. As for masons, plumbers, plasterers, and bricklayers, the clergy were hopelessly outclassed.[8]

This article attracted considerable attention, including an editorial in the New York *Times,* but the indignation aroused does not appear to have had much practical effect. The *Churchman,* which had filled many pages in 1920 with a muckraking series on "The Sweated Ministry: Behind Rectory Doors," was editorializing on the same theme nine years later. The Methodist General Conference did not get around even to recommending a minimum salary until 1928. And the *Congregationalist* was denouncing the skimpy pay of ministers in its issue of June 27, 1929, during the last hectic fever of national prosperity before the chill of depression.[9]

The U.S. Government's *Census of Religious Bodies* undertaken in 1926 unfortunately did not deal with this matter; but such evidence as we have is sufficient to establish my point, namely, that the minister at that time was at one with the public school teacher in receiving the compensation of a salaried employee for ostensibly professional services. It may occur to the reader that poverty and the ministry have been closely associated before; the Baptist farmer-preacher and the Methodist circuit-rider come to mind in particular. But that had been the poverty of the frontier, or at any rate of the rural hinterland. As was observed in connection with Prohibition, the United States had by 1920 clearly passed the dividing line between a rural and an urban civilization. Ministerial poverty now meant the poverty of the city and the suburb, where the folkways of acquired wealth were inescapable; and the psychological consequences of such a state of affairs were disastrous.

I am assuming here that the standing of the clergy, in a

society largely committed to a pecuniary scale of value, would be reflected in that society's determination of how much the clergy was worth in terms of that scale. If this assumption is valid, then that standing was obviously rather low. Furthermore, the society's judgment of the clergy's usefulness was further shown in the fact that in many quarters the clergy's demand for better compensation was not only refused but actively resented.

This is reflected in the tone of the editorials which called for this reform. The editors did not merely point out a neglected area of human need; they found it necessary to answer objection. " 'A preacher should not work for money,' it is true," admitted a correspondent of the *Homiletic Review* and then went on to explain why salary increases were nevertheless necessary.[10] The denominational papers frequently found it necessary to defend the ministers from charges that they were "too worldly" and "in it for the money." An editorial in the *Congregationalist* was particularly sharp toward those who urged the minister to rejoice in the opportunity his poverty offered him to exercise Christian humility: "The Franciscan ideal of poverty is an ideal that might well be confined to those of Franciscan vocation. . . . Let us avoid . . . glorification of poverty, which is too often a sheer horror and an unmitigated curse." [11]

The low estate of the clergy is further reflected in the frequent charge that the minister often had great difficulty in collecting even the pittance due him. A minister's wife wrote of arriving at a church to take up pastoral duties with resources of $1.17 and then having literally to beg the church treasurer for an advance. This church in theory paid an annual salary of $800, "but we never received the whole amount any year we were there." Another pastor said of his income of $600 per year from a backwoods parish that "four hundred came from the Home Missions Board, and came promptly. The other two hundred . . . came on when [the] church treasurer got around to attending to business." [12]

In the smaller churches, of course, this sort of thing often reflected only the poverty of the congregation—although the first writer quoted above went on to express resentment at "smug, self-complacent, well-fed parishioners." Moreover, where one deals with any community service which does not supply an obvious physical need—this applies with equal force to, for example, public education—the line between inability and unwillingness to give financial support to such service is not easily drawn. Then, too, laymen often scrambled cause and effect in discussing preachers' salaries; the minister's mendicancy was assumed to be, not a consequence of the social status which they had granted him, but a cause. The tragedy in such cases was that it soon became both.

The ministry, in the words of Glenn Frank, demanded of its membership the qualities of "a medieval saint, a carelessly courageous agitator, an expert in mental hygiene, and the bustling head of a business corporation"—all for thirty dollars a week and a parsonage.[13] That this demand was not always met should occasion no surprise. There was, in the first place, the sheer physical curtailment of a minister's professional effectiveness which a severely limited income entailed. "Why don't we have a better pulpit?" a Methodist writer asked in 1929, and answered himself: "No money, no books, no travel, no world contact!" [14]

But far more of a restraint upon the pastoral function was the sense of insecurity which such a status gave to the minister in the company of his bourgeois parishioners. One layman remarked of his pastor that "he can't speak with authority to men on Sunday and ask favors of them during the week"; or, as a professor in one of the church colleges put it, men were not turned away from the ministry so much by the hardship of low income as by "the natural self-respect which causes a man to revolt from being an object of pity." "Sacrifices forced upon the clergy," the *Churchman* editorialized, "involve a loss of real dignity that no amount of uncomplaining acquiescence will make up for." [15]

The heart of this matter is that since the Protestant churches' membership was drawn from the upper and middle classes, and since the typical minister had therefore to exercise his spiritual leadership largely within those classes, it became incumbent upon him to order his personal affairs in a fashion which would induce them to accept him as a leader. This included keeping abreast of their living standards, regardless of the cost to himself and to his family. He must belong to civic organizations, entertain, and contribute to charities. James Moffatt, British professor of theology and a translator of the Bible, observed on a visit to the United States in 1926 that American "ministers have few studies and their libraries are depressingly thin. But they all seem to have motor cars." In plain words, the minister was being compelled to live beyond his means.[16]

Ministers were known to be notoriously slow payers on charge accounts. They counted heavily on favors and "donations" from tradesmen. The Association of Congregational Ministers of New Haven, Connecticut, in proposing a code of professional ethics for the clergy comparable to those of bar and medical associations, significantly included in its draft a requirement that "the minister should be scrupulously honest, avoid debts, and meet his bills promptly." [17]

The result was inevitable: an habitual state of shabby gentility. And in the public discussions of the plight of the clergy, the ministers dwelt upon this psychology of well-bred mendicancy as much as upon the physical hardships involved. And well they might, for the effort to keep up with the Joneses, on smaller resources than the Joneses commanded, involved a considerable adoption, in practice at least, of the Joneses' materialist standard of human worth.

This pragmatic "materialism" was just as inescapable for the preacher of the Social Gospel as for the preacher of the *status quo;* therefore it tended to make any thoroughgoing pulpit attack upon that *status quo* seem a trifle academic. So a Marxist observer might expect, at this juncture, that clergymen of liberal persuasion, thus trapped in a very real sense in the "class struggle," would have cried a plague on the unregenerate middle class which used them so ill and carried their ministry into the social classes that were calling for reform. Some, indeed,

disillusioned or exhausted, did break completely with their profession and decline further ministry to *any* social class. But Social
Gospel ministers did not, in any significant numbers, leave
their parishes for the purpose of carrying their ministry into
groups having a more congenial social outlook.

There was, to be sure, some justice in the argument that
after all it was the middle class that needed the Social Gospel;
a trade-unionist did not need to be convinced of the soundness
of the mildly prolabor axioms in the Social Creed of the churches.
On the other hand there was the ever-present danger of pater-
nalism in a Social Gospel which preached uplift of the workers
rather than preaching social action to the workers. This had,
similarly, been a weakness of the prewar Social Gospel, but in
a time of more overt class cleavages such a defect was more
serious. It meant, in particular, a deeper consciousness of social
distance between the churchman and the workman. As Warren
S. Stone, head of the Brotherhood of Locomotive Engineers,
expressed it in 1924, "The main reason why the average clergyman does not understand the workers' problems is because he
does not associate with the workers. . . . The prominent members of his church and the intimate friends whom he invites to
his dinner table are almost invariably persons without any
connection and often without any sympathy for organized
Labor." [18]

The clergy, then, in the decade of the 20's, was committed on
the whole to a ministry to the middle class, but it was a clergy
too low in public esteem to reach even that class effectively with
its message. Probably the editors of the *Christian Century* had
this in mind when they stated categorically in 1926 that "reaction in America does not fear the Church." [19] The pulpit, its
freedom challenged by the pew, demanded "virility" and sum-
moned "our strongest men" to its service, said Lynn Harold
Hough in 1929, for only such men could stand against the pressures of conformism.[20] But could a man stay strong under the
conditions I have just described? And how many strong men
would submit to conditions like these in choosing a career?

Nor was this situation wholly a function of the clergy's economic condition; intellectually, also, their status in America had changed.

"The minister," a prominent urban pastor told seminary students in 1929, "has long ceased to be, saving the lawyer, the doctor, the school teacher, the only learned man in his parish. He is in competition with every kind of printed and spoken word." [21] He presumably needed, therefore, better training for his task than ever before. Yet, judging by the standards of the theological seminaries at that time, he was less well-equipped vocationally than the majority of the members of other professions.

A three-year investigation by the Institute of Social and Religious Research was reported in 1924 in Robert L. Kelly's *Theological Education in America*. "With rare exceptions," the author wrote in summation, the theological seminaries were "not conspicuous as centers of scholarly pursuits"; "goodness rather than intelligence" was "held up as an end in theological teaching." This was particularly evident at the level of admissions; "relatively few seminaries scrutinize carefully the academic training of incoming students in terms of standards usually prevailing elsewhere." Less than one half the students at the one hundred seminaries examined were college graduates; a third of them had never attended any college; and even "among the strictly graduate seminaries which admit only college graduates to the first year, there is no generally accepted definition of a college or list of colleges generally approved." Only Yale, Chicago, Harvard, Union, and a very few other divinity schools were excepted from this harsh judgment.

Courses and teaching methods came in for criticism also on a number of grounds: superannuated and overworked professors; "loyalty oaths" (creedal statements), sometimes of intricate dogmatic detail, exacted of many faculties and of some student bodies; inadequate training in aesthetics (including religious art and architecture), science, and educational methods; and a virtual absence of field work. The *Homiletic Review* followed Mr. Kelly's study with a questionnaire to its own subscribers, which revealed the startling information that in some instances not even the elements of the practical ministry itself were being taught: "We read that some of the seminaries fail to instruct ministers how to administer the sacraments, how to perform the marriage rite, how to conduct funerals, how to receive members." [22]

That all these findings were founded upon fact is witnessed by the reactions to them on the part of the theological schools themselves. The *Homiletic Review* sent another questionnaire to the deans or presidents of 130 seminaries, and in spite of the tendency of any institutional head to view-with-satisfaction when confronted with public criticism, this query drew a surprising number of answers conceding that "there is scarcely any criticism that has been made of theological seminaries that is not in a measure justified." [23] Denominations, also, were beginning to take official notice of the problem; the Presbyterian General Assembly of 1927 adopted a report declaring war upon "low intellectual . . . standards for those entering the ministry." [24]

That the churches were just beginning in the 20's to move for correction of these conditions suggests that they were the victims of a cultural lag from the days of a different kind of American churchmanship. Along the trans-Appalachian frontier and beyond, there had been at one time a widespread prejudice against an educated clergy; the sentiment lingers to this day in parts of the "Bible Belt." But in an age when the other professions, notably medicine and the law, had adopted graduate training for virtually all their membership, this prejudice would not serve. Many clergymen in the twentieth century were still receiving the training of apprenticeship-cum-hard-knocks which in the nineteenth century had also produced doctors, lawyers, and teachers—but did so no longer. And in a culture which paid at least lip service to the value of education, a charge of intellectual inadequacy was devastating. Confronted with the fact of the low social standing of the clergy, men could retort simply, "Is the laborer worthy of his hire?"

As the charge of social and economic heresy brought down upon the minister the wrath of the conservative laity, the charge of professional incompetence brought upon him the condescension of liberals who otherwise might have sympathized with his fight for a Social Gospel. "The ministry," declared Heywood Broun, "is the only learned profession in which a man may close his mind forever at the moment of ordination"; [25] a judgment which was spelled out in more detail by Edwin E. Slosson, director of Science Service:

We are in the midst of the greatest revolution of thought that the world has ever seen. The Einstein theory of relativity, the Planck theory of quanta, the chromosome theory of heredity, the hormone theory of temperament . . . these ideas will influence the philosophy, theology, religion, and morals of the future as much as did the Copernican theory in the sixteenth century and the Darwinian theory in the nineteenth. Such questions would have arrested the keenest interest in the minds of men like Edwards, Berkeley, Calvin, Aquinas, or Paul. A student in engineering or biology will sit up half the night discussing these theories, but your modern theological graduate is bored by them.[26]

There was sharp disagreement with this last statement by some churchmen, who cited in rebuttal the use of sound historical scholarship in Biblical "higher criticism" and the growing awareness of psychoanalytic insights as an adjunct to pastoral counseling. But as one reads samples of this effort to correlate secular and religious knowledge, the superficiality of so many of them moves one to accept the essential soundness of criticisms like Slosson's. The Fundamentalist-Modernist literature tends to be intellectually thin, on both sides of the controversy; liberal "harmonizations" of Genesis and geology are only slightly more edifying than such tracts for the times as *God or Gorilla* and *Evolution Disproved*.

In the judgment of the then President of Union Theological Seminary, "the recent hideous and obsolete controversy between the Fundamentalists and the Modernists came from an uneducated ministry"—which is one more reason why that controversy made the Gospel, social or otherwise, less attractive to those who stood outside the Church.[27] Certainly a preaching message which did not use the new knowledge of the twentieth century authoritatively could not strike home to a congregation among many of whom this knowledge was taken for granted. "No mentally lazy man," a Congregationalist leader warned, "should ever be ordained to the ministry. . . . If our religion is to keep its place as a vital force in the inquisitive world of today and keep the respect of the world's scholarship, the minister must be a first-rate thinker" [28]—on a third-rate income. There is here the making of a vicious circle: intellectual inferiority in the ministry breeds lowered respect for the minister, which breeds a lowered salary scale, which breeds further inferiority.

But an intellectual difficulty of another sort confronted even the most gifted of clergymen: the beginning of a genuine failure of communication between the secular and the religious mind. If the vocabulary of the common-sense empirical world view had changed to such an extent that the minister used it awkwardly, the vocabulary of the Biblical world view was passing out of secular usage entirely. If the minister and the layman would communicate, the layman had some things to learn as well as the minister.

Compare, for example, the casual familiarity with the language of the Bible shown by writers and speakers in nineteenth-century America—as striking, in its own way, as the casual Latin elegance of the literate members of the British upper classes—with the phenomenon noticed by platform speakers and others in our own time, namely, that an audience generally does not recognize a scriptural quotation unless the speaker explicitly designates it as such. Formal theology is in far worse case; the Calvinistic debates of the eighteenth century, which educated laymen could and did follow, now make difficult reading for anyone not specifically trained in their vocabulary. Once in a while, in the 1920's, it was suggested that even the sermon was obsolete and that preaching had become entirely hieratic in character: "Witness the changes in voice, manner of speech, grammatic structure, and so forth, when the preacher steps down from the pulpit. He is no longer the same person." [29] A case in point is the young seminary graduate who began his parish ministry in a slum area of New York City with a sermon on the ontological proof of the existence of God!

There were those in the Church whose attitude toward this

state of affairs was positivistic: very well, let the outdated dis-
course pass from the scene that the message of the Church may
be fully adapted to the needs of modern times. Let the theological seminaries avoid teaching doctrine as such; perhaps, indeed,
they no longer have a place, and should be replaced by faculties
of religion in the secular universities. Let the local church be
a community center, and let the minister be a psychological
counselor. The trouble with this viewpoint was that it would
have adapted the Church clean out of existence. Secularists were
quick to point this out and ironically praised the Fundamentalists for their logical consistency in going all out for ob-
solescence.

The prospect for the pastor in this situation was, to say the
least, discouraging. Even assuming that he was competent and
conscientious, of independent means, and able to break the
barrier of communication, his message would still often be obscured by the triviality of much of what he had to do—"give
the glad hand to the strangers at the church door and . . . teach
Boy Scouts that they should salute the flag—things that a pump-
handle or drill-sergeant could do as well." [30] The churches themselves by that time were deeply tinged with American secular
values, as we observed in our last chapter; and a consequence
was a preoccupation with activity and statistics. "The Churches
in the long run would get further," a former Congregationalist
minister suggested, "if their activities were marked by less
commotion and more insight." [31]

Nevertheless, there were those who refused to respond to the
challenge of an untheological age simply by adjusting to it.
Halford E. Luccock, at a Yale convocation in 1928, denied that
one could "speak healingly" to the modern mood "with a message without doctrine." There was no "place in this picture for
the apostolic business of upsetting the world. This kind of
church would not upset a teacup."

Had he gone on from there simply to exhort a return to
religion, this speaker would have paid one more tribute to
the consciously nonreligious spirit of the 20's. But toward the
end of his address he struck a new note. Frankly accepting the

fact that organized Christianity in the United States was ceasing to be a part of the accepted order of things, he said, in effect, what if it is? The early Church, in the Roman catacombs, had "had its most glorious period in history"; in other words, a religion need not be in the ascendant to be at its best. The Church did not need to "make good," as in an American success story, in order to be the Church. "Our most urgent task is not the extension of Christianity as a conventional majority faith; it is rather the preservation of its essentially Christian quality and purpose." [32]

Such a statement completely changed the significance of the low social standing of the clergy. If churchmen took it seriously, then what was under fire was not a profession but an ideology; thereby, some of the odium on the profession was removed and some of its dignity restored. (Did not something similar to this happen more dramatically with the Russian Orthodox priesthood in the years following the Bolshevik Revolution?) As a spokesman for the American majority, the minister, in George C. Stewart's words, had become "an emblematic figure, picturesquely valuable only at christenings and weddings and funerals"; but as a spokesman for a minority, even for a minority within the Church, he could still claim to practice "the highest, and the broadest, and the deepest of all vocations." His function was as crucial for the lay churchgoer as that of his physician, the teacher of his children, or the arbiter of his political and economic destiny. In the eyes of that lay churchgoer and in fact, the minister might be a financial cripple, inferior in intellectual and general executive ability to the other members of recognized elites, or a remote personality wrapped in archaisms; yet the challenge of the calling remained: "There is no sphere of human life which the vocation of a clergyman does not intersect. He must be apostle, and prophet, and scribe, and scholar, and sage, and seer, and teacher, and pastor, and evangelist, and—God help him!—a saint." [33]

And if he were a spokesman for the Social Gospel, he must turn his attention to areas of the Christian faith which he had overlooked before the war. All species of belief, social and individualistic, Modernist and Fundamentalist, experiential and theological, were under fire; this common fate was prior to the differences among them; thus the liberals in the Church began to lose their impatience with systematic theology in a search for an intellectually respectable Defense of the Faith. The way had been prepared for the rise and flourishing of the brothers Niebuhr—"socially to the Left, theologically to the Right" of the American Christianity of the prewar years.

Postscript: 1971. The concept of the clergy as an embattled and (therefore?) creative minority in a hostile world is a favorite one with many a clergyman, particularly as he moves from the high-level doubts and difficulties posed for his faith in the classroom and the study to the more mundane frustrations of the parish, and the foregoing chapter may betray a considerable insensible absorption of just such an ethos. ("There is something pathetic about this thesis that as the spokesmen for the visible churches obviously became less and less influential in America, churchmen tended to take refuge in a conception of the 'witness' of 'the Church,'" wrote Sidney E. Mead in his 1957 *Church History* review of this book.) The notion dies hard; in his farewell blast "Why I'm Leaving the Church" (*Look*, April 29, 1969), James A. Pike referred to contemporaries who "took an optimistic view of the shrinking of the Church: the faithful remnant would be a hard core of committed, self-sacrificing, courageous witnesses." There have always been, and doubtless always will be, such witnesses, but Pike doubted that they were representative of what was happening to the Church as a whole: "The poor may inherit the earth, but it would appear that the rich—or at least the rigid, respectable and safe—will inherit the Church."

CHAPTER VII

The Impact of

Secularism and War

REINHOLD NIEBUHR inaugurated his productive literary life in 1927 with a book titled *Does Civilization Need Religion?* In characteristic Niebuhrian fashion, his opening sentences threw cold water upon the optimism of fellow American Christians: "Religion is not in a robust state of health in modern civilization," he began bluntly. "Vast multitudes . . . live without seeking its sanctions . . . and die without claiming its comforts." [1] Their religious loyalty was being given to a complex set of forces tending to displace religion and all its works from the scene, a set of forces which in previous chapters I have termed "secularism."

This is a highly controversial word. It is, somewhat unwarrantedly, used rather as a swear word by many churchmen. And secularists themselves often refuse to concede that their dissent from or indifference to organized religion is itself religious in character. Yet it is a useful word, from the very fact that it embraces such a wide spectrum of opinion, all the way from the member of the American Association for the Advancement of Atheism to the man who merely prefers to go fishing on Sunday morning. If the word is not used, then the side of the 1920's which it connotes would have to be described by some such academic barbarity as "nonreligiousness." So I use the word "secularism" without further apology.

It follows that I do not use it in any sense of moral opprobrium. The most striking secularist figure of the 1920's was probably Mr. Bryan's forensic opponent, Clarence Darrow—a man whose writings and actions constitute an integrated humanist pattern, with a richness of ethical motivation and a sensitivity to values which reflect a spirit of high moral maturity, although his world outlook was one in which religion (as usually understood) found no resting place whatever. His secularism was far more challenging to the orthodox than was the somewhat sophomoric God-killing practiced by H. L. Mencken and his followers; men could dismiss the antireligious ire of an *Elmer Gantry,* but they could not dismiss Darrow's Roman naturalist cry that "nothing human is alien to me."

Not that the Mencken type of attack on religion was not devastatingly effective at times. For, as we have already noted in passing, there was much in the religion practiced in the 1920's to make it a fair target. Prohibition, and the identification of Christianity with political reaction and sour asceticism; Fundamentalism, and the identification of Christianity with bigotry and irrationalism; a declining clergy, and the identification of Christianity with social and intellectual ineffectiveness—these called forth the powers of destructive criticism. Intellectuals in the 20's were crusading against a variety of "Puritan" and "frontier" survivals in American folkways, and since some of religion's most spectacular manifestations in that decade were both puritanical and barbaric, religion was inevitably in for some rough handling.

Nor was the power of secularism visible only in attacks upon the Church from outside; it was evident also in the alarm of churchmen at the diminishing power of religion in men's lives. Some of this was no more than the active concern for the faith which has characterized leaders of all ideologies in all ages, but it was another matter when a man of the stature of Harry Emerson Fosdick asserted that "our Christian churches show . . . signs of senility." [2] Secularism to be sure was not an invention of the 20's, for the faith of the fathers had not been quite such an unclouded certainty as was sometimes assumed for purposes of contrast. Nor, in the retrospect of the 1950's, does modern man's loss of faith appear to have been quite so irreversible as writers in the 20's sometimes assumed. Nevertheless, on balance, the relation between church and society had been drastically altered.

From a privileged position in the accepted order of things, Christianity seemed to be reverting existentially to its situation in New Testament times, when the Church had confronted a consciously pagan world. The causes of this swing to a situation in which the Church was once again a stranger in a world it never made are manifold, and a full exposition of them would take us over a broad reach of modern history, back at least to the breakup of the medieval synthesis of church and society (as Mr. Toynbee has done). I propose however to single out a few causes which are of peculiar relevance for the period we are discussing and for the Social Gospel.

Perhaps the most obvious of these causes is the new picture of the world and of man given through scientific discovery. Yet pure science is less of a threat to religion than is sometimes supposed. Other intellectual innovations have struck at the religious world view quite as heavily as have those of Darwin, Freud, and Ernst Mach; the seventeenth-century mystics could have told the modern existentialist a thing or two about the psychological effect of "the eternal silence of these infinite spaces" revealed by a new astronomy. But in their case the eventual product was a heightening, not a diminishing, of religious experience. This would suggest that scientific knowledge itself is probably of less importance as a force making for secularism than are popular extrapolations from it, written with an anticlerical animus not directly dependent upon the science itself.

Of these latter, in the United States of the 1920's, the number was legion. Such an argument could be as cogent as Corliss Lamont's *The Illusion of Immortality* (still required reading for Union Theological Seminary students as an example of the toughest fare the opposition has to offer), or it could be as homespun as that of the itinerant atheist who showed up at the Scopes Trial with a chimpanzee and offered to disprove God to the masses at ten cents a head.[3]

For the most part, when science was appealed to, neither the crusading unbeliever nor the defender of the faith had sufficient grasp on the method and vocabulary of science to know what he was talking about. But faulty argumentation has won converts only too often. The Soviet school teacher who was reported by Sir Bernard Pares to have told her class that thanks to Darwin men no longer believed in God was rather oversimplifying the history of ideas, but many of us know men who have lost their religion through almost as simple an exposure to "science" as this.

But the new scientific discoveries did far more to and for mankind than to provide him with material for religious debate. Entirely aside from theory, there was the direct social impact of technology, which for religion as for all man's other activities was enormously important. In a chapter of his significant study *Religion in Twentieth-Century America*, Herbert W. Schneider has followed out some of the results, particularly of that confluence of the transportation and industrial revolutions which is the modern city.

One of the more subtle consequences of urbanization, for example, is its effect upon religious acts themselves. What is "public worship," Schneider asks, when it is not founded upon a parish, that is to say upon a geographical rather than a functional neighborhood? In a mass civilization, churches are filled not with "congregations" but with "audiences"; "the service is more of a professional performance, less a community expression or folk art." [4] In short, whatever effect urban living has had toward the depersonalizing and standardizing of human relations, it has had also upon religion, since the quality of religious belief is so intensely personal a matter. In the words of a Social Gospel spokesman I have quoted extensively in other connections,

Living in an industrial order which continually denies and thwarts the essential human relations between men makes a real belief in a personal God more and more difficult. . . . The most formidable obstacle to a Christian theism today is not in the intellectual difficulties involved in a belief in a personal . . . God. It is, rather, the psychological . . . difficulty of holding that belief in a social and economic environment in which it is continually denied.[5]

Reinhold Niebuhr in the work we have already cited blamed this difficulty more specifically upon technology:

The applied sciences have created an impersonal civilization in which human relations are so complex, its groups and units so large, its processes so impersonal, the production of things so important, and ethical action so difficult that personality is both dwarfed and outraged in it.[6]

The claim here was not only that a declining belief in God had helped sharpen man's inhumanity to man, but the converse also: human limitation being what it is, man's image of God is only as good as man's image of man.

The most shocking creation of modern technology has been modern war. And, to paraphrase Niebuhr, in our times no groups and units of men have been so large, no processes so impersonal, nowhere has ethical action been so difficult, and nowhere has personality been so dwarfed and outraged, as in war. Consequently, nothing has contributed more heavily to the rise of secularism than has war. The point hardly needs elaboration—the theological problem of the suffering of the innocent, raised originally in the Book of Job, was multiplied so astronomically by the fact of world war that much else besides the strictly religious failures of aspiration by the men of the 1920's is understandable in its lurid light.

That war promotes religious revival is a conceit which some in the churches resuscitate for each new war. In the case of the First World War, the notion is effectively exploded by a study published in 1920 titled *Religion Among American Men*. This report represented careful evaluation of interviews with A.E.F. men overseas, replies to questionnaires, reports from chaplains, letters, conferences, and articles; and it made it quite clear that "trench religion" was in the same category as "death-bed repentance." The composite soldier of this report, did, it is true, almost unanimously profess some form of religious belief, but a belief so extremely vague in content and showing such "widespread ignorance on elementary religious matters" that it appeared to the report's editors that "all the Churches are busily engaged in creating nominal members."

And the men were found, more often than not, deeply critical of the Church even when they professed loyalty to its ideals. The Christianity "preached by the Church" (as distinguished from an aspired-to, "real" Christianity) was called "primarily a selfish thing—the seeking of a personal reward"; or, alternatively, "mainly a negative, prohibitory thing," administered by "an association of trained killjoys." Church members, said the soldiers, did not live up to their professed standards, and their lives were "often peculiarly colorless or narrow or effeminate." The Church was "a convenient institution for the performance of conventional ceremonies, venerable . . . but not much concerned with the real business of life"; "you go there to be married and buried." Much that it emphasized was "unimportant, uninteresting, and not especially relevant"; and the tasks it assigned were often trivial.[7]

Considering that this sample of opinion was obtained through chaplains, to whom soldiers spoke as to superior officers and might therefore have been expected to express themselves with army-wise discretion, this is a remarkable confirmation of the editors' judgment that "America is not a Christian nation in any strictly religious sense." Draftees, then as in other wars, were a fair cross section of Americans, and their criticism of the Church dramatically reflects the onrush of secularism.

To be sure, some of this criticism must have preceded America's entry into the war, but some of it was doubtless stimulated by the trauma of war itself and by the attitude of the Church toward the war. For the Church, rather than doing anything to mitigate the severity of the questions these men asked, gave special point to it by the quality of its religious response to the challenge of war.

In the first place, there is the merely negative fact that the war represented a practical failure of the Church's beliefs. "The final test of ideals," Niebuhr warned, "must include their ability to qualify human action." [8] By this test, the churches had sustained a crushing defeat in the mere outbreak of war. But this was not all. Had the churches gone down with their principles aloft, or, at any rate, treated the war as a grimly necessary compromise, the defeat would have been heavy enough. The full measure of the retreat of the churches is shown in the extent to which they not only accepted the war but went all out in its prosecution. This happened in all the belligerent countries of Christendom, including Germany and the United States.

If it had been possible to sustain the churches' Wilsonian mood of "a truly holy war," of a war "fundamentally . . . between pagan and Christian ideas of the organization of the world," the end of the story might have been different.[9] But the crusade inevitably ground its way to an end, and great was the hangover thereof. The publication by the new Bolshevik government of the prewar secret treaties of the former Russian regime was the first significant act in a movement of revulsion against all "holy wars"; soon, in the United States, men were muckraking the "inside" of the "war system" as furiously as they had once muckraked the "inside" of the capitalist system. And consider what a man of the 1920's, particularly if he had physically participated in the great crusade, must have thought when confronted with something like the following and told that it had been preached in a Christian pulpit in 1918:

Society has organized itself against the rattlesnake and yellow fever. . . . The boards of health are planning to wipe out typhoid and the black plague. Not otherwise, lovers of their fellow men have finally become perfectly hopeless with reference to the German people. They have no more relation to the civilization of 1918 than an orang-utang, a gorilla, a Judas, a hyena, a thumbscrew, or a scalping knife in the hands of a savage. These brutes must be cast out of society.[10]

Such official agencies as the Federal Council of Churches had of course been more restrained. While pledging "support and allegiance in unstinted measure" to the government, the Council had also promised to protect the conscientious objector, looked forward to reunion and reconstruction in enemy lands after the war, opposed vigilantism "toward those of foreign birth or sympathies," and testified "to our fellow-Christians in every land, most of all to those from whom for the time being we are estranged, our consciousness of unbroken unity in Christ." [11]

But unfortunately the performance did not come up to this statement of the ideal. The author of a careful study of the history of the Federal Council (written in 1940) was unable to find "a single instance in which a voice of criticism was raised against any aspect of the government's conduct" during the First World War. "The Federal Council simply accepted what the government did and interpreted it in religious terms to the people of the churches." In particular, the promise to the conscientious objectors was not implemented. Only in 1919, well after the brunt of the legal controversy had been borne by the Civil Liberties Bureau and by the "historic peace churches," Mennonite and the like, which had nothing to lose, did the Council "pass a resolution exonerating the War Department and politely asking amnesty for 'sincere' objectors." [12] Pacifism was an embarrassing subject, anyway; more popular was the preacher who is remembered as having told a group of prospective recruits that "I send you out not to die, but to kill Germans!" [13]

All of this, in the context of the evidence which we found for a militant and effective Social Gospel in the year 1920, makes extremely interesting reading. I have been discussing the roots of the secularism which during the succeeding decade was to be pitted against the Church and all its works, including the Social Gospel. It turns out that one such root lay in a failure of the Church to respond to a major challenge: war—a failure which took place prior to the more successful response of the Church to the social challenges of 1920. This suggests that the immediate background of the 1920 Social Gospel was one of lapse from the standard of criticism of society which had characterized the Social Gospel of the prewar years.

I am not contending that consistency with the Social Gospel tradition would necessarily have required the churches to go all out for pacifism, only that what the churches actually did do in the First World War constituted an abandonment of their independent role vis-à-vis secular society. And without such an independent role, a "social gospel" any more advanced than a mere formulation of that society's current creed is impossible. No wonder the spokesmen for the Social Gospel were beginning to preach of a discontinuity between the Church and the social order, in the hope of rescuing enough of the Church's perspective to save it from becoming a simple mirror of contemporary social trends, good, bad, and indifferent. For unless some such divorce were achieved, one day the ruin of the social order would involve the ruin of the Church, and there would be no Toynbeean "chrysalis" left over to redeem the social order afterward.

There remains one thing further to be said of the import for the postwar Social Gospel of the dynamics of secularism and war: that a chasm had opened between Social Gospel ministers and the secular (and secularist) political liberals of the kind with whom they had at least tacitly fellow-traveled in the kindlier prewar days.

"During the last war," Niebuhr asserted, "moral idealists of rationalistic persuasion, such as Bertrand Russell, Romain Rolland, Henri Barbusse and Bernard Shaw, were more detached in their perspective and freer of war hysterias than any religious leaders of equal standing." [14] For one who has read some of the samples of wartime preaching in Ray H. Abrams's *Preachers Present Arms,* the churches' ringing endorsements of the League of Nations have a hollow sound; and one begins to understand why the secular liberals by 1929 showed such a vast impatience with the Church as Heywood Broun expressed in his column in the New York *Telegram:* "In America the newspaper has become a far more effective ethical and moral instrument than the church. . . . If I were promoting some cause which seemed to me right and true I would rather have the help of one able editor than of a dozen preachers." [15]

Time would come when liberals would look less kindly upon the newspapers and when Broun himself would encounter one Fulton Sheen and eat some of his words, but that is another story. As of the 20's, the combination of the secularist spirit and the behavior of the churches was emasculating the Social Gospel of its moral authority. Walter M. Horton, writing in 1930, summed up the sense of a great many of his generation as they reflected back upon the First World War and its aftermath; and opinions like this, in and out of the churches, must be set against the vigorous and hopeful Social Gospel of 1920 which was described in our second chapter:

We trusted our political leaders, when they told us of the villainy of our enemies, and the unimpeachable purity of the aims by which we and our allies were inspired; and, rightly or not, the impression is now abroad that they betrayed us. We trusted our religious leaders, when they proclaimed their apocalyptic visions of a new heaven and a new earth, whose coming was contingent upon the military victory of the Allied Powers; and . . . we are pretty well convinced that *they* betrayed us. We trusted that God would, somehow, balance the stupendous evils of the war by an equal weight of good, that would immediately accrue to us in the post-war period; and if faith in God is declining today, it is because many feel that *that* faith, too, has betrayed them.[16]

Strangely enough, the Social Gospel abetted this unhappy trend as much as it fought it, to the extent that the Social Gospel itself reflected the secularistic mood. For there was secularism within as well as outside the Church. I have already touched upon this theme, in discussing the displacement of religious by business values in the conduct of church affairs. But, in addition, there were men in the churches who were opposed to the business values but were themselves committed to a secularistic outlook of another kind.

Some advocates of the Social Gospel regarded religion as entirely a matter of ethics, more particularly social ethics, and regarded any religious doctrine beyond this as at best superfluous and at worst an encumbrance. One such writer saw "the dying out of a genuine sense of worship" as a hopeful sign because it was in accord with the trend of social leveling; a rigorously egalitarian democracy must attack theism as "monarchical." Another saw in the "revolutionary change from a supernatural to a natural religion," the hope of the Social Gospel's future, for if the Church "can set up effectively the new set of values, it may again exercise its former powers of social control." [17]

What men of this view usually overlooked was the fact that, if transcendent religious sanction for ethical action became unnecessary, then the Social Gospel, not to mention the Church itself, became unnecessary also. One might just as well become a secular politician, economist, social worker, or labor leader and work for what admittedly were purely secular values through purely secular channels.

It was a searching question which was here posed for the Church. Its answer had to be basically theological. And the search for a new theological basis for the Social Gospel, capable of withstanding the charge that the Social Gospel was by nature secularistic, was to spark the revival of intellectual interest in religion during the 1930's and 40's. But in the meantime, the undercutting of the Church by secularism forces one to conclude that the Social Gospel as it stood in 1920 and the decade thereafter was living on borrowed time.

An Afterthought on Part Two: 1971. In one respect the judgment expressed in the five chapters preceding now seems to me unduly harsh. The confused and ineffective social witness of mainstream Protestantism in the Twenties does not foreclose the possibility that there were creative actions going on within the Church of a kind that would have had to be measured in other ways. What Martin Marty wrote of the ministerial generation of the early 1960's (*Christian Century*, November 7, 1962, p. 1362) may apply also to that of the 1920's: if "in the eyes of the coming generation . . . the image of the ministry is obscured, diffuse, undramatic, purposeless," nevertheless "in hospital corridors, in counseling, in the church study, in the delicate juggle of human relations most ministers lead quietly meaningful and even exciting lives." For perspective, Harry Emerson Fosdick—whose significance for the purposes of this book would lie primarily in his theological modernism, his pacifism, his parish-level experiment in ecumenicalism—stated on several occasions that the most important work going on at Riverside Church was private pastoral counseling. I suspect that this is diagnostic of the way many other Protestant liberals of the day assessed the priorities, at least before the Depression and Roosevelt convinced them otherwise.

PART THREE

THE SOCIAL GOSPEL AND

THE UNIVERSAL CHURCH

CHAPTER VIII

The Background of

the Ecumenical Movement

IN THE retrospect of the five previous chapters, it is clear that the decade of the 1920's was a "Time of Troubles" for the Social Gospel. But before we pronounce that decade a period of unmitigated decline, something further must be said. The fortunes of the churches were not being determined only by businessmen, prohibitionists, secularists, Fundamentalists, and tired liberals. American Protestantism was also being transformed in quite another fashion, through its increasing involvement in the fortunes of Christianity throughout the world. And it was to be of crucial importance for the Social Gospel that the Church, even while it was losing its former pre-eminent position in the secular affairs of the Western world, was at the same time finding itself as a world-spanning fellowship, more truly a "Church universal" than it had been at any time since the high Middle Ages.

We come, therefore, to consider the ecumenical movement,

insofar as it affected the American churches and their Social Gospel. This requires a digression by way of definition, for the ecumenical movement has been many things to many men.

To some, it has meant denominational co-operation for common purposes, as through the agency of the Federal Council of Churches. To others, it has meant the organic merging of denominations or negotiations toward such unions. To others still, it has meant a kind of synonym for nonsectarianism or the kind of religious activity commonly called "interfaith." Some have argued that only such action as has aimed at the creation of a visible Church embracing all Christians, of whatever denomination, is legitimately ecumenical; others would include such inter- and nondenominational work as that of the YMCA and YWCA or the American Bible Society. The Lambeth Conferences of the several Anglican communions—Church of England, Church of Ireland, Protestant Episcopal Church (United States), and so on—are not usually considered part of the ecumenical movement, yet the similar decennial meetings of worldwide Methodism are explicitly named Ecumenical Conferences. Truly we are here faced with a confusion of tongues.

The international aspect of the Church's work does not make it ecumenical, even though the Greek original of this word (οἰκουμένη) means literally "the inhabited world," for the universal Church of Rome definitely is not included in the ecumenical movement, whereas a local council of churches in an American city just as definitely is. Not even the basics of Christian theology set absolute boundaries; the president of the Massachusetts Council of Churches for many years has been a Unitarian. Small wonder, then, that the author of a recent account of the quest for Christian unity declares that "the word 'ecumenical' has deteriorated," in the sense that ecumenicalists are "in danger of losing our grip on the very concept of the thing we are after." [1]

Under the circumstances, for the purposes of this study I shall have to define the ecumenical movement in some such fashion as "all efforts by non-Roman Catholic Christians to achieve church unity," recognizing of course that "unity" itself is a question-begging term. One has no choice but to let the term "ecumenical" serve as a broad coverall, like the word "liberal," and let it define itself operationally as we proceed.

For our purposes, however, the meaning of this movement is a shade clearer, since it is specifically the international and interchurch phases of it which will concern us. The literature of the movement's history helps us. For, although the efforts at Christian unity during the twentieth century have been as various as the religious traditions and nationalities and personalities involved, they fall in the main into two broad categories. Interchurch co-operation for common purposes—social welfare, missions, charities, or any other sort of activity which in no way compromises the theologies, the forms of worship, or the forms of government of the respective churches—is classified in the vast literature of the ecumenical movement as part of the churches' common Life and Work. Interchurch co-operation of a sort which grapples with the diversities of the churches, in doctrine, liturgy, and polity, usually with the eventual hope and intention of organically uniting the churches, is classified as part of the churches' common Faith and Order.

The Life and Work movement, as thus defined, includes joint promotion of the Social Gospel by men of diverse churches; among the matters we have considered, for example, the Interchurch Report on the steel strike of 1919 is a specimen of what churchmen mean by Life and Work. The Faith and Order movement we have not as yet had occasion to discuss, although it should be pointed out that the Fundamentalist controversy definitely (though crudely) raised some basic questions about church doctrine and church fellowship, which is to say, about Faith and Order. At this point in our study, both of these perspectives on the ecumenical movement become intensely relevant. For they presented themselves at first to many churchmen not merely as differences of emphasis but as rivals. The distinction between Faith and Order and Life and Work seemed to some to revive the Reformation controversy over "faith" and "good works" as mutually exclusive ways to salvation. American Protestantism, as for the first time it took account of the world Church, had also to take account of this apparent contradiction;

and since the Social Gospel was involved in the Life and Work side of ecumenicalism, it was confronted with criticism far more searching than any it had faced before, which was to be of crucial importance in rethinking the theology of the Social Gospel. This interplay will be the subject of our next chapter.

Meantime it must be noted that the ecumenical movement, which started among Protestants (although Eastern Orthodox and Old Catholic groups have been drawn in), is a remarkable departure indeed from the historic Protestant tradition. There were, to be sure, ecumenicalist ideas in the minds of the makers of the Reformation, but the outcome of that upheaval in history was certainly not church unity.[2] Until the twentieth century, one would have thought that the very name "Protestant" connoted schism. And over a still longer span of church history, the uniqueness of this ecumenical phenomenon becomes really impressive. As Latourette, Christendom's closest approach to a universal church historian, puts it:

The Catholic Church . . . had succeeded by the close of the third century in bringing into one fellowship the majority of professed Christians. Since the fourth century, however, the drift had been toward further division. Now, in the nineteenth century and especially after 1914, the trend was reversed. Christians were coming together. This was not the triumph of one church over its rivals. . . . Nor was it furthered, as had been the growth of the . . . Church of the first few centuries, by political unity in its environment. It was coming into being in a day when the nations of the world were pulling apart and in the midst of the most world-shaking wars which the human race had ever experienced. It arose from within Protestantism, by tradition and apparently by nature the most divided of the main great types of Christianity.[3]

If "by its nature Protestantism tended towards individualism and fissiparousness," as Latourette remarks elsewhere, this tendency was particularly marked in the history of the Protestant churches in the United States.[4] James Madison attributed much of the vigor of religion in the young American republic to sectarian rivalry in the absence of a state church; whatever should be said of the vigor, the rivalry is undeniable. In the religion of early America, schism was almost the norm. Churches split over slavery; they split over theology; they split over discipline; they split over church government; they split over the possibility of the existence of ice in the summertime. (This last admittedly happened to one of the fringe sects.) Moreover, these schismatic bodies showed remarkable staying power once they had split off. Even in our own age of consolidated farms, schools, newspapers, and corporations, the number of religious bodies in the United States is still growing; at the last count there were 256 (more or less—church statistics, the reader is reminded, are even more elusive than those of governments). That the ecumenical movement could have arisen at all in such an atmosphere is indeed noteworthy. One understands (though one does not necessarily concur in) the assurance with which some ecumenicalists claim divine origin and sanction for their cause.

But in deeper retrospect, even in sectarian America ecumenicalism is historically more plausible than it appears at first sight. Concrete moves in the direction of church unity appear here and there throughout American church history, and the ideal flows along under the successive waves of separatism. The Great Awakening of the eighteenth century, even though it helped to create new schisms and sects, had at the same time the effect of blurring theological distinctions and promoting interdenominational co-operation, in order to reach and evangelize the unchurched masses. Similarly in the course of the Second Awakening at the turn of the nineteenth century there were ecumenical impulses. Members of the Baptist, Methodist, and Presbyterian Churches, for example, withdrew from their parent denominations with the intent not of establishing a new sect but rather of escaping from all sectarian divisions into a simple membership in "the" Christian Church. Shortly afterward there began the development of the societies for interdenominational good works—missions, Bible and tract societies, and the rest—which were so marked a feature of religion in America's National Period.

But it should be noted that where such early ecumenical activities met with success, they were of the species I have described as "Life and Work." The promising venture of the "Christian Churches" just mentioned, confined in the sectarian atmosphere of the times, became only another sect beside all the rest; indeed, it eventually became three (Christians, Disciples of Christ, and Churches of Christ). And, in general, Faith and Order found rough going against the turbulent currents of American religious experimentalism—remember that Mormonism, Adventism, and Spiritualism all date from this period. Consequently, by default, the beginnings of the ecumenical movement in the United States were evangelical, missionary, and social, rather than theological.

Intellectually, this preference for Life and Work over Faith and Order dates from Samuel Schmucker's *Overture on Christian Union* (1842), which specifically came out against doctrinal unanimity as a prerequisite for common Christian work. To be sure, the Evangelical Alliance, a loosely organized Protestant "International" founded in London in 1846, adopted a creedal statement in order to limit its membership to those who held what were considered orthodox Christian views, but the statement was so doctrinaire that it became increasingly a handicap, particularly in the United States. When Josiah Strong, author of the early muckraking book, *Our Country,* and pioneer of the Social Gospel, became secretary of the American branch of the Evangelical Alliance in 1886, he swung its emphasis toward social service.

This climate of pragmatic avoidance of theological differences for the sake of co-operation in Life and Work continued to mark the progress of the ecumenical movement in America for another generation. It largely determined the form of American participation in the nascent International Missionary Council, and, domestically, it characterized the rise of the Federal Council of the Churches of Christ in America.[5] This, the first institution in the nation's history which was empowered to speak and act for the nation's churches as a whole, was founded with an explicit intention to further the rise of the Social Gospel, which by that time had become a major part of the Life and Work of the American churches.

The ecumenical movement, which was thus rising into institutional existence in the United States, belonged, of course, to a wider current in world Christendom. I have already mentioned the fact that the Evangelical Alliance was founded in London; the Bible and tract societies, and the YMCA and YWCA also, were world-wide—or, at any rate, West-wide—organizations. Even this larger Western parochialism began to melt into something more inclusive as the international missionary movement blossomed at Edinburgh in 1910; for the unexpectedly effective witness there of spokesmen for the "native" or "younger" churches foretold that the Christian churches' Life and Work in the twentieth century would be truly ecumenical, in the literal sense, its leaders being drawn from the entire inhabited world.

Significantly, the next great step toward Christian ecumenicity took place under the stimulus of the world peace movement. American churchmen had been attracted to this cause from time to time, and (ironically) during the half-dozen years before the outbreak of the First World War their interest was particularly strong. The newly established Federal Council of Churches, especially, contributed to the growth of this kind of Life and Work. Charles S. Macfarland, on becoming chairman of the Council's Social Service Commission in 1911, went to Britain and Germany with the intention of organizing ecumenical-pacifist sentiment in those countries. It seemed a promising field for action, since there had been some experimentation in German-British pulpit exchange already, and the American peace conferences of 1910 and 1911 had drawn a number of German and British delegates. Taking advantage of this apparent drift toward world brotherhood, the Federal Council's Commission on International Friendship, together with the Church Peace Union, called a conference to meet at Constance, Switzerland, in July, 1914.

Of course, the still small voice of the churches' peace plan was drowned in the thunder of the German General Staff's Schlieffen Plan. The conference was never held.

Yet precisely at this point the development of the ecumenical movement takes a different turn, not merely from previous Christian history but from the history and fate of world society. For the purpose of the conference was not abandoned. The British and American delegates to Constance held a rump conference in London and founded the World Alliance for International Friendship Through the Churches. Even while pastors of its constituent churches were preaching *"Gott mit uns"* at one another, this organization held together. It even managed to get some of the belligerents together at Berne in August of 1915, at a conference which included British and German as well as Danish, Dutch, and Swiss delegates. The French pastors were forbidden to attend by their government.

As the war went on and the patriotic pressures became more intense, the leadership of the ecumenical movement of necessity passed to the neutrals, notably Archbishop Söderblom of the Church of Sweden. The United States was active in this capacity through 1916, and its Federal Council of Churches participated in a call for a postwar conference of Christians from all countries, neutral, Allied, and Central Powers equally. Meantime the neutrals carried on alone; there was a pathos in their gatherings at Uppsala in 1917 and at Christiana [Oslo] in 1918, reminiscent of the pathos that surrounded Henry Ford's "peace ship" of 1915, that was going to get the boys out of the trenches by Christmas.

But the church conferences bore more fruit than Mr. Ford's quixotic venture. For this movement, however feeble, however boycotted by governments and by churchmen, preserved at least a spark of Christian fellowship across No Man's Land. In spite of all her failures, the Church was more successful in this respect than any secular organization; one has but to remember the ignominious collapse of the ideal of world comradeship which had been embodied in the Second Socialist International.

Nor was this all a matter of sermons and conferences. Concrete measures were taken, for example, by churchmen from

Allied countries to keep alive missions in Africa and Asia which had been cut off from their founders and supporters in Germany. And, after the Armistice, the churches recovered their perspective more quickly than the leaders of nations. The World Alliance for International Friendship Through the Churches met on September 30, 1919, shortly after Versailles, with all the major Protestant belligerents represented—six years before Germany was considered respectable enough to be permitted into the secular League of Nations.

Here, in short, was a real response to the real challenge—the only existential answer which the Church was able to give to the bitterly searching questions which secularists asked about the First World War. And the answer made the Church ask itself a further series of questions about its own approach to secular problems.

Peace, considered as one of the Social Gospel's practical aims, had been the Social Gospel's most spectacular failure. The only vestige of success, while the war was still in progress, was this international movement I have just described. But at the same time, as a national institution on the home fronts of the various countries, as we saw in the case of the United States in our last chapter, the Church had shown itself to be as much an instrument of men's passions as any other organization. *Its failure had been denominational; its success had been ecumenical.* This fact was to lend tremendous impetus to the ecumenical movement in the succeeding two decades. The feeling was growing among churchmen that the Church's sorry condition in the modern world could be remedied only by enabling it to transcend the particular and relative interests which were subordinating it to their own service—interests of nation and of denomination. This is a great deal of what is meant by the ecumenicalist motto, "Let the Church be the Church!"

With the close of the First World War, the ecumenical movement's need to articulate an ideology was strongly felt. Consequently, exploratory conferences on Life and Work and on Faith and Order were scheduled to meet in Geneva in 1920. Americans had participated, through the world missionary movement and through the Federal Council, in the growth of Life and Work; through the initiative of Bishop Charles Brent and others they had played no small part also in the genesis of Faith and Order. Thus, American Protestantism—including its Social Gospel—passed institutionally into the larger stream of world Christendom; and the Social Gospel both influenced and was influenced by the men and movements that were pointing toward an eventual World Council of Churches.

Postscript: 1971. Historical judgments are forever being set aside by further history—a fact which, incidentally, has the profoundest theological implications. "The universal Church of Rome," I wrote in the draft of this chapter published in 1956, "definitely is not included in the ecumenical movement." Then, two years later, quite unexpectedly came Pope John. His successor's renewed emphasis on the rigorous distinctiveness of certain of Rome's doctrines did not alter the fact that during the brief pontificate of John XXIII windows were opened between Catholic and Protestant, Catholic and Jew, even Catholic and atheist, that will probably never again be fully closed. On the Protestant side, the *Christian Century* in its lead editorial for March 18, 1970, announcing a pending merger with a British religious fortnightly whose ancestry was in part Roman Catholic, recalled the days "when the Century regularly took a very hard line toward Roman Catholicism." The old Chicago-based liberal weekly expected "no watering down of critical issues" such as "the papacy or population policy or parochial schools" in its new, transatlantic format, but it did anticipate "facing these issues together in a new way as Christian brothers and sisters," out of a conviction that the issues which had come to matter most "in Christian faith and life now cut across all ecclesiastical borderlines," including the one which for centuries had divided all other Christian communions from Rome.

CHAPTER IX

American Belief

and the World Church

HENRY SLOANE COFFIN told the graduating class of 1915 at Union Theological Seminary that "we care not whether it be by our theological interpretations or by some other that the Gospel of Christ is proclaimed; whether it be by our ministry of by some other that His redemptive Spirit touches the nations, provided only that the new social order comes." [1]

As the ecumenical movement became an institutional reality, many Americans carried into its councils Dr. Coffin's point of view; and they stirred a storm of controversy. For the fact that some of them really did not care by what means the new social order came disturbed European Christians profoundly. The question of by what theological interpretations the Gospel was to be proclaimed, or by what kind of ministry it was to be preached —questions, in short, of Faith and Order—were for Continental churchmen of the utmost importance. Consequently they launched a thoroughgoing attack upon the American Social

Gospel at the level of its theology. Since these men spoke neither out of the social limitations of the American businessman nor out of the intellectual limitations of the American Fundamentalist, their criticism was the most relevant and challenging in the Social Gospel's entire history.[2]

Insofar as the American Social Gospel had a foundation in systematic theology, it was predicated upon a reinterpretation of the doctrine of the Kingdom of God. The prayer, "Thy kingdom come on earth," had been interpreted as a moral imperative for men to go out and transform the social order. True, the makers of this theology, and most notably Rauschenbusch himself, had at times expressed some caution about this; the Kingdom was, after all, the Kingdom of God, and so the initiative in its achievement must be an act of the Divine Will. But the practitioners of the Social Gospel, according to their European critics, ignored this caution; they acted as if the Kingdom were something to be achieved purely by human means, and by secular means at that.

To conceive of man's salvation as being achieved by social work, political reform, trade unionism, or revolution, rather than by the grace of God (so the argument ran) was to change one's concept of the nature of God. The theology of Horace Bushnell had prepared American Christians to believe in an indwelling, immanent God Who participated in the collective life and actions of men and therefore did not have to be approached through the transcendental aloneness of a "conversion experience." Such a God, for the friends of the Social Gospel, operated in and through history, with the help of men, to bring into existence His Kingdom on earth.

Not so, replied the Continental critics; God is set over against, is "Wholly Other" than, His creation, and therefore stands outside of history and judges it. Hence the coming of the Kingdom is synonymous with God's judgment upon all of man's works; it is a shattering, catastrophic, eschatological act in which the participation of man is rescued from complete insignificance only by his being a child of God.[3] It is a far cry from this judge-God to the partner-God of the pragmatic American Kingdom-builders. Finding such a God too much for purely human purposes, to paraphrase Voltaire, men had had to invent a lesser one; and the theologians of the Social Gospel had rejected the transcendent Creator-Judge-God in favor of the God described by William James in his Gifford lectures—limited, finite, and one Who could fail in His purposes without the active co-operation of man.

James's purpose in so declaring the power of God to be limited had been essentially moral: to provide man with sufficient incentive to do battle for the right (assuming that if he believed in an omnipotent God he would lie down on the job). And such, the European critics said, was what the Social Gospel's champions had done to the idea of Godhead; they preached a "God ethicized." Ethics, which in any orthodox account of Christianity is a product of religious teaching, had been made its cause. "Ethical conduct," Rauschenbusch had said, "is the supreme and sufficient act"; thereby, said the critics, divine and human purposes became identified.[4]

This they considered as disastrous even when the human purposes involved were constructive. For, with God's transcendence, His Otherness, undercut, there was nothing to prevent men opposed to the Social Gospel from seeking to bend Him to their purposes in the same way. "God is no longer conceived of as active and dynamic Will, judging, guiding, and saving humanity, but rather as the totality of the inherent qualities of the universe and of humanity as the power of inward reason and goodness"—and many other men besides Christian theologians in the days after the First World War were finding the inherent qualities of the universe and of humanity perilously frail reeds to lean on.[5]

Much the same criticism made against an ethicized view of God was made against an ethicized view of Christ. I have remarked upon the quest by the theologians of the early Social Gospel period for "the historical Jesus"—for His "real," which was to say, ethical, teachings, stripped of their theological accretions, so that they could be brought to bear upon the social problems of the world. Some European theologians conceded that the results of this search had done much to sharpen the stern moral imperatives in those teachings for Christians who had escaped from their inconvenient severity behind a screen of dogma. But also, the same theologians added, by dismissing or watering down the dogma of the Incarnation the liberals had undercut the very Presence which gave the ethic its power. The religious and the ethical meaning of Christianity, said European theology, were emasculated unless men declared with Karl Barth that "this man was God." For only a God Incarnate could solve the central ethical problem, which was man's own attempt to become God, that is to say, the problem of "original sin."

Here 'we come to the least popular, for modern men, of all the uncomfortable and uncongenial components of the new theology. "The modern mind can easily confess its ignorance —is it not always seeking to abolish ignorance? . . . It can confess its feebleness—have we not dedicated ourselves to the worship of Power? But its *guilt?* Never!" [6] "Sin" was something one exorcised on a psychoanalyst's couch, not in church; the feeling of guilt, rather than guilt itself, was to be purged; one sought not redemption but cure.

Moreover, original sin was individual sin, and this was something which the Social Gospel thought it had gotten away from. It had, true enough, a concept of sin, but this had been collectivized: "sin is not a private transaction between the sinner and God," Rauschenbusch had said. Rather, "the sinful mind is the unsocial and anti-social mind." [7] Ethical failure was social, and the remedy for it was social also; individualist salvation was as outmoded as individualist economics. To all of this the European—and some American—critics made stern reply. For the first time in generations, serious intellectual credence was being given to the thesis that individual men were "sinners in the hands of an angry God."

The Europeans found striking resemblances between the Social Gospel's collectivized interpretation of sin and salvation, and the social ethics of John Dewey. Hence, at times they did not bother with elaborate theological analysis, but simply dismissed the Social Gospel as one more deplorable example of American pragmatist *aktivismus*. And, indeed, the socialization of these doctrines was pointed up by the fact that the American conception of religious experience continued to be individualistic. "The varieties of religious experience" for William James and his followers were varieties of personal and private experience. The result was that the art of corporate worship continued to be neglected in the United States, and the Europeans were provided with another basis for attack upon the Social Gospel: the fact that its theology neglected to work out any formal doctrine of the Church.

The American church was to a large extent a social rather than a religious fellowship. It was, to be sure, a means whereby individuals might worship together, but this act was not thought of in the same corporate way as in the liturgical churches on the Continent. A revival meeting was obviously a "collective" experience of the most vivid sort, yet the pressure of it was toward an internal, individual decision. And the other form of nineteenth-century American Protestant worship, the "prayer meeting," came down essentially to individual testimony. The "communion of saints" was an article in the Creed which made little sense in the American religious tradition.

The Social Gospel had inherited this low-church attitude, with the result that a vital part was missing from its theology and program. Ministers preached the Social Gospel; Conferences and Assemblies passed resolutions promoting it; boards and agencies collected and published facts; but the concrete accomplishment of social justice was left almost entirely to secular agencies: government, labor unions, political parties. The question of the Church's direct function in society, which depended upon the answer given to the question of what one considered the Church from a theological standpoint to be, was hardly discussed at all.

But the men of the Faith and Order movement, by very definition, took the question of the nature of the Church far more seriously. Such matters, for example, as how extensively churches could co-operate for common purposes if they rejected one another's sacraments or ministry as unscriptural, were of tremendous importance for them. Yet they were addressing themselves to the same general ecumenical question which, under the name of Life and Work, was attracting the attention of the friends of the Social Gospel. Therefore, if Americans, who had been so instrumental in launching the ecumenical movement, were to continue to enter into a world Christian community, they would perforce have to take up the theological problem of the nature of the Church, and, thereby, be confronted with all the other European criticisms of the Social Gospel.

Americans were often simply bewildered by this entire business. It should be remembered that theology, for many if not most of the practicing social-gospelers, was incidental; the great theological formulation came, indeed, in 1917 after the movement was well under way. A systematic liberal theology had preceded the Social Gospel, but comparatively few Americans knew it; they rationalized their religious liberalism not in the language of the theological Germans (Ritschl, Harnack) but in Spencerian terms (John Fiske) or by way of a philosophy of religion rather than a theology (Borden P. Bowne). Many American churchmen equated any sort of theological reasoning with medieval attempts to count the angels dancing on a pinpoint. Bishop McConnell in his reminiscences of the Lausanne Conference on Faith and Order in 1927 observed that "the first question at the conference was that old abomination as to which is the true church." [8] That this question was no more than an "old abomination" was a fairly widespread reaction among American clergymen of McConnell's generation.

Some of this was pragmatic impatience with what they considered pointless discussion that interfered with positive social action. Indeed, because much of the European criticism was coming from German Lutheran circles, some Americans dismissed the whole movement as an instrument of political reaction, which linked doctrines of an authoritarian God and a hopelessly unattainable Kingdom with a reminder to organized religion that it ought to stay in its place.

This rebuttal somewhat missed the point; Karl Barth, for

example, could hardly be charged with having arrived at his position through *social* conservatism when he could say in 1916 that "the greatest atrocities of life" were "the capitalistic order and the war." [9] The European critique of the American Social Gospel did not call either social reaction or social radicalism "good" or "bad" in this connection. Moreover, the time was to come when an American theologian was to be preaching on the theme of original sin and at the same time be heading the New York City chapter of Americans for Democratic Action; for the Social Gospel was destined not so much to refute these criticisms as to incorporate them.

For the most part the European critique of the Social Gospel made little domestic impact in the United States during the 20's; Barth, for example, was not translated in this country until 1928. Its influence in that period must be traced through contacts with American religious leaders who attended the international church conferences at Geneva, Stockholm, Lausanne, and Jerusalem.

These leaders were not without some preparation for this debate. Every dominant idea generates some kind of minority report; Faith and Order had always been a concern of some Americans. In a negative way it was a mainspring of Fundamentalism. The Lutherans had never lost sight of Faith and Order; nor had the Anglicans, who had escaped the schisms of the other Protestant bodies in the main because of the firmness of their conviction that order was integral to faith. As for the ecumenical movement in the United States, it showed a marked Life and Work orientation in its beginnings. But its advocates also contended that the goal of church unity had something to do with the Church and was not simply an adjunct to the moral improvement of secular society.

Consider, for example, the preamble to the Plan of Federation which became the constitution of the Federal Council of Churches—"WHEREAS: in the providence of God the time has come when it seems fitting more fully to manifest the essential oneness of the Christian Churches of America in Jesus Christ as their divine Lord and Savior . . ." [10] This clause, for all the more purely social stated purposes which followed it, tied the nascent Council back to a source in transcendental faith. As the clause stood at the start of the 1905 meeting which adopted this plan and founded the Federal Council, it did not include the word "divine"; this addition was proposed from the conference floor and adopted unanimously, with the practical effect of excluding the Unitarians on grounds of Faith and Order from fellowship with the Council even before it had come into existence. But the Quakers, thanks to a generous semantic latitude in their use of the term "divine," stayed in.

When the Federal Council entered into the deliberations of the growing world church, its delegates thus had some grounding in Faith and Order to set off their concern in the Church's Life and Work. And every international conference involved them in this issue more deeply.

At the Geneva preliminary conference on Life and Work in 1920, for example, there was present a "fraternal visitor" from the Greek Orthodox Church. The breaking of a thousand years of isolation on the part of its Patriarch at one stroke broadened the ecumenical basis of the movement beyond Protestantism, and, as a consequence of this renewed contact, the Federal Council in 1923 created its own Committee on Relations with the Eastern Churches. The contact with the East, in turn, helped to bring the Church of England into full relationship with the ecumenical movement, and it considerably eased the mind of the Episcopal Church in the United States, whose association in the Federal Council had been undertaken with the utmost hesitation. These groups—Orthodox and Anglican —were liturgical, priestly, sacramental churches; they could in no wise be mistaken for the social-club-cum-gymnasium-and-kitchen which Europeans accused the American churches of being. Their inclusion added a churchly and theological bent to the deliberations, both internationally and in the United States, and the nature of the discussion was profoundly changed. Ultimately, this would be reflected in a change in the nature of the American Social Gospel.

The Geneva postwar conferences of 1920 were a preliminary

to the serious work of the ecumenical movement. The first World Conference on Life and Work duly convened in Stockholm in 1925, its five hundred delegates representing one hundred religious bodies from thirty-seven nations. Its task was stated to be the defining of the social function of the churches; the result was that for the first time American church leaders had to reckon with the new "crisis-theology" in a full-dress debate.

The prime issue at stake was the Social Gospel's definition of the Kingdom of God. "Nothing could be more mistaken or disastrous," said one German leader, "than to suppose we mortal men have to build up God's Kingdom in the World. . . . We can do nothing, we have nothing, we are nothing." The kinship of this with the discussions of social versus individual gospel then going on in the United States is obvious. But so extreme a statement as this, prompted perhaps by the political defeatism of Weimar, was too much for the majority of the delegates; "if we give up fighting for reforming the world," declared a Danish bishop, "then the world will reform us." [11] The official Message voted by the conference (and drafted incidentally by another of the Germans) came out solidly for the Anglo-American concept of Life and Work. Indeed, it expounded what any of the Americans present could recognize as kin to their own Social Gospel: human rights over property rights, responsibility of the total community for social welfare, the international and interclass character of the Church. It closed "with an appeal addressed to Christians, to youth, to teachers and scholars, and to the workers of the world"—like a baptized Manifesto.[12]

The debate was carried a step further at the World Conference on Faith and Order at Lausanne, Switzerland, in 1927. This gathering heard a ringing defense of the Social Gospel by Bishop Francis McConnell of the United States; but, also, the Europeans' discussions of their differences on theology, the creeds, church polity, and the nature of the Church, ministry, and sacraments—differences some of which were here definitively "nailed down" for the first time since the great councils of the Middle Ages—quickened the interest of Americans in the whole question of Faith and Order. It was after Lausanne that Barth and others of his school began to be translated and discussed in the United States, and it was also after Lausanne that Richard and Reinhold Niebuhr began to be heard from as, in effect, mediators between the European theologians and their own countrymen.

One other world ecumenical conference of note took place in the 1920's: that of the International Missionary Council at Jerusalem in 1928. Missionary work had been considered an unambiguous "common purpose" when the Council was founded; but missions could no longer be discussed in isolation. The growing military adventurousness of Japan was fraught with consequence for the flourishing mission field in China. Gandhi in India was simultaneously a political challenge to the British government and a religious challenge to the Christians. The daughter-churches in the Far East were beginning to demand autonomy from the Western churches under whose auspices they had been founded, raising some knotty questions on church order as they did so; and shortly the same cry was to be heard from Africa. At Jerusalem, as at Stockholm and at Lausanne, American and other churchmen found themselves involved increasingly in complex issues of Faith and Order, Life and Work.

Meantime, back at home in the United States, general ecumenical sentiment was on the increase. Traditionally, the opening gambit in such discussion had been, "We are for church union, but—"; now, however, there was coming to be a note of distinct disapproval of denominationalism as such. This had occasionally been expressed before; at the founding convention of the Federal Council of Churches a delegate had "stirred up a hornet's nest" by characterizing denominational differences as "bird-tracks in prehistoric mud," but by the end of the 20's this sentiment was a growing consensus in the Church.[13]

There were some who on this issue could be termed "maximalists" (if I may be permitted a Russian political phrase); they saw no visible alternative between a thoroughgoing sectarianism and full organic union of all the denominations, from Catholic to Quaker, in one world-spanning Church of Christ. (How the Church of Rome was to be induced to join the team without insisting upon being its captain was not quite clear.) Others stood for more modest approaches to interchurch fellowship, through local councils of churches and the like. In any case, the general idea of church unity was definitely "in the air." Ecumenicalism was preached from the pulpit, in the church press, and through the new medium of the religious radio broadcast (which for practical reasons connected with national programming almost had to be ecumenical). It was witnessed in a quickening tempo of church mergers, also; most of these simply reunited branches of the same denomination, as in the Lutheran unions of 1918 and 1931, but one of them—across the border in Canada—brought together six hundred thousand Protestants from denominations differing fairly sharply on matters of Faith and Order. And as this process went on, the two streams of Life and Work, Faith and Order began to fuse.

This meant a considerable change in the character of the American Social Gospel. Originally, the liberals in the churches had been for church unity on strictly pragmatic grounds: a united church was a more effective weapon for social action than a divided church. Social gospelers also criticized the denominations for their perpetuation of class differences: rich and poor men's churches, white and black men's churches. Men like H. Richard Niebuhr wrote of *The Social Sources of Denominationalism;* theological differences between the churches were less important for practical purposes, he said, than divisions of nation and race. Denominationalism "draws the color line in the church of God; it fosters the misunderstandings, the self-exaltations, the hatreds of jingoistic nationalisms . . . in the body of Christ; . . . it seats the rich and poor apart at the table of the Lord." [14]

This is a Social Gospel, Life and Work argument: the existence of separate denominations is in a sense a social rather than a religious evil, and its abatement (for example the lowering of the color line in church) would constitute a general social reform. But, at the same time, it is a theological, Faith and Order argument, in that it declares secular rather than religious forces to be dominant in keeping the churches separated: the denominations "are emblems . . . of the secularization of Christianity," insofar as they "follow the fortunes of the world." That the Church can only accomplish its task if it "has transcended the divisions of the world" is a Social Gospel argument; but those divisions in the Church, that is to say, figuratively in the Body of Christ, are not a social but a religious failure.[15] In adopting ecumenicalism as part of its program, *the Social Gospel adopted Faith and Order*—and the Social Gospel would therefore never be the same again.

The greatest change, functionally, in the Social Gospel, as a result of this impact of the Faith and Order movement, was that the social gospelers began to stress the importance of the Church itself as an agent of reform. The Church's social destiny was not simply to recruit leaders for trade unions and peace societies. In such matters as race relations within the Church, and above all the development of the Church as an international fellowship, Christians could accomplish tremendous social reforms simply by laboring to hold the Church up to its own ideals. To preach a sermon on race relations was good; to throw down the barriers between white and Negro at the communion table was far better.

Hereby, there was removed from the Social Gospel a logical contradiction of long standing. The pre–World War I liberals had attacked the individualistic ethics which had ruled American business in the heyday of the entrepreneur, but they had not turned their new socialized ethics backward upon the Protestant faith itself. Their individualistic conception of religious experience had been basically inconsistent with their socialized conception of political and economic experience. Critics, as we have seen, had argued that they lacked any doctrine of the Church; now, at last, they had such a doctrine. Thenceforward it would be less likely that the liberals in the Church would fall into the trap of working for social reform according to secular criteria only superficially connected with Christianity.

Whatever else this "new" Social Gospel was—and I shall

have criticisms of my own to make of the ecumenical outlook upon church and society, in a later chapter—it did represent a counterattack to the challenge of secularism, and to the challenge of international anarchy which secularist and believer alike had failed to meet. In particular, such a view called a halt to the growing secularization of the Church itself, by restoring what the Rauschenbusch Kingdom-theology had tended to blur: the distinction between church and world.

From this new perspective, it was important to dissociate the visible Church's motives from those of purely secular reformers, even when their objective was the same. That is to say, the Church should pursue a given social aim for its own reasons rather than for society's; otherwise, its distinctive witness as the City of God over against the City of Man would be lost. The danger of "ethicizing" one's idea of God, the European critics were saying, was that the ethics in turn too readily adjusted to passing pressures of society, without the absolute frame of reference as a check. A more Church-centered Social Gospel was envisaged as a corrective to this.

"The religion which is socially most useful," Reinhold Niebuhr remarked in one of his characteristic paradoxes, "is one which can maintain a stubborn indifference to immediate ends and thus give the ethical life of man that touch of the absolute without which all morality is finally reduced to . . . self-assertiveness"—including the assertions of political liberals.[16] Little of this viewpoint had penetrated into the Social Gospel in action by 1929, as will be seen in our next chapter, but it was a Social Gospel thus evolving in a "neo-orthodox" and ecumenical and Church-centered direction which was to confront that quickening of the political awareness of Americans —the New Deal.

An Afterthought on Part Three: 1971. It is no longer as evident as it seemed in 1956 that a "new" Social Gospel, committed to Faith and Order and "evolving in a 'neo-orthodox' and ecumenical and Church-centered direction," in any noticeable way has "called a halt to the growing secularization of the Church itself." Harvey Cox, in his book *The Secular City,* criticized the Church in 1965 in language which would also have fitted the Church in 1925 (compare above, pp. 66, 82) :

The colossal staffs, astronomical budgets, and cavernous facilities of the organized churches today themselves provide the main obstacles which prevent that church from fulfilling its calling. . . . The crisis of the organizational churches is not, as we often hear, that they have a splendid institution which is simply being steered in the wrong direction. If this were the case, then a minor palace insurrection in denominational headquarters might win the day.

As for the influence of European formal theology—of "faith," as distinguished from "order"—upon American belief, we may still say that it was considerable; indeed, some of the "crisis-theology's" bitterest critics argued that its Continental origins were a major key to what was wrong with it, forgetful that their own (rationalist or romantic) liberalism had also had Continental origins. On the other hand, the ideas that came to fruition in America in men like Reinhold Niebuhr were not altogether a European transplant. Sidney E. Mead, in his profoundly critical review of this book for *Church History* (December, 1957), quoted one of my sentences descriptive of the Niebuhrians' views—"The same religious scruples which enjoined one from equating the Kingdom of God with any given social order nevertheless required one to become involved in the social struggle" (below, p. 229)—and noted that what had seemed to me at the time "new and different in America" in this religious insight could have been said with equal appropriateness of Abraham Lincoln! Paradoxically, it turns out that this "European" critique of American liberal Protestantism also articulates one of the most deeply rooted strands in American thought.

122

PART FOUR

THE SOCIAL GOSPEL

AND THE NEW DEAL

CHAPTER X

Legacy: The Social Gospel in 1929

IN ENTITLING the discussion of social Protestantism in the 1920's "The Social Gospel Under Fire," I may inadvertently have given the impression that the fire was not returned, that the history of the Social Gospel in the 20's was an affair entirely of passive martyrdom. This was of course not the case. Even in the retrospect of that discussion, the condition of social liberalism in the Church as of 1920 appears healthier than that of social liberalism outside the Church in that same year. Nor should it be assumed that this condition suddenly ceased to exist in the 20's, any more than it had suddenly arisen in the 90's. While the various adverse waves which I have described were sweeping across Protestantism, men continued to preach and practice the Social Gospel.

The Federal Council of Churches, in particular, if anything grew in importance during that period, not only in its role abroad in the coming world church but also at home in the business of the Social Gospel for which it had been founded.

Together with the National Catholic Welfare Council, it campaigned against the open-shop "American Plan" in industry; it entered the fight against the twelve-hour day in steel; it took part in the struggle for a Child Labor Amendment to the United States Constitution. Of no less significance were its fact-finding studies of strikes, its social research work, and its dissemination of a Social Gospel point of view through its Information Service (founded 1920), and, later, its Social Questions Bulletin.

Nor was this all an institutional show. In addition to the kind of Social Gospel propagated in the Council and by resolutions of denominational legislatures, the message continued also to be spread by great preachers. During this period E. Stanley Jones was extending the Rauschenbusch Kingdom-theology, making its socially revolutionary implications more vivid, more apocalyptic; Kirby Page was free-lancing in behalf of a socialistically oriented pacifism; Harry F. Ward was feeling his way toward a synthesis of Marxism and Christianity; while Francis McConnell carried on the prewar pragmatic social-reform tradition of the Christian progressives.[1]

The fate of the Social Gospel as of 1929, therefore, must be seen dialectically in terms of the interaction between the men and movements here mentioned, on the one hand, and all the adverse forces and circumstances listed in Part II of this study, on the other. One would expect to find it weakened, and it was so regarded by some outsiders; W. A. Visser 't Hooft, the Dutch theologian, wrote in 1928 that "the social gospel as it presents itself today is less absolute in its denunciations and affirmations, less hopeful of the immediate realization of its ideals and on the whole less aggressive in its attitude." [2] But this was one man's opinion; one could as readily cite Kirby Page or McConnell on the other side. To take the pulse of the Social Gospel in 1929 we must go once again to the denominational press.

One finds, at times, echoes of the older, stronger Social Gospel in journals of all denominations. The *Churchman* celebrated its 125th year of publication with a deluge of congratulatory messages from the secular liberals, one at least of whom found in the "religious and cultural" press, free of circulation and advertising pressure, the last hope for an American journalism independent of the capitalist order. The *Congregationalist* flailed the police and the repressive forces in the city where it was published in editorials like "What Price Silence?" (on the Sacco-Vanzetti case) and "In Darkest Boston." The *Baptist* published an obituary of Victor L. Berger, Socialist leader, warmly commending his moral courage and his "clean and carefully reasoned advocacy" of "a thoroughgoing and constructive socialism." [3] Other, similar examples could be cited.

But, on the whole, this is not the impression one takes away from intensive reading in the church weeklies for 1929. It is not simply that their general tone is (in Visser 't Hooft's words) "less absolute . . . less hopeful . . . less aggressive" in advancing the Social Gospel; there is revealed something far more damaging for liberalism than simply loss of fire. In these editorials, articles, and official opinions there is a new note, not found to anything like the same degree in 1920, of adjustment and acquiescence to "things as they are."

One continually encounters articles which begin in a fashion which would lead the reader to expect a blast against the social order—and which end by letting him down with an unexpected thump. For example: the *Baptist* began the New Year of 1929 by asserting that "everyone knows that . . . control has passed to the man with the bank book. He governs business. He governs politics. He governs the city, the state, and the nation. . . . He governs the press, the schools, the church, and industry." The rhetorical conclusions from such a premise might usually be fairly predictable—a complaint that "something ought to be done," at the very least, and at the most a call for socialism. But not in the pages of the *Baptist* for the year of our Lord 1929.

It turns out that this all-powerful financiers' "government is fundamentally democratic, for it rests on the consent of the governed. The people wish to have it so, and they are entitled to their wish. This is not an outcry against bank government" —only a reminder to this system of its social responsibility "to the democracy out of which it seems to have grown." Even the control of the Church by business was defended: "Why not? Control of the economic life of a community means always control of . . . all its organized life. . . . Are the churches therefore hypocritical? No. They are merely sensible. They recognize realities. They act within the approved limits of their light and liberty." [4]

What a far cry from the tradition of Baptist democracy! And what a far cry from the demand, heard even as late as 1920, that the money-changers be driven out of the temple!

The *Churchman,* praised by Oswald Garrison Villard of the *Nation* as being identified "with the social advance of great masses of our people," was refreshingly free of this kind of capitulation.[5] Its 1929 file is a record of enthusiastic partisanship in the major disputes of the day. Yet even the *Churchman* would at times make disappointing reading for a secular liberal, for a different reason: a loss of sense of the *proportionate* importance of social issues. For, while in 1929 it had much to say about the struggle to unionize the South, and about civil liberties, and about ragged patches on the garment of prosperity, and on the whole said them very well, one is struck by the fact that the one topic it returned to again and again, the "social evil" which it headlined most prominently, was the quality of motion pictures.

Admittedly, the cinema of the early days of the sound track did not make the most edifying contribution to the national culture. But for a journal with the *Churchman*'s reputation for aggressive liberalism, this crusade against "objectionable" movies strikes one as decidedly a comedown. One begins to understand how subtle and pervasive in the thinking of the Church was the influence of Prohibition, to which the psychological relationship of such a "crusade" is fairly clear.

If one finds this moralist misproportion influencing a journal published in a nonprohibitionist church, consider its effect upon the *Baptist,* the *Christian Advocate,* the *Congregationalist,* and the *Presbyterian Advance,* all organs of dry churches.[6] These papers devoted quantities of space to the problem of the Demon Rum, such that the modern reader's disagreement with the prohibitionist premise is displaced by wonder at the relative importance the matter was assumed to have. The climax of this sort of thing was an editorial in the *Christian Advocate* entitled "The Leader Leads":

Mr. Hoover has taken his rightful place as a moral leader. He is seeking to give the nation the sense of direction it so sadly lacks at the present time. . . . His position on the most important issue of the times greatly enheartens all who still believe that democracy has within itself the forces of its own redemption.[7]

What was this "most important issue of the times"? World peace, as the pacifist aura of that Briand-Kellogg period might suggest? Sore spots of idleness and violence in the nation's prosperity? The social blindness of a get-rich-quick civilization? No; it was law enforcement, and in particular the enforcement of the Volstead Act. A sad decline in the Social Gospel here—for farewell to all social reform begins in pursuit of the wrong kind.

Not only had the denominational journals succumbed to reaction and to lack of social proportion by 1929; they also show a marked tendency to anachronism. All of these papers printed sermons, articles, and editorials on social issues, many of them with some literary or journalistic merit and some of them distinguished by real eloquence, but oftentimes such eloquence was directed to a state of affairs which had long since ceased to exist. The Federal Council's 1929 Message for Labor Sunday, for example, argued the points which it chose to make well enough, but hear the criticism of a thoughtful contemporary:

The reader happens to live in the State of Massachusetts. In years before the war the Massachusetts legislature passed progressive laws concerning child labor, women's labor, night work, the length of the work day. At that time our cotton mills had not begun to move South. At present our progressive legislation feels a bit lonesome.

A criticism of this sort implied a disjunctive Social Gospel, not in contact any more with contemporary problems. The Federal Council's Message, our critic continues, "stood for the right," but "its 'right' had been right for some time and was not very new." The document might, indeed, have been written before the First World War. It did not take account of the industrial problems peculiar to the kind of prosperity which characterized the year 1929. "The new and shiny . . . program of rapid work, mass production, high wages, quick scrapping of the inefficient man and the inefficient tool . . . must raise some problems concerning the slow man and the old man and the nervous man, which are yet to be dealt with." [8] In other words, an effective criticism of the capitalism of the turn of the century was worse than useless as a criticism of the capitalism symbolized by Henry Ford, worse because it left the churches and the Social Gospel far in the rear of what was actually going on.

Anachronistic, also, was the survival of middle-class attitudes toward labor. From time to time there appeared articles of "discovery" with titles like "What a Minister Learned from Labor," in which, with a condescension that merits the Marxist epithet "petty-bourgeois," a clergyman found "latent creativeness" among workers and was "amazed" to learn that some of them sought cultural improvement: "Here and there were workers who had haunted the second-hand book stores and built up a fine library!" [9] That exclamation point shows how perilously far apart the churches and labor were drifting.

When one passes from the field of labor relations to that of race relations, one finds this anachronistic tendency even more marked. Mass migration of Negroes from the crossroads villages of the South to the city slums of the North had created a new cultural milieu for Negroes, and in it there had taken place in the 1920's what is sometimes known among the race's intelligentsia as the "Negro Renaissance." They had already, before the war, begun to reject the standards for social progress associated with Booker T. Washington as hopelessly out of date. The older pattern had been one of educational and economic advancement within the limits set by white supremacy; the new, as symbolized in the founding of the National Association for the Advancement of Colored People in 1909, was to take the form of political and social action against segregation. But the churches were unusually slow in responding to this changed situation in which the American Negro had begun to cry, "If separate, then unequal—away with separation!"

The denominational papers did, to be sure, applaud Mrs. Hoover's reception of the wife of Negro Congressman Oscar De Priest at the White House (although there was nothing new here; Theodore Roosevelt had started that particular precedent). But they did not explore the implications of the existence in the North of a segregated and compact Negro community (Chicago's) which could send one of its members to Congress. In such places as Cincinnati, Chicago, Philadelphia, New York, Springfield (Massachusetts), and such Southern cities as New Orleans and Houston, the churches were accomplishing a great deal for the Negroes, giving economic relief, teaching urban folkways, promoting social welfare, and so on; but apparently they were doing nothing whatever about what the American Negro was coming to have most on his mind, namely, the problem of finding himself culturally as a Negro and as an American.

The churches' response was further slowed by the existence of strong, autonomous Negro denominations which embraced the overwhelming majority of colored churchgoers. There had been some justification for this at the outset; the separation of Negro from white worshipers had often been "a forward step from an association without equality." [10] At least two such churches, the African Methodist and the African Methodist Zion groups, had been established as a conscious act of independence by founders who withdrew in protest from the parent white denomination after having been forced to worship in segregated balconies. As the earliest spontaneous Negro social movement in America's history (turn of the nineteenth century), they had served a highly useful purpose, particularly in developing the first Negro administrators (bishops and board secretaries). But the twentieth-century leaders of these churches, like other members of the Negro middle and professional classes, too often had a vested interest in the continuance of segregation which obscured the real social aspirations of Christian Negroes.

131

On the other hand, in those white denominations which had Negro members, these were almost invariably organized into separate Negro parishes and conferences and synods. (The exceptions were usually individual Negro families who belonged to local churches with an overwhelming majority of white parishioners; one found this sort of arrangement from time to time in New England.) Consequently, there was not, in the churches, the constant concrete interracial contact without which discussion of "the Negro problem" is academic. Even the militant liberals like Francis McConnell seemed to deal with this matter in a superficial way, and Negro leaders within the "mixed" churches often showed similar limitations of horizon.

Thereby, the Church lagged behind both secular social history —which was moving inevitably in the direction of integration —and behind its own canons of moral judgment. If all men are brothers, then the ecumenical movement had implications for denominationalism's class and race divisions in America. Yet that movement was in for a bout of ethical contradictions when ecumenicalism came up against the triangle of Northern white, Southern white, and Negro churchmen. The special challenge of race to the Social Gospel and to the ecumenical movement would come to a head in the 30's.

Meantime, there was a more immediately fatal lapse on the Church's part than its lagging on the score of industrial and of race relations: its fixation, with all the rest of America, upon the illusion of perpetual prosperity.

Hindsight is altogether too easy here; perhaps one ought not to censure the churches for failing to prophesy what was about to happen to the big bull market and the full dinner pail. And yet, it is amazing how close the church editors came in their criticisms at times and still managed to miss the point. Rural depression, regional and technological unemployment, lack of sufficient distribution of the national income, the overinflated stock market, the evils of the Smoot-Hawley Tariff then pending in Congress—all of these were observed and discussed in the church press. But nobody seems to have added them all together.

The *Christian Advocate* attacked "the easy and false assumption . . . that there are no hungry, no unemployed, no destitute and miserable"; the *Presbyterian Advance* pointed to "large areas in rural America where the economic outlook . . . gives the lie direct to national prosperity," but the fashion among practically all such writers was to regard these phenomena simply as deviations from a prosperous norm. James Myers, notable trouble shooter for the Federal Council, visited Ohio coal-mining towns in the winter of 1928–1929 and exclaimed, "Is this America—and prosperity?" The wrath of the Social Gospel was kindled in this instance by the feeling that poverty in America was abnormal under the prevailing economic conditions. "The work is here. The workers are here. The tools are here. Unemployment is absurd." [11]

Social reform, the men of '29 felt, was a matter of adjustment within a framework of permanent prosperity. The problem was not "full employment," in the post-World War II sense. Rather, it was one of personal and class adjustment to a system whose continuation was taken for granted—the sytem of which Fred Taylor and his stop watch remain the most hideous symbol.

The result was that when, in 1929, the Social Gospel was applied to the problem of economic justice, it was applied in a manner which prevented it from getting to the heart of the problem. The mechanics tinkered with the truck engine while the truck itself approached the edge of the cliff. On November 7th, when the stock market had already crashed, the front cover of the *Congregationalist* was an impressive photograph of a wheat field ready for harvest. For all the criticisms which might be made, this was "America the Beautiful, and never more so than now." [12]

There remains one aspect of the Social Gospel which cannot be dismissed as submissive to reaction, for it drew the fire of the right wing; nor as disproportionate, for it dealt with the most urgent practical problem of twentieth-century man; nor, at first thought, as anachronistic, for it represented tremendous evolution in the mind and heart of the Church. I refer to the strong condemnation of militarism and war.

In view of all that has happened since then, and particularly in view of the changes in church opinion, it is well that the reader of the 1950's be reminded how widespread and how thoroughgoing this feeling was in 1929. It reached far beyond the confines of the "historic peace churches" (Mennonites, Brethren, Society of Friends) to reach large numbers of people in all the major denominations.

The Federal Council of Churches had helped to start this trend, through its disarmament lobbying at the Washington Conference of 1921. Its slant had switched from "enforce peace" to "outlaw war," and by 1929 a large number of antiwar resolutions were on record in the proceedings of denominational legislatures as well. Some of these resolutions nonpacifists could endorse, notably the near-unanimous condemnation of military training in schools and colleges, but others went a good deal further.

In March, 1929, there was convened a Study Conference of the National Committee on the Churches and World Peace, which called upon the churches thenceforth to condemn "resort to the war system"—not merely "aggressive" or "preventive" war, but war per se. They were asked "to refuse, as institutions, to sanction it or be used as agencies in its support"—which, taken literally, would have automatically outlawed service flags and prayers for the armed forces. This was admittedly the product of a temporary interchurch body in the moment of afterglow of the Kellogg Pact, but the denominations' own separate pronouncements on war were becoming increasingly stiff and sharp. It is noteworthy that the Southern Presbyterians, for example—representing a region not particularly characterized by pacifism—voted at their General Assembly of 1929 that "the Church should never again bless a war or be used as an instrument in the promotion of war." [13]

To be sure, some of this was simply a reflection of bad conscience on the part of the churches for their bloodthirsty behavior in the First World War, coupled with realization of how much that behavior had done to advance the cause of secularism. As a writer in the *Baptist* put it,

The darkest and most disheartening phenomenon in the last thousand years was the impotency of the Christian church in the World War. . . . The Church did not delay the war. . . . The Church did not shorten the war. . . . The Church did not mitigate the brutalities nor reduce the atrocities of the war. . . . This was a Christian war, a war fought by so-called Christian nations. . . . All of its instruments of destruction had been shaped by Christian hands, and all its methods of slaughter had been conceived in Christian brains. . . .

The World War gave the Christian Church the heaviest blow it has ever received. . . . Since the war . . . religion is everywhere scouted because the Church . . . cannot do the things which humanity needs to have done.[14]

In this sense, the churches could afford to be pacifist because they had nothing to lose. Their prestige was already sufficiently low, as I have shown in other chapters, that if anything they stood to gain by endeavoring to live down the First World War. But this definition-by-vacuum is not enough to explain why the churches made so much of this part of the Social Gospel when they were making so little of the rest. Elsewhere, we saw the Church trimming, adjusting, losing relevance, swinging from its revolutionary function of prophecy to its conservative function of priestcraft. Here, in contrast, at first glance the Church appears to have placed itself in the lion's den.

Congressmen and military men were beginning to brand the Federal Council as "Communist" for its antiwar opinions; its secretaries and officials were beginning to appear on DAR blacklists and such scholarly compendia as Mrs. Dillings's *Red Network*. Moreover the bankers and factory managers who sat on the churches' boards of control were, as often as not, American Legionnaires, and the American Legion could never forgive the churches their opposition to military training in the schools. In addition, there was an economic, quasi-Marxist implication in almost any liberally oriented pacifism—the argument that the "merchants of death" were the only ones who really wanted war—which could and did get speakers into trouble. Surely pacifism is an exception, one would think, to our generalization about the 1929 Social Gospel; it attacked the *status quo,* and it was profoundly relevant to the present and prospective ills of the world.

But on closer inspection, this pacifist perspective does not appear so clearly courageous and radical as the same perspective would appear in, say, 1950. The reason is that the secular *status quo* itself in 1929 was infused with a surprising amount of pacifism.

The subsequent history of the Hoover administration and of Mr. Hoover as former President may obscure a fact of crucial importance for understanding American public opinion as of March, 1929: a member of the Society of Friends had just been inaugurated as President of the United States. Quakerism, at that period, was most prominently associated with nonpartisan relief and rehabilitation in Europe during and after the war; and it was on this record, more than on his Secretaryship of Commerce, that Hoover had been commended to the American people.[15] Nor did Hoover disabuse his admirers of the prospective picture of his administration which was thus built up. He even did a little pacifist muckraking, accusing shipbuilders of promulgating propaganda against international naval disarmament (which they were), and his inaugural address took so strong an antiwar line, with an eloquence distinctly unusual in Hoover, that a Congregationalist leader used it as the text of a responsive reading for use in Armistice Day worship services.

The present-day reader who has experienced within a little over a decade the Second World War and the Korean War should bear in mind that we are dealing here with an era after the signing of the Briand-Kellogg Pact and before the depression and Hitler, an era when the Soviet Union was swinging into a seemingly peaceable routine of "socialism in one country" and when a man who had served time as a conscientious objector in the First World War was Prime Minister of England. And the conclusion which many in the churches drew from this situation in 1929 was that "the pacifist has suddenly become the patriot." "Human nature may not have changed; but human opinion has changed," the *Churchman* declared; "only five years ago anyone 'talking peace' was the target of every sort of vituperation," but now "we have stepped into a different intellectual atmosphere. Any parson can now preach against war and retain his job." [16]

This throws a very different light on the pacifism of 1929 as an indication of the condition of the Social Gospel. For, far from being a headlong attack on the *status quo,* pacifism was interpretable as conformity. More recently, we have had a similar swing in the status of an opinion from heresy to comparative acceptability, namely, pro-Russian sentiment just before and just after the "summit conference" of 1955—an episode which makes a little clearer what really was the case with 1929-style pacifism.

Of course, pacifism made of sterner stuff than this was abroad in the land. But those who staked their pacifism on public approval built it on sand. (I draw no parallels regarding the aftermath of the summit conference; the reader may draw his own if he wishes.) A depression and a wave of totalitarianism would make short work of that kind of peace sentiment; as an acceptable part of the *status quo,* pacifism was due for a short life. Indeed, it really fitted the mood of the United States only for the brief period between the inauguration of Hoover in March and the stock-market crash in September. In the rest of the world it is doubtful whether it fitted at all.

Meantime one must conclude that the churches' views on international affairs, like the rest of the Social Gospel, had been vitiated by adjustment to a norm. Indeed, they had lost such awareness of the need for collective security as had been evident in their League of Nations talk of 1920; the World Court, rather than the League, was the instrument they now relied on. World law and world opinion, rather than world power, would be the basis for the outlawing of war. The point of view came to be that the foreign policy of Senator Borah, which was less difficult to put into effect than that of Woodrow Wilson, was also more moral. True, the Kellogg Pact, which embodied this reliance on world opinion, was coolly appraised by the *Wall Street Journal* as "amiable futility," but *that* opinion was shrugged off by the liberals as characteristic capitalist cynicism.[17]

The strength of this faith in world public opinion among churchmen is best seen by an illustration. Since the accession of Stalin (1926), the Soviet government had begun to broaden its antireligious activities beyond the former state church of the tsars. The Baptists, who had made more missionary headway in Russia than the other evangelical Protestant groups, were particularly hard-hit, and the *Baptist*, official organ of the Northern Baptist Convention in this country, resolved to do something about the persecution of their Russian co-religionists. There being no United States embassy in Moscow at the time through which to lodge a formal protest, the editors seriously suggested that American Baptists write letters to Joseph Stalin. "Stick to one subject, namely, the relief of our brethren," they tactfully advised; "make the terms of your petition simple, respectful and direct." A few weeks later they printed a specimen response to their appeal:

Dear President Stalin:
The congregation of the First Baptist Church of Cedar Rapids, Iowa, United States of America, approved the following resolution at the morning service, July 28, 1929: "Be it hereby resolved that this congregation vigorously protest all forms of religious persecution now being carried out by the Government of Russia." [18]

The fact that such action as this was taken in all seriousness —personal appeals to the Man of Steel—may help the reader to understand why so much faith was placed in the possibility of outlawing war by the pressure of public opinion. And in spite of the anguished cries about "Bolshevism" which had been heard in the United States from the moment of the October Revolution, it is strikingly apparent from this letter what a great deal American citizens, in and out of church, had yet to learn about the moral enormity which was the totalitarian state.

In due course a pacifism would evolve which grimly took this into account, but it would not be a pacifism that rested its case on the fact that the Briand-Kellogg Pact was the law of the land. Meantime the shallow optimism about the international scene which had already begun to appear in Social Gospel discussions back in 1920 had triumphed to such an extent that European theological objections to so easygoing a view of human nature become more understandable.

Only once, in all the issues of all the journals examined for 1929, did I discover a churchman asking the really relevant question: what was going to become of all this pacifism when the skies darkened?

Precisely what things which the churches did in the last war will they refuse to do in case of another war? Will they refuse to take sides, to promote war morale, . . . to pray for the success of "our cause," . . . to prepare hospital supplies, to send gifts and letters of encouragement to the soldiers, to denounce "the enemy" and pacifists? . . . In spite of all pacific resolutions, there is a shrewd suspicion that they will do next time just what they did the last time—and not only that they will do so but that they mean to do so.[19]

For in espousing pacifism on the basis of its being, or seeming to be, majority sentiment, rather than on the basis of its being in their eyes an inescapable deduction from Christian premises, the advocates of the Social Gospel were repeating the same old psychological error which had dogged them in domestic affairs even before the war—that of assuming that exhortation plus the good will of all reasonable men would be sufficient to accomplish social change. When the reasonable men began to act unreasonably, they did not know where to turn.

There was growing in the Church, as I have previously shown, a sense that Christianity as an actively motivating faith was becoming a minority viewpoint in a "pagan" world. Some, believing this, were prepared to take the consequences; they could face being out of step with the majority in perfect equanimity. But at the same time the institutional church in other quarters was reckoned as one of the signs of conformity, and there were many who were unprepared to lose the social influence which they believed to flow from that conformity—so would drop pacifism, as they had already begun to drop liberalism, when the situation seemed to them to call for it. The American Protestant church had a great deal to learn about herself, socially as well as theologically. In the meantime it was the tragedy of countless men of good will—Mr. Hoover being not the least of these—to be "moral men in an immoral society."

Part of what American churchmen had to learn in order to adapt the Social Gospel to the needs of the interwar world was in the realm of theology, but part was external. There was needed a shattering demonstration that the *status quo,* even in liberal times, was not good enough to stand on as a social creed. Matters external to the Church—strikes, want, political clamor—had played a role in shaping the direction of the original Social Gospel. Now, by 1929, the Social Gospel, which had still seemed valid and viable in 1920, had so far run out of steam that another terrible lesson of the same kind was required to break the mold of churchmen's minds. That lesson was furnished by the great depression of 1929.

Postscript: 1971. Robert Moats Miller, in *American Protestantism and Social Issues 1919–1939* (Chapel Hill, 1958), views the Social Gospel's legacy from the 1920's somewhat more favorably, and his chapter "A Dissenting Report of the Churches in the Twenties" should be set against the foregoing pages for comparison. Another testimony to the continuing vitality of Protestant social liberalism during the Twenties may be found in J. Theodore Hefley, "Freedom Upheld: the Civil Liberties Stance of *The Christian Century* Between the Wars," *Church History,* XXXVII (June, 1968), 174–194.

CHAPTER XI

Preparation: The Social Gospel

in the Great Depression

THE crash of 1929 and its aftermath were a psychological as well as an economic event. "Depression" meant not only "hard times," in the simple financial sense, but a deep, continuing, and pervasive spiritual gloom.

The onset of this malaise should not be dated too closely. The historian's temptation here is to treat the morning of October 24th, 1929, like the drop of a curtain, rising a few weeks later to reveal a changed social landscape—as if there had not been serious instabilities before the crash and as if the transition into "hard times" did not take an appreciable time afterward. Economic ups and downs do not, of course, occur with the satisfying chronological neatness of Marathons and Waterloos and Gettysburgs.

On the other hand, as the Korean War demonstrated, the American people are sometimes remarkably mercurial in the way they react to crisis. The psychological transition from "prosperity" into "hard times," consequently, was rapid. And once the depression settled in, it tried the spirits of Americans more sorely than even the war had tried them. For the war had been "over there"; one could fight it and leave it and come home; but now "God's Country" itself was the seat of the trouble. Too, the war had seemed, in 1917 at least, to be something right and meaningful and worth undergoing, but what began to happen a dozen years later was so patently meaningless that it broke men's hearts.

But if the depression broke their hearts, it opened their minds. The social illusion that prosperity was permanent, to be sure, was replaced by the social illusion that prosperity was just around the corner. But the corner moved farther off as the months passed. The School of Hard Knocks was in session, and men learned.

As the number of those who walked the streets swelled by the million, the Church began to learn too. Budgets fell off; pastors found themselves spending more and more of their time finding work for unemployed parishioners; the churches began to be called upon for charity in amounts so enormous as to strain their resources. Missionaries began to come home; religious papers were published less frequently. A district official of one of the churches unctuously told the ministers in his charge that from thenceforth they would have to learn to get along on "nice, nourishing stews." [1] The resulting clamor found its way into the denominational press; by 1932, most of these journals were fully aware of the crisis, and their response to it was a remarkable tribute to the educative power of misfortune.

Of course, there were those in the churches—as in the nation —who could not learn. Throughout the years of "hard times" the notion was abroad that the depression would go away if citizens turned their backs and pretended it was not there. Furthermore, owing to the middle-class nature of the Protestant churches, a relatively high proportion of their membership did not really suffer at all; indeed, they could take a certain moral satisfaction from a mild enforced asceticism.

The editors of the *Presbyterian Advance,* for example, which in 1929 had preached a lukewarm Social Gospel, never quite got the point as to what was going on. After all, they reasoned, the depression was not so bad, compared with other lean years America had been through; for instance "there have been no great strikes"—a sign, they felt, of the greater degree of brotherhood in America in their more enlightened modern times. Occasionally, the stubborn and incredible facts broke through —after all, by 1932 churches as well as banks were closing— and an understanding article would appear and concede that "people are breaking, physically and spiritually." But these writers always bounced back with a whistle in the dark. Really, they philosophized, "the 'Depression' has a wonderfully cheering side." [2]

But other churchmen, including other Presbyterians, found less to cheer about. The Presbyterian General Assembly received from its Committee on Social and Industrial Relations a report declaring that the depression was no holiday; it was "an emergency of unprecedented magnitude," brought on by "incompetency and wrongheadedness." Furthermore, it was an opportunity to learn and unlearn some painful lessons about capitalism: "The world's economic system stands today distraught and bewildered in the presence of a crisis precipitated by the very principles upon which it had been assumed general prosperity was based." [3]

If these Presbyterians found the prevailing economic system "distraught and bewildered," the Episcopal *Churchman* found it "rotten to the core." This journal had been less affected by the sag in the Social Gospel during 1929 than most of its contemporaries; it consequently had less lost ground to cover, and its 1932 Social Gospel blazed forth with all the old vigor. Its perennial feud with the movies continued, but was pushed into a more proper perspective of one-paragraph squibs. And its frequent anticapitalist editorials were sometimes so furious as to border on Marxism.

The depression, also, had changed its line of attack somewhat. The *Churchman*'s old support of government intervention in the economic life now took the form of a vast impatience with

Hoover's hesitancies: "In the name of humanity, in the name of Christ, let us have done with red tape and apply ourselves to feeding the hungry!" Here was foreshadowed the humane tough-mindedness expressed a few years later by Harry Hopkins: "Hunger is not debatable."

One standing policy the *Churchman* reversed completely. Its Social Gospel in the 20's had sounded a strong ascetic note, in conjunction with attacks on "materialism." In 1929 it had cried, "The country has been made rich beyond endurance." But by 1932, it had swung completely around to the consumer's point of view: "Luxuries have actually become necessities, and who can degrade them again to their old status? It avails little to remind the poor that Grandpa had no automobile." [4]

Far more impressive as an object lesson in education, because it had more ground to cover, was what happened to the *Baptist*. The reader will recall from our last chapter that in 1929 this journal had been endorsing the existing economic order in a manner startlingly at variance with the Social Gospel point of view; it not only approved "free enterprise," it approved outright business domination of society. It did dislike stock speculation, but only because a Baptist journal would dislike gambling of any kind; it did not carry this feeling over to business outside of the stock exchange itself. (The crash it greeted with satisfaction; the gyrations of Wall Street offended the denomination's frugal Calvinist tradition, and of the plunging market of October and November the *Baptist* tartly observed that "even a devil's dance cannot last forever.")

But events were moving fast. The membership of the Baptist Church reached lower into the economic strata than that of any other major denomination, and their official journal was always remarkably sensitive to what rank-and-file Baptists were thinking. Within a few weeks after the crash the editors' illusions about the benevolence of plutocratic control were dispelled. In mid-December of 1929 the editorial writer scanned the new-used-car prices quoted in the morning paper, reflected on them, and wrote with quiet sarcasm: "The preacher may not know business, but he ought to have sense enough to know when the storm blows his house down. . . . Yes, somewhere, at bottom, business is 'fundamentally sound.' " [5]

By 1932, the *Baptist* was well back to its old stand for the Social Gospel. Moreover, this was a Social Gospel which had shed some of the vulnerabilities it had shown in its early days. The editors for one thing now recognized that the transfer of social privilege involves the use of social coercion, a fact which the right and center of the old Social Gospel had not always faced up to. If this necessitated taking sides within the body politic, they knew which side they were on: "We can be . . . sure that in any fair conflict between rich and poor, Jesus could be found on the side of the poor." Also, this rejuvenated Social Gospel had shed much of the old Baptist asceticism. Part of this journal's proposed remedy for the 1920 high cost of living had consisted simply in consumer belt-tightening; how different the editors sounded in 1932 when discussing "Charity or Federal Aid": "To call a thing a disreputable name is not argument. . . . Called by any name, federal aid . . . to . . . the unemployed could not possibly be so destructive to the self-respect of the recipient as . . . what we are now doing." [6]

A Congregationalist leader put this particular matter more trenchantly: he described the psychology of the man "too proud to accept charity" as a distinct hindrance to effective relief and blamed it upon "the damnable American myth which says that any person who is honest, thrifty, and industrious can always earn a comfortable living." But the Church, as well as the social order, was at fault for the creation of this myth, said the editors of the *Congregationalist,* and it was high time that the Church got away from stereotyped denunciations of "materialism" in the sense of "mammon-worship"—exhortations which had been highly relevant in the 20's but which made little sense in the era of "Brother, can you spare a dime?"

Should we under these circumstances be talking about the false god of money, and the false god of things, or should we be frankly recognizing and emphasizing the *need* of money and the *need* of things? . . . Instead of decrying our bigness and our productive power and our nationalism, ought we not to be sounding the note of a determination with our immense resources to meet every need and right every wrong? [7]

The Methodists in 1932 were distracted from their Social Gospel task by anguish at the imminent passing of Prohibition, in which they had had a large stake, but among them, too, the pressure of events was awakening social perspectives. "Hunger in America startles us," confessed a contributor to the *Christian Advocate,* and a national condition of "famine in the land of plenty" compelled Americans to "rethink through our capitalistic theories of economics, perhaps face square up to state control of industry."

Elsewhere in Methodism there was ferment also. Delegates to the 1932 General Conference of that church assembled to hear their senior bishop begin to read the Episcopal Address. "As he began to stress the social implications of Christianity, signs of approval multiplied. When he declared, 'We know now that the Kingdom of God cannot be built upon the poverty of the many and the absurd and cruel wealth of the few,' there was a burst of applause"—applause, be it noted, from men who were well enough off financially to attend a national convention in Atlantic City. At the Conference's end, the delegates voted to send Bishops McDowell, Hughes, and McConnell to Washington to urge federal unemployment relief and then rushed through a report from their Committee on the State of the Church which a reporter described as a "wholesale condemnation of the present social order, and the acquisitive principle on which it was based." [8]

The correlation between this new critical vigor shown in all the denominations and their experience of depression is quite clear. Church as well as nation was in a bad way; it was a year of "empty altars and diminished missionary funds." A number of denominations—Presbyterian, Baptist, Dutch Reformed, Disciples, Methodist, United Lutheran—were in legislative session in 1932, and "over nearly all of these meetings rested the pall of the depression. There was . . . very great conservatism with reference to policies and projects. In some bodies there were forebodings as to the future of missionary work." The Methodists confessed in humiliation that they could not afford to pay their bishops. The Congregationalist national body did not meet that year at all.[9]

Thus it is not surprising that some of the freshly aroused criticism was turned inward. In addition to their revived concern in the secular world, the reformers moved to reform the Church. Such a homely but vital matter as the ministerial salary question, for example, now got the attention it deserved, and in the next few years the churches got more seriously to work upon pension and equalization schemes. In a remarkable upsurge of self-criticism, the *Christian Advocate* turned its disapproval of unethical business practices to focus upon the business practices of the Church itself:

Before the Crash, the Church had no ethical message that seriously interfered with the practices men were employing to make money [because] the economic morality of the Church, speaking generally, was not sufficiently different from prevailing practices to make any one inside or outside the organization at all uncomfortable. . . . We [must] consider . . . just what the sources of our income are, and whether or not money is going to tie our lips and prevent us from speaking the message that must be sounded forth from every pulpit if the Church is not to fail society. . . . We can honestly face up to all our own economic practices from our treatment of the sexton in the humblest church to the way we organize and conduct our vast business enterprises.[10]

Even more important, in this trend toward internal reform of the Church, was the waning of extreme prohibitionism. The smokescreen which had drifted over the Social Gospel was beginning to lift. External political circumstances helped; Governor Roosevelt was wet, but Al Smith was wetter, and FDR's convention victory over Smith helped to dissipate some Protestant objections to the party of Rum and Romanism, and smoothed the way for the social-gospelers to bow gracefully out of the Republican camp. The GOP did its best to hold them, through a suitably ambiguous platform plank, but President Hoover undid all the good work by a speech on that prohibition plank which spread "disappointment, chill and dark" in dry circles. "In 1928," the *Congregationalist* complained, "millions of drys voted for Hoover on the one argument that he was dry and would not budge. He has budged."

By budging, Hoover opened the way for wet liberals and dry liberals to get together again. The journal just cited made this change of heart explicit in its own case; it had supported Hoover in 1928 and now withdrew that support on the ground that "the factors that determined our attitude four years ago are not now present." A reader of this paper went further: "The Church elected Hoover. We bragged about it. Some of us have been honest enough to admit the error. This year, let us be as true to the cry *for* bread as we were to the cry *against* beer four years ago." [11]

Awakened to the misproportions in its own financial affairs and in its political judgment, the Church also showed in 1932 an impressive and heartening awareness of what was wrong with intrachurch race relations. Perhaps this was the most important social advance of the year.

A Southern Baptist leader inadvertently touched off a wave of both criticism and self-criticism by declining to sit at a banquet table in Rochester, New York, presided over by the chairman of the Baptist ministerial association for that region, who was the pastor of a Negro Baptist church. The discussion began with a spate of *tu quoque* letters, but rapidly passed beyond that stage. A ringing article in the *Baptist* demanded to know, "In how many cities is there any vital fellowship between Baptist white and colored ministers? . . . In how many Baptist [local] churches is there any inter-racial fellowship?"

There was dawning among white churchmen a realization that "inter-racial fellowship" involved more than simply being nice to Negroes at controlled gatherings arranged for that purpose. "Brotherhood is no idle sentiment; it means social equality," declared a later commentator on this Baptist discussion. He spelled out the significance of the Church's tacit approval of segregation with unwonted bluntness, concluding, among other things, that the Church by upholding antimiscegenation laws "contributes to bastardy." [12]

For white men in 1932, strong self-critical talk like this was needed; for Negroes, action based upon it was more convincing. It was perhaps with this in mind that the Episcopal Bishop of New York, William T. Manning—never one to do things by halves—forced the door of All Souls' Protestant Episcopal Church in Harlem (whose vestry had padlocked it, ostensibly for "repairs"), officially declared the church to be under the charge of its rector, and preached a sermon supporting the rector's decision to admit Negroes to services and membership on equal terms with white parishioners. It was an issue which had been hanging fire among New York City Episcopalians for several years.

The Methodists drew applause from Negroes at their General Conference of 1932 by providing that no such national gathering should thereafter "meet except in cities where there is no segregation of special racial groups, no discrimination in hotels, elevators, and restaurants, and where there have been specific instructions given to all employees to treat the representatives of every race with equality and courtesy." To protests that this action would make it virtually impossible to hold a General Conference in any city in the United States, the resolution's sponsor replied: "If no city would meet these conditions it would be better for us not to meet at all." [13] The Church was regaining its nerve; it was once again willing to embark on a course of action on the ground that it was right rather than on the ground that it met with majority social approval. A theology that revived Augustine's distinction between the Church and the World was beginning to bear fruit.

But the rekindled Social Gospel of the last year of the great depression was not confined to the righting of wrongs within the Church, nor to negative criticisms of the World. There was also some serious thinking about the kind of new political and social order the social gospelers specifically wanted to see.

The 1928 plenary meeting of the Federal Council of Churches

had decided that the Social Creed of the Churches, adopted in 1912, was long overdue for revision. At the time, what they had in mind was the addition of statements on world peace and on race relations, but in the ensuing four years came the depression. So when the revised version of the Social Creed came to the floor of the 1932 meeting of the Council, it was a transformed document.

Clauses from the old 1912 Creed—reduction of working hours, industrial safeguards, opposition to child labor, et cetera —were retained, but ambiguous phrasing was sharpened. Thus the Creed's vague first clause, "practical application of the Christian principle of social well-being to the acquisition and use of wealth" was spelled out as "subordination of speculation and the profit motive." Again, the bare "right to organize" theretofore conceded to labor was extended by addition of the words "for collective bargaining and social action," thereby getting beyond the thinking of that element in the Church which had believed that it is all right for workers to organize unions so long as they do not use them for anything.

More significant were the wholly new clauses: II, "Social planning and control of the credit and monetary systems and economic processes for the common good," and XI, "Economic justice for the farmer in legislation, financing of agriculture, transportation, and the price of farm products as compared with the cost of . . . commodities which he must buy." [14] A quiet revolution had taken place in the Church which would help to prepare Protestants for the social transformations of the New Deal.

As a least common denominator, intended for the longer-run social aims of the churches, this was impressive enough; what a church group could do and say under the pressure of short-run, contingent, emergency considerations could be even more so. The most remarkable Protestant social document of the pre-Roosevelt era originated on the floor of the Northern Baptist Convention of 1932; it opened with affirmations the like of which had rarely been heard in that or any other church's history:

150

That all wealth and all labor power are intended by the Creator for the highest good of all people; that from the cradle to the grave all members of the community are bound to do their best for the common good, and reciprocally are entitled to the best that the community is able to provide for its members in common; that the normal standard of living for any is that which is practicable for all; . . . that those members of the community who perform their duty within the community, acquire thereby a rightful claim upon or within the community for a normal living; and that no person can establish a rightful claim upon or within the community for more than a normal living.[15]

This is not the usual vague church plea for "brotherhood"; it is a sweeping economic and social equalitarianism. They used the phrase "cradle to the grave" in 1932, a full decade before the Beveridge Plan; but more startling was the spelling out of the frankly Marxist "from each according to his ability, to each according to his needs." The coincidence did not go unremarked; this was a majority, not a unanimous, report. That the Baptists adopted it after hearing even this much of it is a real tribute to the sense of social urgency that the depression had helped to create.

From this statement of ideals, the document passed over to the question of "How?" "Civil government," it answered itself, "is the sovereign agency for the promotion of the general welfare. To it belong all the rights of property and power necessary to accomplish the purpose of such an agency." But this sovereign agency could only achieve this purpose if certain other things were also true. So this Report proceeded to an assertion of social optimism; not the "prosperity-is-around-the-corner" optimism of Hoover, but the more robust sort that was to be communicated to the nation on the 4th of March next by a new President:

The people have the natural right to hold, and can safely be entrusted with, the power of democratic control over their economic life.

Distribution can be so coordinated as to supply the needs of all.

There need be no dispossessed class sinking into servitude, poverty, ignorance, vice, and misery.

Only then, after this trumpet blast of affirmation, did this document pass on to condemnation of the existing American economic system:

It has exalted personal possessions, privileges, and power above personal virtues and personal service.

It places an excessive and naive dependence upon competitive private trading as a method of distributing goods and services.

It endows the ownership of property with special economic and political power.

The relationship of the Church itself to the reforms necessary to redeem this "predatory national economy" would vary. Some desirable changes "lie on the very surface, obvious to common sense"; others "must be turned over to experts in political and economic science and in practical management." But even from the latter the Church cannot excuse herself from concern and action. "A sound society must use its own skills to cure its own ills, but the pervasive influence of Christianity ought to create in society the ability to distinguish between wholesome skills and vicious ones." And churchmen were bound to insist that "the government . . . shall not evade its supreme responsibility."

All of this was so far beyond the sterile social vs. individual gospel debate of the 20's that it begins to appear that the depression was not so much the cause as the opportunity for the Social Gospel to come to maturity. In effect, what the Baptist Convention was doing in accepting this report was to go on record for the New Deal a year before it was born. I do not mean to imply that most Baptists by 1932 were New Dealers in embryo, only that, for the time being, the teaching function of the Church (as Baptists understood it) was swung around to support of the social ideals which the following year were to be imperfectly crystallized in the New Deal.

But when the Northern Baptists adopted this report, they endorsed certain phrases and slogans which were shortly to ring in Republican brains like fire alarms. Indeed, some of these phrases and slogans, particularly concerning the role of the gov-

ernment—"control," "co-ordinate," "inquire," "give the public
. . . assistance in arriving at reliable judgments"—were to give
some of these same liberals cold chills when they were put to use
in the 50's in a nonliberal administration. In accepting the New
Deal before its time, the social gospelers were also accepting its
defects.

One member of the committee which brought out the Baptist report sensed this, from a theological rather than a political
perspective, and concurred separately: "Agreeing fully with the
indictment of selfish society and with the thesis that Christians
have vast social responsibilities, but not agreeing . . . with the
argument that unregenerate humanity can be molded into a
society that can be called the Kingdom of God, I sign the report."

Christians have vast social responsibilities, yet humanity is
unregenerate! We have heard much of this in more recent years,
in that paradox of political left and theological right by means
of which Reinhold Niebuhr and his followers have synthesized
the European "crisis-theology" with the American social concern. Indeed, by 1932 the European critique had begun to penetrate beyond the few specialists and to have a broader influence
in the American Protestant churches. "Many who cannot understand this strange dialectic theology know that it is saying something which they have long dimly felt," wrote Henry P. Van
Dusen the following year.[16] And in 1932, this interpenetration
of European and American theology took a sudden surge forward as Niebuhr dropped his first real bombshell. Into the
implicit ethical monism of the old Social Gospel he injected the
ethical dualism of *Moral Man and Immoral Society.*

Niebuhr had learned some things in the course of the depression too.[17] Beliefs he had groped for in 1927 now emerged in
stark clarity. *Does Civilization Need Religion?* had cast some
preliminary taunts at the "conceit of religious people . . . that
a vigorous statement of the ideal ought to result in its realization," and at a religious liberalism which failed to "do justice
. . . both to the essential harmony and to the inevitable conflict in the cosmos and in the soul"; now, in *Moral Man and*

153

Immoral Society, this criticism burst forth in a manner that split asunder the world-view of the older Social Gospel.[18]

"The thesis to be elaborated in these pages," he wrote, "is that a sharp distinction must be drawn between the moral and social behavior of individuals and of social groups, national, racial, and economic." To be sure, the Social Gospel had always warred against an individualistic interpretation of social ethics; this had been the whole point of Rauschenbusch's *Christianizing the Social Order.* But Rauschenbusch's generation had sought to transfer an effective ethical motivation from the realm of individual action to that of social action. Society cannot be reformed by reforming individual members of it, they asserted —but society as a whole is capable of reform. Not so, said Reinhold Niebuhr; the discontinuity between individual and social morality is more radical than ever the men of the old liberal Social Gospel had thought possible: "Individual men may be moral," he admitted, "in the sense that they are able to consider interests other than their own in determining problems of conduct, and are capable, on occasion, of preferring the advantages of others to their own. . . . But . . . these achievements are more difficult, if not impossible, for human societies and social groups."

But if this is true, then a Christian ethical perspective on the social order would seem impossible; indeed, just such an assumption—the moral relativity of all human institutions—was involved in the European attack upon American Christian liberalism. Quotations abound in Niebuhr himself which would seem logically to justify withdrawing all support for a Social Gospel. "There are constitutional limitations in the genius of religion," he writes, "which will always make it more fruitful in purifying individual life, and adding wholesomeness to the more intimate social groups, such as the family, than in the problems of the more complex and political relations of modern society." [19]

One can easily go on from this to Barthianism: if Niebuhr is right in saying this, the Social Gospel cause is lost, and Christians may well leave all tinkering with the social order to "reforming busybodies who suffer from a lack of humor," as Karl Barth once put it, and get on with the central business of preaching the Word of God to any individual who is moved to listen.[20] But this is just what Niebuhr did not do, in the individualist way that Barth had in mind. Instead, he came up with a radical new theory of Christian social action.

There are at least three lines of departure from a judgment that moral man is trapped in an immoral society. One may withdraw from the moral relativities to the realm of the Biblical absolute, with Barth; one may overcome the moral relativities, seeking an apocalyptic answer—bringing in the Kingdom of God by storm; or one may use the moral relativities, pragmatically, in a "crusade for the relatively better." Somewhere between these latter two lies a Marxist or quasi-Marxist brand of Christianity, and this, in 1932, was the road taken by Niebuhr.[21]

In this view, society is "immoral" because its principles of operation are geared to the preservation of power for those who rule it, i.e., the bourgeoisie; and since its institutions are corrupt, the only human beings capable of "morality" are those who have no vested interest in society to corrupt them, i.e., the proletariat. Only they, therefore, are capable of bringing about even approximate social justice; and, hence, the only force that can bridge the gap between moral man and immoral society is a thoroughgoing socialism. What Reinhold Niebuhr had done here was not to abrogate the Social Gospel of the center but to revive the long-slumbering Social Gospel of the left.

It is no accident that *Moral Man and Immoral Society* was published in the year that followed the establishment of the Fellowship of Socialist Christians, whose Manifesto was published to the world on November 30, 1931, declaring

that a Christian ethic is most adequately expressed and effectively applied in our society in socialist terms. . . . Recognizing the fact of the class struggle, they support the aggressive assertion of the rights of the exploited and disinherited. . . . They believe that it is not impossible to secure sufficient ethical insight among all classes of society to prevent the class struggle from issuing in the violence of class war. . . . They see little prospect, however, of such a develop-

155

ment if a constantly increasing number in the privileged groups do not . . . recognize the extent of covert and overt violence inherent in the present order and its maintenance.[22]

The signers of this document, who included Niebuhr, John Bennett, and Buell Gallagher, were, as is usual with Christian socialists, a middle-class lot; they pledged themselves, for example, to "encourage one another in rigorous self-discipline in the matter of income and expenditures, in the effort to practice [Christian economic] principles in our present society." They also pledged themselves "to support the Socialist Party or such other party as may embody the purpose of socialism as the political organization most nearly approximating a political expression of Christian ethics for our day," and men like these unquestionably played a major role in the 800,000-vote last rally of the American Socialist Party in the election of 1932.

But it was a sharper, bitterer socialism that Niebuhr stood for than most Christian socialist clergymen had been wont. It was antiprogressivist, for "civilization has become a device for delegating the vices of individuals to larger and larger communities"; it was antimoralist, for moralists lacked "an understanding of the brutal character of the behavior of all human collectives"; and it was anti-Fabian, for "conflict is inevitable, and in this conflict power must be challenged by power."

Here, for the first time, an American Christian of the political left made a clean break with the prewar theology of the Social Gospel. He asked the question which most of the followers of Rauschenbusch had never put to themselves, namely, "*How* is the Kingdom of God to be achieved on earth?" and answered it, frankly, "By force." Consequently, it would not be the Kingdom of God at all, but a human social order adjusted to the realities of the human social situation. In programmatic terms, this came out as Marxism.

Niebuhr was attracted to Marxism in this period because it, also, made war upon the illusions of middle-class Christian liberals. He praised Marxist "realism" in seeing "how inevitably special privilege is associated with power"—which is to say, how inevitably society is immoral. Furthermore, in espousing

Karl Marx he by no means committed himself to the gradualistic version of Marxism. The conclusion drawn from his chapters on "Justice Through Revolution" and "Justice Through
Political Force" is a tossup: "The contrasting virtues and vices
of revolutionary and evolutionary socialism are such that no
purely moral choice is possible between them."

On the other hand, he did not absolutize the Marxian socialist state as a goal either, for by Niebuhr's definition no social
order could be ideal. Man's concern "for some centuries to
come" would be, not an "ideal society," but "a society in which
there will be enough justice, in which coercion will be sufficiently non-violent to prevent his common enterprise from issuing into complete disaster." [23]

In pre–World War I years all of this would have been called
into question quickly enough, far more so in the years following the Ten Days that Shook the World. Unfortunately, any
socialism of the 1930's, Christian or otherwise, had to define its
position with respect to the Russian Revolution. So Niebuhr
and men like him, by reviving the Social Gospel of the left in
so aggressively Marxist a form, inevitably also called into being
a Social Gospel of the *far* left—something which in the gentler
days of Washington Gladden would have been almost incon-
ceivable.

This should not be misunderstood. In the 1930's, general
sympathy with the aims of the Russian Revolution, and willing-
ness to adapt Russian social experiments to meet the challenge
of the American depression, did not necessarily constitute
"fellow traveling," in the treasonable sense that that term
acquired in the late 1940's. Christians in particular, of the
sort who had been accustomed to deprecating "greed" and
"mammon-worship" in this country, even as they drew back in
horror at Soviet brutalities, were moved in spite of themselves
to sympathy with a system which claimed to have abolished the
profit motive.

The denominational journals for 1932 returned again and
again to the topic of Russia. They were fascinated by it; an
official atheist creed in conjunction with a program which

claimed to achieve their own ethical goals—the Kingdom of God, in short, without God—disturbed and challenged them. And the dreary fact of the depression in America was never far from their minds. "There is hunger in Russia this winter, too," said a writer in the *Baptist*. "But Russia's hunger is quite evenly distributed, while the frigidity of the American business system continues to separate a desperate farmer from desperate hunger in our cities." Men like this, while rejecting Soviet autocracy and police methods, were quite willing to "wish Russia well in her experiment and we are ready to learn from her success or failure." [24]

The nation's experience of Senator McCarthy is so fresh in our minds that it is difficult for us to remember that in the 1930's these words were not particularly shocking. The Red Scare of the 1920's had lapsed; the Red Scare of the 1940's was yet to come; and as a corollary, free discussion of the Soviet system was taken for granted. The *Congregationalist*, discussing the "farm strike" which centered in Iowa in 1932, advised that "we forget the Communists and other very improbable sources of danger." To conceive of the Communists as a very improbable source of danger, in the hydrogen era, may take some imagination, but the evidence of the sentiment's existence in the 30's is there to be read.

Nor was this, of course, confined to the Church. "Why should Russia," Stuart Chase asked at the close of his book, *A New Deal*, "have all the fun of remaking a world?" [25] The use of the word "fun" in this connection speaks volumes about the temper of the times. And the liberals in the churches, to the extent that they concurred in this sort of thing, concurred in something which (along with other things the Democratic Party is less anxious to forget) was to be a living force in the minds of the Americans who created the New Deal.

As for Reinhold Niebuhr himself, his Marxism was and had to be a passing phase. Marxism, together with the Christian liberalism which Niebuhr rejected, presupposed "moral man," and hence, after the Revolution, "moral society." Niebuhr already rejected the latter; as his understanding of the human situation became more pessimistic he would reject the former. The theology which was going to revive in intellectual America the doctrine of original sin would have no place in it for Marxism, which for all its catastrophic revolutionary apocalypses was by comparison with neo-orthodoxy wildly optimistic.

This change lay in the future for Niebuhr and the Church. He had not yet been made to see that social action in America was still possible short of social overturn. Moreover, he did not yet understand the dynamic of the Soviet state.

He criticized it, to be sure, but in terms of method, over-emphasis, overcompensation (e.g., vindictiveness in the pursuit of class enemies). He tended to identify, and to confuse, the revolutionary élite with the working class—to assume that dictatorship of the proletariat meant dictatorship by the proletariat. He had his reservations—he saw "very considerable" abuse of power by Communist bureaucrats, which was "bound to grow" as the purer revolutionary idealists were "supplanted by men who have consciously sought for the possession of power." But, on the whole, he criticized Russia not for being a "police state" but for imperfectly and inadequately fulfilling the Communist ideal.

This would pass; the absolutistic pretensions of the Soviet state would in due course drive him, and men like him, into a forthrightly antitotalitarian position—a development of the utmost importance for the Social Gospel. But that position was yet a few years away; in the meantime Niebuhr's inclination to revolutionary Marxism as much as any of the rest of his thought marked and molded the Social Gospel under the early New Deal.

It marked and molded Reinhold Niebuhr, also; a man who has undergone the experience of looking at the world through Marx-colored glasses is not the same man afterward. Niebuhr's Marxist experience was to contribute toward another aspect of his thought, which was to stir further controversy in the Church —his militant antipacifism.

In 1932, Niebuhr was still a member of the pacifist Fellowship of Reconciliation, but the handwriting was on the wall. "The middle classes are wrong," he wrote in *Moral Man and Immoral Society*, "in their assumption that violence is intrinsically immoral. Nothing is intrinsically immoral except ill-will and nothing intrinsically good except goodwill." [26] The chapter surrounding these words was filled with more of the same Nietzschean antinomianism, and to a reader who bore in mind the Christian compulsion of the ethic of love, the language of this justification of violence seemed startling and even terrifying. Niebuhr and the Niebuhrians in reply could only point to events in the world, which were also startling and terrifying.

The series of disarmament conferences and moratoria and naval holidays which had begun so auspiciously at Washington in 1921 was coming ingloriously to an end at Geneva in 1932; the atmosphere of the Briand-Kellogg Pact was melting away. The world public opinion which Senator Borah had counted on to keep the peace had broken in confusion the moment a nation became sufficiently desperate to flout it. Japan, already in possession of Manchuria since September of 1931, hesitated briefly when the League of Nations adopted the "Stimson Doctrine," and withdrew from Shanghai on the eleventh of March; it was the first victory for "world public opinion" in the Age of the Dictators—and the last. Two weeks later, the Japanese government gave notice of withdrawal from the League of Nations and proceeded without further interruption along its course of what might be termed international *laissez faire*.

What did all this mean for the churches? It meant that the easy, socially acceptable pacifism of the Hoover-Kellogg era was gone, never to return. Resolutions against war, which continued, did not have at all the same implications as they had had in a time when pacifism seemed itself to be part of the *status quo*—and social gospelers knew it.

"If Geneva fails," the Washington correspondent of the *Christian Advocate* predicted—referring to the 1932 Geneva Conference on naval disarmament—"Germany will rearm," and then there would unfailingly be an arms race and a war.[27] And, of course, there was. Consequently, pacifism no longer meant self-righteous obedience to an antiwar treaty to which one's country was a signatory. It meant, rather, such things as the pathetic letter which the Japanese Christian leader Kagawa addressed to Chinese Christians in that year: "Dear Brothers and Sisters: I want to ask your pardon for my nation. . . . Pardon us, especially, because our Christian forces were not strong enough to get the victory over the militarists." [28] Pacifism meant the robust awareness of being in dissent, which men like Kirby Page showed; it meant, also, the tough-minded, thoroughly political behavior of Mohandas Gandhi, who demonstrated that nonviolent resistance could explode with a psychological violence all its own.

Unfortunately, it meant also a blurring-over of moral distinctions in international matters; it is far easier to oppose all war on principle if one assumes that in any given conflict both sides are equally at fault. There was among pacifists, therefore, a nearly fatal lack of understanding of the nature and reality of aggression. Under the circumstances, it is not at all surprising that a current set in among Protestant liberals to carry them back toward nonpacifism.

Yet it was not quite the same kind of nonpacifism which had made preachers present arms in the First World War. The feeling lingered that in that conflict the Christian pulpit had disgraced itself. Furthermore, the point of view expressed in *Moral Man and Immoral Society* tended to cut the nerve of any attempt to absolutize the social order, either in a pacifist or a militarist direction. If man was not going to bring in the Kingdom of God by enacting Kellogg Pacts, neither was he going to bring it in by making war to save the world for democracy.

To fight or not to fight now became a choice of relative evils instead of a choice between good and evil; the Christian nonpacifist would never again go to war in the mood of the YMCA secretary or the Boy Scout. The editor of the *Congregationalist* expressed this sober point of view when he wrote that he was not a pacifist—but took no credit for the fact:

I am never quite sure that a Christian should not be ashamed of being anything less [than a pacifist]. If under any conceivable circumstance [war] should be necessary or unavoidable, I would rob it of every suggestion of glory. . . . If we must train men for war we should do so with full recognition of the grim and terrible thing we are doing.[29]

But this Christian nonpacifism did not convince everyone. The Niebuhrian tendency to relativize, some Christians felt, was so overdone in this case as to negate the Christian ethic entirely. Possibly some of them read the reflections on violence in Chapter VII of *Moral Man and Immoral Society,* and to Niebuhr's charge that any pacifism unwarrantedly absolutized a social-ethical program, they could reply in his own words:

The absolutist and fanatic is no doubt dangerous; but he is also necessary. If he does not judge and criticize immediate achievements, which always involve compromise, in the light of his absolute ideal, the radical force in history . . . finally sinks into the sands of complete relativism. There is only one step from a rationally moderated idealism to opportunism, and only another step from opportunism to dishonest capitulation to the *status quo.*[30]

Niebuhr was of course talking here about socialism, rather than pacifism, but the argument is transferable, and by many pacifists it was transferred. The consequence was that in the moment that the schism in the Social Gospel over Prohibition began to be healed, another and more grievous schism opened over pacifism—more grievous for the reason that men on both sides of this controversy could and did continue to think and speak in terms of political liberalism, although the "old" political liberalism, absolutist and optimistic, the heir of the "old" Social Gospel, tended to be pacifist, whereas the "new" political liberalism, relativist and pessimistic, tended toward the nonpacifist position. As the nation divided between isolationism and interventionism, churchmen were to divide also. The Social Gospel, beginning to flare up in all its old power, was also beginning to confront the most serious challenge in all its history.

CHAPTER XII

Impact: The Hundred Days

and Afterward

THANKS to the fact that the Constitution had been drawn up in a time when it had taken weeks to reach the nation's capital, there elapsed between the election of 1932 and the arrival of the Roosevelt administration nearly four months, and they were the months of winter. If the nation did not talk quite so wildly of revolution as in the short, cold days of the winter before, it was in almost as desperate a physical plight. And the liberal press was remarkably pessimistic about the prospect of any improvement. The pages of the *New Republic* for January and February of 1933 make instructive reading in their gloomy prediction that the new President would be another do-nothing conservative. For desperate intellectuals, then as now, hope for the future was a species of disloyalty.

The Social Gospel press, also, shared in this anticipatory skepticism. Its acknowledged leader, the *Christian Century*, was bothered by Roosevelt's glibness; it disapproved of "Cactus

Jack" Garner; and, in view of FDR's big-Navy views, his imperialistic role in Haiti during the Wilson administration, and his "airy sarcasm" on the subject of disarmament, it feared Roosevelt's foreign policy. As for domestic policy, "both Mr. Hoover and Mr. Roosevelt are conservatives," the *Century* had declared during the campaign. Such differences between the two men as the editors observed they ascribed to temperament: "both are conservative, but Mr. Roosevelt may be characterized as a loose conservative."

Thus, moved by no enthusiasm for either candidate, yet constrained to choose between them by the gravity of the situation, the *Christian Century* delayed taking a stand as long as possible. Finally, unwilling to move sufficiently far out of the existing two-party system to support Norman Thomas and professing to see in the Republican candidate "a sense of responsibility and a high quality of intellectual integrity which can hardly be claimed for his opponent," its editors despairingly announced their support of the candidacy of Herbert Clark Hoover. Reinhold Niebuhr promptly wrote them a letter attacking this choice, but he, as a leading light of the Fellowship of Socialist Christians, had been for Thomas, and as between Roosevelt and Hoover he shared the *Century*'s despair.

The depression and the winter wore on, and, in the course of their clutching at straws, the liberals in the churches began to thaw. The *Christian Century* relaxed a little when it contemplated the free hand that the new President had been given by his heavy electoral majority and by the "insignificant core of positive commitments in so large a volume of talk." It relaxed a little more when Roosevelt indicated that he would continue the "Stimson Doctrine" in the Far East, and again when he disclosed his proposals for the Tennessee Valley, and yet again, be it noted, when he announced the appointment of Cordell Hull, a stern dry who had opposed the Democratic Party's repeal plank. On March 1, 1933, the *Century* editorialized on the subject "The New Pilot Comes Aboard," in a tone hopeful and expectant (and prophetic) "that the government of the United

States may be a very different affair in 1937 from what it is to-day." [1]

Then, together, came the bank panic and the inaugural.

Wilson had spoken with a more literary eloquence; Bryan had been a more cathartic emotional experience; Adlai Stevenson was to set forth the issues with far greater cogency; but it is doubtful whether any other speech in American history fell upon the nation with greater immediate psychological impact than the first inaugural address of Franklin D. Roosevelt. There had been other times when despairing men had waited similarly for a simple, convincing resolution of grievous social issues, but Webster and Clay and Lincoln had not had the radio. Herbert Hoover had had it and had scarcely known what to do with it; his best speeches, oratorically, were not to be delivered until the Republicans' lean twenty years were nearly over. Franklin Roosevelt had it and used it; he had the office of the presidency and used that, also. A Danton calling for audacity, and showing it himself in a measure that made men cheer (and some men weep), he set the nation on its ear—and the people in the churches were as astounded, bedazzled, and enheartened as all the rest.

Even the weather was on the politically lucky FDR's side that March day: a gray drizzle which broke clear just in time to give dramatic point to his optimistic words. "Calm, courageous, confident of himself and his country," editorialized the *Christian Advocate* under the title "Clouds and Sun," Roosevelt spoke in "the ringing tones that ears were aching to hear. . . . In twenty minutes he had done the country a world of good"; and the editors exultingly predicted "that this is the decisive month of the depression; that the worst will soon be over." [2]

As March and April and May passed and the sun continued to shine and the Congress to make hay, the liberals in the Church felt that once again the sources of social evolution had been tapped. "Why *not* change our form of government?" The *Christian Century* ebulliently asked, its former unhappy skepticism forgotten. And the *Churchman* saw in the New Deal

165

"qualities of spiritual reality which have already remade the national psychology. . . . No one in the church . . . who has preached and thought these many years in terms of the social gospel . . . can experience anything but sheer joy." [3] Statements such as this show a sense of relief not only for the improvement in the national situation but for the improvement of the situation of the churches as well.

The times had been hard for church as for state; church buildings had closed, church assemblies had been postponed, missionaries had been recalled, benevolent funds had been curtailed or exhausted. But the Church's troubles, as we have seen in earlier chapters, were of older standing than the depression. Secularism had been riding high; church membership in some instances had been lagging behind population growth; the number of theological seminary graduates was "appreciably smaller" than in the previous generation; and many churchmen attributed this situation in part at least to the Church's record of capitulation to the *status quo*.[4]

Now, with the guardians of the erstwhile *status quo* seemingly on the run, a favorable atmosphere had been created for a "new deal" within the Church itself, a "new deal" which would include a more expansive Social Gospel. No longer was it as "dangerous" to preach the Social Gospel from a Christian pulpit as it had been in 1929. If the prophetic preaching of Rauschenbusch had done its bit toward establishing an ethical frame of reference for the New Deal, the New Deal in its turn had created at one stroke a more spacious atmosphere for the intellectual and political rejuvenation of the Church.

Pundits have occasionally argued that the New Deal was no "revolution"; the government's efforts toward recovery both under Hoover and under Roosevelt, they say, were so radical a departure from the policy of inaction in the depressions of 1837 and 1893 as to constitute a bond between the Hoover and Roosevelt administrations more important than any ideological difference between them. But there was at the very least, as between Hoover and FDR, the difference between reluctance and enthusiasm, and in the eyes of the hard-pressed American people this was the difference that really mattered. The sentiments of a clergyman of lifelong Republican convictions are typical: "I voted for Roosevelt because I thought he would *do* something." [5]

So it is not surprising that many men in the churches responded to Roosevelt's quickening influence. Some social gospelers accepted the New Deal with all the ardor of the young New Dealers in Washington (though perhaps with less of the manipulative cynicism that some of the latter showed). Benson Y. Landis, the Federal Council's equivalent of a brain truster, summed up the transformation in a book whose title was soon to be applied to the New Deal by friends and enemies, *The Third American Revolution;* F. Ernest Johnson, another Federal Council leader, declared in *Economics and the Good Life* that the New Deal embodied what the Social Gospel had stood for all along. "This IS a New Deal," the *Churchman* exclaimed, applauding FDR, Frances Perkins, Harry Hopkins, John Collier; "we had become so accustomed . . . to the continuous slide down hill . . . that it hardly seems possible we have challenged gravity and are now walking up—perhaps even running." [6]

The New Deal also dissolved more of the prohibitionist ice which had kept some churchmen in frozen wedlock with Hoover. Such men did not, at once, abandon their dry hopes, but Prohibition's political and psychological importance for these men continued to recede. C. Oscar Johnson, President of the Northern Baptist Convention, is reported to have told FDR during a White House visit at the time of that church's annual session (which in 1933 happened to be in Washington): "Baptists are back of you 96.8 per cent. We cannot go the other 3.2 per cent"—referring, of course, to 3.2 beer. [7]

Once faced with a *fait accompli,* when Utah completed ratification of repeal in December, it was no more difficult for even an unreconstructed dry to reconcile a general support for the New Deal with a dislike for the liquor policy of FDR and the Democratic party than it was for an unreconstructed Southerner in the same period to go along in spite of misgivings about Harold Ickes and Henry Wallace and Eleanor. If the Republicans retained a lingering campaign issue here, they killed it for good in 1940 by nominating as FDR's opponent a man whose brother was vice-president of Seagram's.

The good will of the churches for the early New Deal was of course in part simply the general good will for national recovery, which was in somewhat the same category as being "against sin." The real test was to come when the honeymoon was over.

Structurally, national recovery took the form of a vast mass of legislation, poured forth from the Congress during that breathless "hundred days" the like of which the republic had never seen before, but, pre-eminently, it was embodied in the National Industrial Recovery Act. This measure became the law of the land on June 16, 1933, and shortly after Congress had adjourned the realm began to be peppered with edicts, codes, and Blue Eagles, all issuing from the nest of the energetic General Hugh S. Johnson. The denominational journals in due course displayed the Blue Eagle at their mastheads, with the accompanying slogan "We Do Our Part"; and their treatment of that redoubtable bird is the real measure of the Social Gospel as applied to the early New Deal.

The attitude of churchmen toward the NRA, at first, ranged from enthusiasm to the more sober feeling that this was the remedy for depression which the administration had chosen to try and it simply had to work. "The plan may conceivably have flaws," said the *Christian Advocate,* in the number which first showed the NRA label, "but this is no time for criticism." [8]

Others worried about the problem of maintaining support for the program. They recognized that recovery had thus far been based more upon a surge of public confidence than upon any specific action of the government and that, after the glamor of the emergency had worn off, the President's enthusiasm would not be enough to carry a program of social change by itself. As the *Churchman* put it:

The history of America is a long, pitiful tale of deflated moral enthusiasms. We work our way into a state of altruistic ecstasy only to suddenly collapse like a busted balloon. . . . Right now, when we are all broke, we are strong for the reorganization of the social order. . . . Tomorrow, when new riches are within our grasp, shall we still be whooping it up for . . . collective altruism?

A few weeks later the same journal again warned that the President's fireside chats, and the popular confidence which they generated, would not suffice to make the NRA codes a success; the key to success or failure was the good faith of the business community. "If the industrial leaders have their fingers crossed when they sign, before the ink dries the code becomes a scrap of paper." The prospect was not good, for the predepression record of those industrial leaders was "a sad, sordid story of cruelty and chicanery." [9]

Thus, enthusiastic as the churches were for the professed social objectives of the New Deal, they were not swept away. Churchmen could be just as impatient as socialists with FDR for attempting to save American capitalism from the consequences of its own folly, and the doubts as to NRA's economic workability were succeeded by doubts as to its political wisdom in the first place.

On September 28th, the *Christian Advocate* published an important contribution to the development of church thinking about the NRA. This article was prompted by efforts of General Johnson to mobilize pastors, as "natural community leaders," to urge their congregations to subscribe to and uphold the recovery program. The Church dared not be wholly neutral about the NRA, the writer felt; that would be "entirely too certain a demonstration of the divorcement of religion from life, an indictment already laid against the Church." But General Johnson was stepping into dangerous territory. The writer recalled the government's effort, so largely successful, to mobilize war sentiment through the churches in 1917; he, for one, was not in the mood to subscribe thus blindly to another mobilization, even in the cause of national recovery. The Church should at any rate take a long, hard look at the program before putting a Blue Eagle on the steeple; there were certain pointed questions about the NRA which it was the minister's duty to ask, in and out of the pulpit.

The most momentous of these was the one which Washington itself could hardly have answered at the time: was the recovery program conceived of as a temporary emergency measure, or as a permanent change in American life? If permanent, how were the problems of wage-price parity, coercion, the abrogation of the old legal-constitutional apparatus, et cetera, to be handled on a long-term basis? If temporary, what was to be done toward permanent recovery?

The "moral gains" resulting from NRA, this writer believed, were "undeniably apparent"—"age-long abuses have yielded to sharp Federal pressure that for long years have resisted every other kind of attack." But, if the NRA were a temporary expedient, would not these evils return as conditions more nearly approached normal? On the other hand, if the NRA were permanent, was it the right kind of permanent institution to do the job? NRA was "quite frankly an attempt to patch an old system on new pieces of cloth," and hardly filled the bill as an agent of social reform. It, and anything else which Washington might accomplish, had "been made possible only because of . . . thorough disgust with the present archaic capitalist system"; and insufficient thinking had been done in Washington toward what in due course should take that system's place.[10]

Such serious expressions of doubt in the churches toward the central piece of recovery legislation, mingled with general approval of the social reforms men expected from the New Deal, show that at least some of the liberals in the churches were running far ahead of Roosevelt in their thinking. For the NRA, in historical retrospect, looks a good deal less like what the well-wishers of the New Deal thought it was at the time. Indeed, its demise and the enactment of a new sort of legislation centering upon the Wagner Act are now considered by many historians to be the turning point between a "first" and a "second" New Deal, a shift from emphasis on recovery, with the co-operation of big business, to emphasis on reform, with punishment of big business for having failed to respond to FDR's efforts at recovery. The men of the Social Gospel, then, did not fixate at the Blue Eagle stage; they kept before them the aim of general social overhaul which had been called back into the Church's consciousness by the experience of depression.

"General Hugh S. Johnson, industrial administrator," said the *Presbyterian Advance,* as early in the NRA's career as August of 1933, "calls for 'a truce on selfishness.' We move to amend by substituting 'war' for 'truce.' " [11] Their feeling was all too justified; as the NRA swung into action, it did not seem merely ineffectual as a means to social justice, it seemed positively illiberal.

The codes themselves appeared simply to legitimatize existing private arrangements on prices, marketing, and so on, to the convenience of big business, "the substitution of legal for companionate marriages in the realm of private monopoly," as Walter Lippmann put it.[12] "Not in many years have monopolistic tendencies in industry been so forwarded and strengthened," Clarence Darrow's review committee reported to the President in 1934; "the code has offered an opportunity for the more powerful and more profitable interests to seize control of an industry or to augment and extend a control already obtained." [13] Neither were the act's benefits to labor organization working out as planned. Administrative interpretation of the famous "Section 7a," the collective-bargaining clause, made separate rather than collective bargaining possible and paved the way for the breaking up of union locals on a "divide-and-rule" basis. The labor press began to refer to the initials NRA as standing for "National Run-Around."

Churchmen discovered this situation as quickly as any other category of citizens. In the fall of 1933, *World Tomorrow,* the radical Christian paper edited by Kirby Page, pointed out that the National Industrial Recovery Act's minimum-wage provisions had had the unexpected effect of aggravating the unemployment problem. This worked particular hardship upon colored workers—the traditional "last hired, first fired"—who

171

were often dismissed from work en masse on the assumption by employers that whites were more efficient and thus "worth" more in terms of the new, higher wage scales. The article concluded, "The Blue Eagle has been spoken of as a 'predatory bird,' and local Negro humor in Alabama has interpreted it as the 'Negro Removal Act.' " [14]

"Merely to 'restore the system to its normal functioning,' as we have been advised to do," the Methodist bishops warned on November 24th, "is to trifle with a terrible catastrophe and assure its return." [15] After the joyous atmosphere of the spring of 1933 and the trenchant criticism of the winter of 1932, liberal churchmen could not long rest content with halfway patchwork like the NRA. The Social Gospel was quite prepared to turn farther left.

Moreover, it was foreseen in the Church that even the degree of social reform possible within the framework of the NRA would soon be imperiled. As early as June 21, 1933, with the ink scarcely dry on the Recovery Act the *Christian Century* prophesied:

About six months hence . . . some unit in the old laissez-faire industrial order will refuse to submit to the regulations of the new planned economy. Some cotton mill in the south, for example, may refuse to accept forty hours as the maximum working week for its employees, or $25 as the minimum weekly wage. . . . In some such fashion as this the issue will be put up to the supreme court. . . . The nation is being carried forward into an hour when its fate rests on the word of nine men.[16]

And in due course, in the summer of 1935, the nine men heard the now-celebrated "sick chicken" case and struck down the NRA.

By that time, however, the climate of opinion had swung generally from recovery to reform, and the death rattle of the Blue Eagle was drowned almost immediately in the birth cry of the Wagner Act. America was by then on the move from the "first" to the "second" New Deal, whose legislation was destined to outlive Roosevelt, the depression, and two wars. Men of the Social Gospel could take credit, during this era of transition, for keeping the eyes of citizens in the churches focused on social reality.

Nor was the NRA the only target of criticism. As Protestant liberals drew back from recovery-by-monopoly, they also expressed opposition to abundance-through-scarcity. The plowing-under policies being pursued in the Department of Agriculture convinced some secular liberals, but they outraged many men of the Social Gospel. Innocent for the most part of formal economic theory, including the economy-of-scarcity rationale which underlay the AAA, they saw it simply as a matter of not feeding the multitudes when food was available. "It seems little short of blasphemy against the bounty of nature and the labor of man," declared the *Congregationalist,* and, also, "futile"— like "the smashing of machines a century ago" (in England).[17]

On the eve of another winter the Methodist bishops, remembering the horrors of 1931 and 1932, blasted plowing-under in these terms and criticized the administration for insufficient boldness in distributing national wealth. When bishops could thus go beyond the program of a government already being denounced as "radical," it was evident that they were beginning to live down the scandal of their colleague, the dry potentate James M. Cannon.

But, unfortunately for the future of the Social Gospel, if most of this criticism had the effect of clarifying and sharpening the reform purposes of the New Deal, one line of attack was destined to confuse the debate considerably.

On August 10th, 1933, the *Christian Advocate* editorially exclaimed: "Recovery, what sins are committed in thy name!" Usually, when Methodists talked this way, they referred to "booze"; sometimes, as we have seen, to the Blue Eagle, but on this occasion the editors had something else on their minds:

Battleships are indeed a costly toy. . . . As objects of "lasting usefulness" [in the language of the public-works programs] they have had their day. Even their social usefulness is challenged, and the only "lasting" feature is likely to be the interest on the bonds which build them. That debt will be alive when the cruisers have gone to Davy Jones's locker.

In Congress, this would have been dismissed as another partisan squawk about "government spending"; but this criticism was in pacifist, not penny-pinching, terms:

When peace-loving people joined the agitation for government expenditure for unemployment relief, they thought of highways and bridges and forests and irrigation and power projects, to make this a better country to live in. They are against spending relief funds for making machines for killing people.[18]

Pacifism had entered into and become a vital part of the Social Gospel. It was receding a little, with each blow struck overseas, but it remained a formidable force in the Church nevertheless. Consequently, as the Administration's "militarism" moved toward the fore, pacifism would constitute a challenge to that administration—and, by inference, to all of FDR's record including the New Deal.

The day of breach was yet in the future; the men of the Social Gospel would share in the electoral triumph of 1936; but their day of glory was to be a short one. The signs were present to be read. For the United States was not the only country in the world to have enjoyed a "hundred days" during the spring of 1933. The other was Hitler's Germany.

But in the meantime, if the churches had done their bit toward creating a receptive atmosphere for the New Deal by the kind of message which they preached in 1932 and 1933, the New Deal had done a great service for the churches in return. As the trend toward smokeless factory chimneys and closed banks and lost farms came to a halt, so also did the trend toward empty treasuries and closed churches and curtailed benevolences and recalled foreign missionaries.

More important yet, the churches shared in the psychological breath-catching afforded to the nation. The depression as I have observed before was a psychic as well as an economic phenomenon, and so was recovery. The effect upon the work and morale of the Church was comparable to the effect upon the nation. Once again board secretaries dared to think in terms of long range plans of a kind other than retrenchment;

once again the life of the Church quickened and rid itself of paralyzing thought for the morrow.

Church legislative gatherings took on a new tone. "An unusually large number of official and national meetings were scheduled for 1934," writes the editor of the *Yearbook of American Churches,* and "nearly every body found its agenda concerned with discussions of the social implications of religion." [19] Several denominations created new machinery to implement the Social Gospel; for example the Northern Baptist Convention appointed a Commission on Social Action, and the General Assembly of the Presbyterian Church in the United States—significantly, for this was a Southern denomination—set up a Permanent Committee on Social and Moral Welfare. But by far the most interesting of these new agencies arose among the Congregationalists, in the form of the Council for Social Action.[20]

The Council for Social Action came into being in a general upsurge of Congregational social concern, mingled with a feeling that what the denomination was doing to advance the Social Gospel was inadequate from a structural point of view. Arthur E. Holt wrote of the existing Social Relations Commission (the CSA's predecessor) that its own personnel felt that the growth of denominational social interest was commendable but that "the present provision for this interest is in no way commensurate with its importance to the life of the church." The Department of Social Relations should "be lifted to the rank of a major society in the denominational structure." [21] Letters to *Advance* (which had inherited the *Congregationalist's* function of public forum) showed support of the idea and evidenced an uneasy social conscience in the local churches; the era when the local First Congregational Church could as readily have been named the First Republican Church was vividly remembered.

The same sentiment carried over into the denomination's General Council, which in 1934 passed a remarkable resolution pledging "to work toward the abolition of . . . our present competitive profit-seeking economy." Congregationalists as a class were better off economically than Baptists, and this resolution created even more of a furore than the vividly egalitarian Baptist statement of 1932; indeed, the reverberations of this celebrated "profit-motive" resolution among alarmed Congregationalist laymen have never died down to this day. It was this kind of General Council which, "believing that the Church will find itself as it loses itself in the struggle to achieve a warless, just, and brotherly world," launched the Council for Social Action.[22]

Of course the general idea embodied here had abundant precedent, clear back to Washington Gladden's Committee on Capital and Labor established by the Congregational national body in 1892. Gladden's group was transformed into a permanent Labor Committee in 1901, which in due course, under such men as Graham Taylor and H. C. Herring, evolved into a Commission on Social Service. In a sense the agency created in 1934 was simply the descendant of these.

But in one important respect the Council for Social Action differed both from its own predecessors in the denomination and from similar agencies in other churches. A group whose leaders act as official spokesmen for their denomination is often tied to a lowest common denominator of social consensus. (This can amount at times to nothing more, politically and socially, than agreement to oppose the President's sending a government representative to the Vatican—the one political issue which seems to unite all American Protestants, right, left, and center.) On the other hand; a freewheeling organization which takes the liberty of stepping on the toes of vested interests is usually an unofficial organization lacking the formal blessing of its denomination, and it will not receive the denomination's backing when its gets into trouble. The Council for Social Action, by contrast, was distinguished by its unprecedented combination of official standing with freedom of action.

Furthermore, this freedom of action was expressed in a markedly partisan way. "The complexion of the CSA," said a former director, "was 'New Deal liberal.' Roosevelt and the

New Deal were the political expression of our stand." [23] To be sure, there were other denominational organizations that stood in or to the left of the New Deal; for the period of the 30's the highly contentious Methodist Federation for Social Action was particularly noteworthy. But the uniqueness of the Council for Social Action is that it was deliberately created by representatives of an entire denomination, with the conscious realization by many of them that they were placing it in advance of their own middle-class thinking. This is a striking illustration of the deep impact of the Social Gospel: men who could not bring themselves to move toward political liberalism personally paid it the respect of giving it in their church a voice which was both unfettered and authoritative.

The autonomous situation of the CSA did much, in a subtle fashion, for pastoral morale. By giving a special institutional sanction to the Social Gospel, the Council gave the social gospeling Congregational minister a much-needed psychological support in his relationship with the bourgeois laity. "I never felt myself a representative of a large body of opinion in the church," reminisced Dwight J. Bradley, Director of the CSA for the years 1938 through 1944. "I was employed to be a spokesman for the Gospel." [24]

Here one more of the views of the prewar religious liberal—his insistence upon functional continuity between minister and layman—was quietly dropped. It is significant that this man's predecessor, Hubert C. Herring, had been a sociologist in religion, of the tradition of the "old" Social Gospel; Bradley, however, was a Niebuhrian. Perhaps, after at least a decade of feeling less than equal to the laymen in their congregations, it was inevitable that some "ministers" should turn into "priests," that is to say, should come to stress the religious and social uniqueness of their function. This hieratic feeling was cast over all that they did, including preaching the Social Gospel; and thereby their ministry of that gospel both gained and lost.

It gained in affirmativeness, in formal theological understructure; it lost in that it threw still another screen between the secular and the religious vocations, enabling the layman to tolerate a vigorous Social Gospel without accepting it. Many Congregationalist laymen seemingly wished "to be sensitized to their involvement in corporate sin but not granted the grace for their extraction from it," writes the CSA's historian. As often happens, what had been intended as a spur to conscience became a substitute for it: "Twentieth-century Congregationalism chose the year 1934 in which to vindicate its prophets by declaring that their voice was in a sense the voice of the Church. It cannot be claimed that the action was in any sense a declaration of intention by the many to join the prophetic band." [25]

It represents, nonetheless, a tremendous change in the situation of the Social Gospel from the 20's, when inconvenient social ideas had been suppressed rather than admired at a distance. At least the Word was now free to be sown, however stony the ground. In a rather subtle fashion, the Social Gospel had now become "official," i.e., an inescapable part of the Church's total message, to a degree that had never been possible, even in the liberals' heyday before the First World War.

By implication, much the same change in prestige evolved for the Federal Council of Churches. There was a time when this body could not have gotten away with an all-church endorsement of the Social Gospel if the churches had known what it was up to. "It was fortunate," C. S. Macfarland observed in 1936, "that in days of experimentation, the Council was not tied so closely as now to the denominational machinery. . . . I am not sure that the Council would then have survived denominational direction." [26] But by the 30's it was an entity in its own right which made everything it said and did count in the life of the Church, including its Social Gospel. If, as with the CSA, this represented on the part of the rich young rulers a grudging tribute to a philosophy they had no intention of sharing, it also represents an augmentation of the teaching function of the Church.

And the Federal Council was the chief carrier, in the United States, of the ecumenical movement; consequently, as that movement continued to gather prestige, some of that prestige was cast upon the Council and thereby upon the Social Gospel. I turn, therefore, to discuss the ecumenical movement as it developed during the years of the New Deal.

Postscript: 1971. Was the Federal Council's commitment to the New Deal truly an "augmentation of the teaching function of the Church," or was it—despite the anti-Roosevelt fulminations of Republican businessmen—in essence only a modernized rationalization of the *status quo?* That the Council held its ground on the Social Creed of the Churches is historically important, Donald Meyer argues (in *The Protestant Search for Political Realism,* 1960) ; "Had this one most formal, most conspicuous social-gospel covenant been broken, the pressures toward sealing off the passion [for religiously-premised social reform] in sectarian enclaves and beyond institutional frontiers could have been overwhelming." On the other hand, to formalize the Social Gospel in terms which were then equated with the goals of the Roosevelt Administration, as in Dwight Bradley's confession that the "teaching function of the Church" as carried on by *his* organization was "New Deal liberal," meant to place severe restrictions on such men's critical horizons—however acute may have been their perception of specific measures such as NRA.

Meyer points out that during the Thirties Paul Tillich was showing that the basic conflict in modern civilization was not so much between moral man and immoral society as between "concrete man" and "abstract society," a conflict the significance of which the New Dealers, with their casually collectivist responses to Hoover's "rugged individualism," never quite grasped. Perhaps we can learn here from the out-and-out reactionaries. Reviewing this book for the politically and theologically far-Right journal *Christian Economics* (November 27, 1956), Irving E. Howard concluded that although I had "written of the Social Gospel sympathetically," I had "unwittingly sketched the rise of a power philosophy within American Protestantism," and had shown how social actionists of the Niebuhr stamp made it possible "to give Christian sanction to a big militaristic government in the name of One who was nailed to a cross by Militarism and Big Government."

* PART FIVE *

THE CHURCH, THE WORLD,

AND THE FAITH

CHAPTER XIII

The Ecumenical Movement

in the 1930's

THROUGHOUT the decade from 1930 to 1939, the ecumenical movement in the United States progressed from strength to strength. Depression, wars, and politics seemed neither to hasten nor to slacken its pace; church unions and other ecumenical gestures occurred regularly throughout the ten years.

The year 1930 saw the American Lutheran Church born and closer relations established between the Episcopal and Eastern Orthodox communions. The Congregational and Christian Churches' merger, authorized in 1929, duly went through to consummation in 1931. Conservative and liberal ("Orthodox" and "Hicksite") Friends achieved a species of functional union in 1933; the Evangelical and the Reformed Churches united in 1934. The Northern and Southern branches of American Methodism produced an acceptable Plan of Union in 1935, debated it in their regional and national conferences during the following three years, and ended a near-century of separation in 1939.

To many observers, Protestantism seemed thus to be turning High Church—not in its creed and worship, as yet, so much as in its structure. It was a trend strongly counter to what many had hitherto considered the essential genius of Protestantism. It was certainly counter to the irrepressibly schismatic tradition of American Protestantism, even though it had been launched and given shape in very large measure by American Protestants. A discussion of why this movement should have captured the imagination of Christendom in the twentieth century is in order.

In the first place, such a movement had become physically possible. Merger, union, consolidation have accompanied and followed the Industrial Revolution in many other fields besides religion.

This factor is a strong element in, for example, the changing nature of the American church press. The *Christian Century,* with its authoritative standing in the Church and its mailing list of a quarter of all the ministers in America, probably emerged in its leading position less on account of the ideology of the ecumenical movement, which it stood for, than on account of the decline of its denominational contemporaries. The latter can in turn be laid to the same doleful economic conditions that affected secular publishing to make the continued existence of a multitude of low-budget, low-circulation journals less and less possible. The *Baptist* inherited six different subscription lists when it was created in 1920; yet its circulation dropped from around 40,000 to a mere 8,000 in 1932, at which time it was absorbed into the *Christian Century*. Six regional Methodist *Christian Advocates* had to be merged into one publication, with four regional editions—essentially a boiler-plate solution of the problem. Some papers suspended publication; the survivors found it impossible to continue appearing once a week as one or two of them had been doing for a century or more.

If this bowing-out by starvation is "ecumenical," it is ecumenical only by default, but there was, inescapably, a residue of the ecumenical movement that came down to no more than this. Local church unions, and even common action at higher levels, at times were prompted by considerations of sheer economy.

Nevertheless, church members in the past had shown themselves willing to make incredible economic sacrifices for the prepetuation of rivalries. They were now evidently less willing to do so than ever before in American church history. To this economic factor, as a proximate cause of the ecumenical movement, we must add a psychological element: the Church felt the need of unity because it was, more than ever before, on the defensive.

It was a defensiveness that was not without good reason. "It must . . . be recognized," an ecumenicalist leader confessed in 1937, "that the church . . . although founded by a Carpenter, has lost its hold on most of the carpenters of the world." [1] In at least one-seventh of the world, those who had not been sufficiently able to call the workingman "brother" had lost the struggle for his allegiance to those who cultivated him as "comrade." And by the 1930's this rivalry had taken a new and even more dangerous form; the rival cause was no longer simply a revolutionary movement out to steal away believers, but a government out to crush an internal enemy.

Nor was this a Communist threat alone. The struggle was precipitated in Germany when the Christians of that country awoke to the fact that Hitler was in process of foisting a *Reichsbischof* upon them; in Japan, when Christians learned that the state Shinto cult meant business; in a Mexico which, like Russia, was trying to secure the gains of a revolution against a church which was implicated in the old social order. Within the democratic states, there was the subtler assault of the scientific and liberal secularism which I have discussed in an earlier chapter. That Christians should have sought to close ecumenical ranks against attacks as serious as these would seem an elementary dictate for self-preservation:

We must minimize our differences, magnify the cardinal tenets that unite, and consolidate our common spiritual resources, if we are to stem the tide of secularism that is sweeping across the world. No compromise of essential values is involved in joining with evangelical Christians in every nation and presenting a solid front against the common enemies that oppose the Church everywhere.[2]

Still, in other times, the Church had survived against opposition and pressure, and had positively thrived on persecution. Furthermore, it had done so in some instances under conditions of schism. To the economic and psychological elements at work here, therefore, we must add a social and political factor. For at least some of these adverse forces beating in upon the Church were not a danger to the Church alone; they were a threat to the world.

Negatively, the ecumenical movement in this sense amounted to creating a common social front against social evil. As political liberalism turned solidarist and nationalist in movements like the New Deal, so the Social Gospel turned solidarist and institutionalist through the ecumenical movement. Positively, the movement was an expression of the generalized and secularized ideal of the brotherhood of man, a counterpart of the League of Nations or perhaps of the socialist Internationals. "The solidarity of mankind is being hammered into us. . . . Mankind must be one or we will soon be none, and Christianity must rebuild the world on the basis of brotherhood." [3] This socially pragmatic ecumenicalism was the species embodied in the category of Life and Work.

Still, European Christians who rejected out of hand the notion that men could "do something" about their disordered world, or could "Christianize the social order," were involved in the ecumenical movement also. The external social conditions which shaped a program of Life and Work are not fully explanatory; history must also invoke as a causal factor the religious and theological motives of Faith and Order.

To many Christians, the issue of the ecumenical movement came down in essence to an issue of belief, namely, that the Church was the body of Christ and that its rending by schisms was a sin. It was this feeling, for example, quite as much as social considerations, which generated the moral force that pushed the Protestant Episcopal Church into the Federal

Council in 1940 after twenty years of debate; there was increasingly a sense that the two High Churchmanships—Anglican and ecumenical—were somewhat in each other's way.

At the other or Low Church end of the Protestant spectrum, the Congregationalists were rethinking their traditions in terms of Faith and Order also, so that a speaker at their legislative session of 1938 could address his confrères on "The Holy Catholic Church and the Communion of Saints"—a topic from which his Puritan ancestors would have shied away as "popery." By 1940, a prominent leader of this denomination could declare that the traditional Congregational concept of completely autonomous gatherings of free believers was theologically and thus in a sense even morally in error:

One simply cannot . . . use the plural, Churches, to explain our oneness. In the quiet of my study I therefore crossed the Rubicon which some of you have long since left behind you: I wrote a prayer for the Congregational and Christian *Church*. It seems unreasonable for us longer to permit ourselves to be robbed of the fine connotations of this word.[4]

From a traditional Protestant point of view there were great dangers in statements of this kind; it was but a step from declaring church union to be "the will of God," as one Methodist leader did when the branches of that church were joined, to declaring that church division was rebellion against the will of God; and some Protestants saw in the ecumenical movement the danger of Protestantism's becoming a sorry double of Rome.

On the other hand, to be able to assert that "notwithstanding the tragedy of our divisions . . . there exists an actual world-fellowship," in an era like the twentieth century, was and is a very real accomplishment.[5] If in the ecumenical movement there existed the danger of a lack of moral balance on account of self-righteousness, the same is true of any force capable of commanding men's allegiance. The shortcomings of the ecumenical movement must be seen in the perspective of the shortcomings of the world, to whose challenge it was in several ways—physical, psychological, political, and religious—a response.

There seems to be some justice in the Federal Council's judgment that as of 1940 the united visible Church was in a sense already an accomplished fact: "A real unity within the churches . . . already exists. It is not something which has to be created; it has only to be recognized and expressed." [6] During the years of the New Deal, that recognition and expression took place most vividly at the international level, in the church conferences at Oxford, Edinburgh, and Madras.

It will be remembered from previous discussion (Chapter IX) that the two ecumenical areas of Life and Work, Faith and Order, tended to overlap whenever one examined them searchingly. In the 30's, this overlap was to be institutionally embodied. A joint body of thirty-five eminent Christians, chosen by continuation committees from the Life and Work Conference at Stockholm and the Faith and Order Conference at Lausanne, presented for the consideration of world conferences at Oxford and Edinburgh in 1937 a Constitution for a World Council of Churches.

A visible Church was beginning to emerge not only in organization but in emotion and intellect. Common worship services, for example, had been virtually impossible at Stockholm in 1925; they were in some respects the key to the success of Oxford in 1937. Protestant theology was changing, in a direction which would make the men of Faith and Order abandon some of their misgivings about Life and Work. The delegates to Stockholm, except for certain of the Germans, had retained essentially the theology of the prewar American Social Gospel, which is to say a theology which asserted that the Kingdom of God would be achieved in history. But since that time had come the depression, Manchuria, Hitler, Ethiopia, Spain. In a chastened fashion the delegates to Oxford and Edinburgh moved toward a theological consensus which fully accepted human limitations and was therefore not quite the consensus of the older liberals. Consequently, this consensus could embrace those who had remained theological conservatives all along.

But this is not to say that these conferences let slip their

188

grasp on the Social Gospel, particularly the one at Oxford, which met to carry forward the debate on Life and Work. Its very composition constituted a species of social action. Delegates from the missionary churches of Asia and Africa attested to the rising of the colonial world. Chinese and Japanese delegates made a special point of their fellowship together even though the China Incident was a week old when the conference convened. At the same time, the presence of Eastern Orthodox and Old Catholic delegates bore witness to the principles of Faith and Order.

Much of what came out of the Oxford Conference would have been recognizable to any New Dealer, or even to a later, post–World War II liberal; its section on Church, Community, and Economic Order came out for full employment, universal educational opportunity, social security, and conservation. Particularly did this World Conference on Life and Work take note of the special problem posed by the modern totalitarian state, and, because of the cultural direction taken by at least one such state, the problem of the modern myth of race. Plenary addresses again and again attacked parochialism of race or nation.

But note that this is not quite the old Social Gospel, which would have discussed social-ethical issues without bringing in the Church itself as a term of the discussion. For the older social-ethical issues had not constituted a direct challenge to the Church; they had been seen rather as an indirect rebuke to the Church for not having "done something" about labor relations, world peace, and so on. But the new issues, particularly that of the totalitarian state, struck not only at Life and Work but also at Faith and Order. The old American Protestant and British Nonconformist fear of the Church's meddling in the state was suddenly reversed; in the New Order a-building in Europe, separation of Church and state was being denied by the state. A Church which had managed to accommodate to a Bismarck and a Wilhelm found that the Continental antisocial theology had its outer limit when confronted by a Hitler. Barth himself, driven from his pulpit into Switzerland, had to blunt and modify that part of his message which dissented from the Social Gospel.

There were two noteworthy absentees from the Oxford Conference: the Church of Rome and the German Evangelical Church. There was nothing, short of entire surrender to Catholicism, that the conference could have done about the former. But to the German Evangelical Church it addressed a striking message:

Though your delegates are absent, the very circumstances of their absence have created a stronger sense of fellowship than ever before.

We are . . . greatly moved by the afflictions of many . . . pastors and laymen who have stood firm . . . for the freedom of the church of Christ to preach his gospel. . . . We call upon the churches throughout the world . . . to rejoice that once again it has been proved that a faith born of sacrifice is counted worthy of sacrifice.[7]

The pressure of Hitler had produced a heightening of self-consciousness in the Church as an institution. External social events had thus once again marched together with internal theological developments to change the Social Gospel and oblige it to involve within itself some doctrine of the Church.

The Nazi dictum of state-over-church was seen as a particularly severe case of the secularist dictum of world-over-church. This thesis that the world is essentially secularist and anti-Christian appears throughout the conference. Reinhold Niebuhr set the tone on Oxford's second day with a characteristic address on "The Christian Church in a Secular Age." Again and again speakers expressed the idea that "American Christians had more in common with their fellow Christians in Germany or Japan than with their fellow Americans who do not share the Christian understanding of life." [8]

The strategy of churchmen, over against such a secularized world, was considerably changed from the days of Rauschenbusch. Rather than counsel social reform primarily through secular channels, the Church as such was to become involved in the struggle, and in its own terms rather than in society's. The gist of the Message which Oxford released to the world was that the failure of Christians to redeem secular society, as Rauschenbusch and his allies had hoped they would, was compensated for by success in Christian fellowship per se, across national, racial, colonial, and class lines. Moreover it was claimed that any attempt at solution of the world's problems which did not take this special function of the Church into account would fail:

Because community is sought on a wrong basis, the intensity of the search for it issues in conflict and disintegration. In such a world the Church is called to be in its own life that fellowship which binds men together in their common dependence on God and overleaps all barriers of social status, race, or nationality.

The old attempt to reform the world simply by telling the secular reformers what *they* ought to do was now distinctly subordinated. "We do not call the world to be like ourselves, for we are already too like the world." To carry out this high calling of transcending the barriers of race and nation, it particularly behooved the Church to destroy those barriers to the extent that they existed in its own fellowship—not the denominational barriers alone, but those which marked churches off as white and colored, rich and poor, ethnic, national. "The first duty of the Church, and its greatest service to the world, is that it be in very deed the Church." [9]

If Faith and Order had thus entered into the Life and Work of the Church, Life and Work had also permeated Faith and Order. Two weeks after the close of the Oxford Conference, many of the same delegates convened at Edinburgh to hear William Temple, then Archbishop of York, launch the Second World Conference on Faith and Order in the terms of the "new," church-centered Social Gospel which had been the theme of Oxford:

How can [the Church] claim to bridge the divisions in human society —divisions between Greek and barbarian, bond and free, between black and white, Aryan and non-Aryan, employer and employed— if when men are drawn into it they find that another division has been added to the old ones—a division of Catholic from Evangelical, or Episcopalian from Presbyterian or Independent? A Church divided in its manifestations to the world cannot render its due service to God or to man. . . . In part our progress [in ecumenicity] is due to the pressure of the needs of the world.[10]

The previous World Conference on Faith and Order, at Lausanne in 1927, had listened to a stirring exposition of the Social Gospel by Francis McConnell, but McConnell had complained afterward that the Europeans had not understood what he was talking about. Now, the "pressure of the needs of the world" had changed the picture entirely. One of the conference committees took its cue from Temple and set the Faith and Order problem in the context of Life and Work: "We speak of unity, brotherhood, concord, and renewing power to those who are torn by caste divisions and colour prejudices, or are speaking of the class war—but we cannot overcome our own rivalries." [11]

Indeed, the external stimulus of a divided and revolutionary world probably played a part in the immense advance even in purely theological matters which Edinburgh represented over Lausanne. The latter conference had had considerable difficulty in coming to a "sense of the meeting"; churchmen had been in sharp disagreement even about the nature of their disagreements, and only one committee had completed an acceptable report. But at Edinburgh, many more areas of theological agreement—and sharper definition of the areas of really essential disagreement—were found. The conference closed with a unanimous Affirmation of Union which was solemnly repeated as a religious rite in the closing service of worship—an act which, it was generally agreed, would have been intellectually and emotionally impossible at Lausanne.

With such unprecedented consensus in Faith and Order, and with the new international consensus on the theological basis for Life and Work, it is not surprising that both Oxford and Edinburgh ratified the draft constitution for a World Council of Churches. This was a hazardous enterprise, for it faced the same kind of catastrophe which had surrounded the birth of the ecumenical movement a generation before. The first session of the provisional committee to set up the World Council was scheduled for 1938—in Hangchow, China. Japanese aggression ruined that plan; the conferees had to settle for neutral Utrecht, instead. But Utrecht also, two years later, was to be a place of shattered buildings and shattered hopes as the Second World War smashed once again the Christian hope of peace in our time.

But, as in the First World War, the ecumenical cause survived and eventually prevailed. "Contacts were kept alive between the leaders, even on opposite sides of the battle line." [12] Work was done among prisoners of war during the conflict, and an impressive chapter was written of Allied aid to the "Orphaned Missions" from the Continent. The churches were at work among the refugees and were rebuilding the churches of former enemies almost as soon as the fighting stopped. In 1948, the heirs to the Life and Work and Faith and Order movements met in another Dutch city and witnessed to "Man's Disorder and God's Design" by establishing the World Council of Churches.

It was still a precarious affair. New national and ideological rivalries had replaced the old, and the East-West debate at Amsterdam between Czech Bishop Hromadka and John Foster Dulles put the World Council under stress at its very moment of birth. Nevertheless, the consummation of a World Council of Churches, with member churches that spanned the Iron Curtain, in the face of the growing absolutization of secular loyalties on the hither side of that curtain, bore witness to the continued working of the creative and redemptive Spirit indwelling in the Church of Christ.

Having thus set forth the ecumenical movement's case, it becomes the writer's duty to enter a minority report.

When the World Council of Churches was founded in 1948, the Fundamentalists felt it necessary to establish, in competition, an International Council of Christian Churches. Ecumenicalists, perhaps rightly, discount this group as being out on the theological and political far right, and as representing a very small fraction of the Christians of the world; but, in the light of the ecumenical movement's claim that it is a work commanded of God, the bare existence of a rival group of Christians is worth noting. Within the United States, furthermore, there exist relatively numerous groups which had and have nothing to do with the ecumenical movement, either internationally or through the Federal (now National) Council of Churches. A Southern Baptist attended Edinburgh, but primarily in the role of critic, and the antiecumenical bias of the Missouri Synod Lutherans was and is considerable.

The existence of such opposition cannot be laid exclusively to stubbornness or backwardness. In spite of what the ecumenical movement has meant for contemporary Protestantism, it remains possible to contend that its answers to what is wrong with the world, or with the Church, are not final, and that certain of its implications carry considerable potential danger.

The reader will perhaps already have glimpsed what I have in mind, namely: that the Niebuhrian "new theology's" crusade against the absolutizing of any and all human institutions can be turned upon the Church itself. Such a phenomenon as the World Council of Churches, once it is an institutional reality and not a transcendent hope, also becomes relative. It therefore contains the danger of being equated, in the minds of its enthusiasts, with "the" Church of Christ and of becoming subject to precisely the kind of critique which Protestantism historically has leveled at the Church of Rome. Niebuhr himself prophetically warned at Oxford that

a profane Christianity falsely identifies the Church with the Kingdom of God. Since the historic Church is always touched with human finiteness, is subject to sociological forces and pressures, and is victim of the prejudices and illusions of particular ages, any tendency to obscure or deny this fact becomes the final and most terrible expression of human sinfulness. Of that sin no Church has been free.[13]

Within the period covered in this study, the years between the First and Second World Wars, there occurred one remarkable instance of just such an ethical absolutizing of an ecumenical objective—remarkable in that it caused the Social Gospel to divide against itself. It involved the largest union of churches which has yet taken place in any country, that which yielded the 9,000,000-member Methodist Church out of Northern, Southern, and antiepiscopal fragments of the original American Methodist movement. The division of the Social Gospel to which I refer turned upon that most painful of social sore spots, race relations in the United States.

The American delegates who "came to Oxford talking about *our churches*" and went home "talking about the Church" took home with them also, presumably, the Oxford Conference's judgment that the churches' call to "immediate Christian action" included the reform of their own institutional life.[14] Some of this proposed reform gave churchmen deep satisfaction. We have seen, for example, the financial stringency churchmen had labored under even during the boom years which ended in 1929; there was great rejoicing at home, therefore, at Oxford's pronouncement that "there should . . . be a reasonable uniformity in the payment of those who hold the same spiritual office" and that it was "not tolerable that those who minister to the rich should be comparatively well off and that those who minister to the poor should be poor for that reason alone." But other Oxford summonses to the home churches had more the effect of a red flag—in particular, the declaration that "against racial pride or race antagonism the church must set its face implacably as rebellion against God. Especially in its own life and worship there can be no place for barriers because of race or color." [15]

We have already noted how grievously far behind the churches had lagged in this aspect of their Social Gospel. Even the Federal Council of Churches, the great ecumenical agency of American Protestantism, shared in this lag; its pronouncements on race, between 1920 and 1940, very often got no further than the "separate but equal" formula, which our highest court has struck down. The Council did found a Commission on the Church and Race Relations in 1921, which after the crash labored in behalf of Negroes on specific economic issues; for example, it sought to interest them in consumer co-operatives.

(And, of course, this Commission condemned lynching, but in theory everyone condemned lynching, even in the states which observed lynch law.) But the problem of the color line in the Church—the problem so crucially posed by Oxford—the Council did not feel competent to tackle, except to foster Negro-white pulpit exchange on "Race Relations Sunday," a date in the ecclesiastical year whose very observance is a sardonic and tragic mockery of human dignity.

The reason for stressing the point is this: among those denominations which by the 1930's accepted the moral obligation to seek ecumenical relationship were some whose mutual divisions were regional; and churches of predominantly Northern and predominantly Southern white membership respectively partook of Northern and Southern attitudes on race. What would happen to ecumenicalism, and to the Social Gospel, when a partially integrated Northern church and a lily-white Southern church sought to unite their memberships, and race became the point of controversy which was keeping them divided?

When, in 1932, a Southern Baptist leader "as the representative of four million" of his coreligionists declined to sit at a banquet table in a Northern city presided over by a Baptist who was a Negro, Northern Baptists unhappily considered the ecumenical angle: "We pray for union [of the Northern and Southern Baptist Conventions], but the implications of this incident give us pause." [16] Similarly, when the Methodists adopted their rule that General Conferences should be held only in cities where equal treatment of white and colored delegates was promised, before the gavel descended on a motion for the previous question a delegate managed to shout: "What about its effect on Southern Methodist union?" [17]

The Methodist problem was more acute than the Baptist because Methodist union was far more imminent. Northern and Southern Methodists had already come to many working agreements. They were using the same hymnal; they were jointly operating certain foreign missions. In 1924, they had made a serious attempt to ratify a Plan of Union; in 1935, they prepared to try again. Theologically and organizationally, these churches faced no insurmountable difficulty in mediating their differences. The problem lay in the fair-sized body of Negro Methodists who had belonged to the united ancestor-church when it split over slavery in 1844.

The Negroes in the Southern church, under the "Black Code" situation in the unreconstructed Southern states as of 1866, had found their situation in the Church intolerable; they had therefore been set apart in a new and autonomous denomination, the Colored Methodist Church. In the Northern church, on the other hand, the Negro Methodists not only remained members of the denomination but continuously bettered their position in it.

They began more or less as wards of the white annual conferences. Gradually they achieved, first, control over their own annual conferences; then, fully equal status of their ministers with white clergy in the deliberations of the General Conference; then, the election of one of their membership as a missionary bishop to Africa; and, finally, in 1920, a formula whereby the mixed General Conference elected both white and colored bishops for the work of the church in the United States. There remained a great deal of segregation in the Methodist Church, most Negroes being grouped in their own local churches, annual conferences, and episcopal areas, but all of these arrangements were subject to legislative rearrangement by the General Conference at any time.

In other words, while the Southern church moved away from interracial relationship and became more "lily-white" than it had been before the Civil War, the Northern church was moving steadily, albeit slowly, toward integration. When serious talks began between Northern and Southern Methodists looking toward union, therefore, the raising of a race issue between them was inevitable. Southern churchmen were often no more given over to sweet reasonableness on this matter than Southern Senators; in 1911 Bishop Collins Denny of the Southern church flatly declared that if the General Conference of a united Methodism "should elect a Negro Bishop to preside over the whole

Church, there would be no Methodism in the South for him to preside over." [18]

The Southern solution to this problem sounded, to Southerners, simple and workable: one united Negro Methodist denomination, and one united white Methodist denomination. But this the Negro members of the Northern church bitterly resisted. Then, a compromise was proposed: that "regional" conferences, six in number, be created within one united Methodist Church—one of the "regions" consisting of the great bulk of the Negroes, the others being based on geography. These "jurisdictional" conferences would also elect the bishops, thereby freeing Southern white delegates from the odium of participating in the balloting for Negro bishops at the General Conference of the whole church.

The constitutional pros and cons need not detain us here; what is relevant is the fact that the Negro Methodists continued to protest and resist, while the Northern white Methodists accepted the compromise. What kept up the Negro opposition, so that their delegates to the Northern General Conference voted 36-11 against the Plan of Union with the South, was the feeling that segregation had been made a constitutional part of the church's structure, and that the Plan was therefore an immense step backward. What stimulated the Northern white support, so that their delegates voted 459–47 for the Plan of Union, was the driving force of ecumenicalism.

White leaders, driven along by "an almost irresistible enthusiasm for unification," endeavored to explain to the Negroes that their status would be better, not worse, under the united church, because the Plan assured them of "their own" local and regional leadership.[19] A few Negro leaders, borne along on the same current, also rationalized their way into support of the Plan. But among Negro Methodists generally, and equally so in the Negro secular press, the protest was clamorous. Inasmuch as Southerners defended the Plan on the ground that it not only preserved but actually promoted segregation, the clamor would retrospectively seem justified. Even if it were not, however, the fact remains that a substantial minority in the church felt (and still feels) that it was wronged as a group and that this feeling was overridden by the church majority on ecumenicalist grounds. The fact suggests that the ecumenical movement needed, and needs, closer ethical scrutiny than Protestants have usually given it. The further fact that some ecumenicalists I have talked to deny that the Methodist union was "really ecumenical" convinces me of this need all the more.

Lewis O. Hartman, the leading spokesman for the small Northern white minority which voted against union with the South, summed up the conflict as being one "not . . . between an absolute good and an absolute evil," but rather between "two 'goods,' one the great desirability of keeping clear of the very appearance of the evil of race discrimination." Some of his fellows, mindful that they must accept or reject the Plan of Union as a whole, put the ecumenical consideration first as a greater good; this particular delegate and forty-six other white men cast votes of "nay" on the ground that they could not bring themselves "to endorse unification at the price of the Negro." [20]

Since the majority was arguing that a united Methodist Church would be a stronger force for improvement of the secular world, and the minority was arguing that even for the sake of unity the Church could not afford to reverse the national trend toward race equality, it is clear that *both sides were appealing to the Social Gospel*. In this case, the ecumenical movement, which had been called into being in part to fulfill the Social Gospel, had instead had the effect of splitting it asunder.

Yet Bishop Hughes, in summing up the work of the ratifying conference of the Northern Church, called the union with the Southern Methodists "the blessed example that may providentially result in other needed mergers in Protestantism," and he assured the delegates that their "overwhelming vote . . . has been succeeded by an increasing assurance that in this great matter we have done the will of God." [21] Assurance that in great matters it has done the will of God has been a stumbling-block to the Church on many, many occasions: the Albigensian Crusade; the Inquisition; Prohibition in the United States. The more chastened view of the neo-orthodox pessimists needed to penetrate a good deal farther into the very body of the Church before the ecumenical movement would be an entirely reliable instrument for political and social liberalism in Protestant Christianity in America.

Postscript: 1971. Once again an attempt at prophecy has been confounded by further history. In the 1950's, criticism of the ecumenical movement, whether on behalf of the "neo-orthodox pessimists" or in terms of a theological outlook quite different from theirs (for example, Marion J. Bradshaw's *Free Churches and Christian Unity*, 1954) usually came down to a fear that a monolithic ecumenical "establishment" might effectively crush religious liberty and diversity in the name of its supposed Divine mandate for religious unity. By the end of the 1960's, however, the National (formerly Federal) Council of Churches was being criticized for its *in*effectiveness: "Many ecumenically minded denominational officers have poured vast amounts of time and energy into N.C.C. machinery, only to discover that the machinery can't, or won't, move." The *Christian Century*, for whose editors ecumenism had always been a primary article of faith, took note in one lead editorial (February 11, 1970) of "managerial mythologies" and "intramural strangulation" within the National Council, and wondered whether that body, "like the U.S. Congress," might be inherently "incapable of renewing and restructuring itself." If the Council's most recent board meetings were any indication of its true condition, the *Century* declared, then "conciliarism in America has plummeted to a condition of painful distress, acute embarrassment and operational impotence." The ecumenical movement in the United States, which in the Thirties had appeared to be an instrument for the rejuvenation of Protestantism, had itself in turn come to seem in need of religious revival.

CHAPTER XIV

The Social Gospel

and the Coming of the War

THE historical date of the "end" of the New Deal is one whose exact placement is fairly arbitrary. Some would put it at the crucial court-packing controversy of 1937, the first successful challenge to Roosevelt's authority. A person who has lived through the McCarthy era might well date the end of the New Deal from May 26, 1938, when the Dies Committee was established. Samuel Lubell uses as a terminus the elections of 1938, when presidential attempts to "purge" recalcitrant Congressmen met with failure and the great political deadlock of the mid-century began.[1] Richard Hofstadter chooses the State-of-the-Union message of January 3, 1939, in which for the first time no new legislative proposals were made by the President to the Congress.[2] Others use the outbreak of the Second World War as a terminus, when (in FDR's words) "Dr. New Deal" was superseded by "Dr. Win-the-War," and the prodigal businessman was welcomed back to Washington. In any case, there is general agreement that well before the end of Franklin D. Roosevelt's second term the political force of the New Deal was spent.

This being the case, as the months and years passed after the 1936 electoral landslide there was less and less that liberals, including church liberals, could say about the innovative side of the New Deal; it became a matter of consolidation, of conserving gains already made. After the Federal Council of Churches, in its Labor Sunday message of 1937, had endorsed the upholding of the Wagner Act by the Supreme Court, the specifically New-Deal-prompted Social Gospel appears to have run out of subjects for discussion. Church criticism, constructive and otherwise, passed over to the administration's foreign policy.

The early FDR foreign policy had met with general approval in the churches as a "peace program." The policy of the Good Neighbor; the Montevideo Conference; the withdrawal of the Marines from Haiti; the Tydings-McDuffie Act—these were seen as acts of atonement for American imperialism. The Presbyterian General Assembly of 1933 commended Roosevelt "for his recent vigorous efforts to promote international peace"; the Northern Baptist Convention applauded a declaration that "President Roosevelt may be wrong on some things, but he is right on peace!" ("Some things," among Baptists in 1933, meant booze.) The *Christian Century* went further and made FDR the hero of an international melodrama. His message summoning fifty-four nations to support Ramsay MacDonald's ill-fated disarmament plan seemed to that journal an eleventh-hour move: the President had "thrown himself, and the strength of the United States, across the path of the nations—a path that was leading straight to the abyss." [3]

But what the *Century* meant by the "strength" of the United States, in this context, was the same thing that Senator Borah meant by it. The mere act of uttering a moral appeal to all these nations ("including Russia!—and Japan!—and Germany!") had, the editor believed, mobilized "world public opinion" and prevented war.

On May 17, 1933, the day after the Roosevelt message to the

nations, Hitler spoke on the radio—and talked peace. The *Christian Century* promptly jumped to the conclusion that "nazi Germany is responsible to world opinion," and thanked God that the ten-year pact concluded the following Sunday between France, Italy, Germany, and Britain "guaranteed . . . peace for ten years." One can see in this incident not only that pacifism retained a strong hold on the imagination of the Church in 1933, but that insofar as this pacifism was of the *Century*'s sort it fully accepted the pre–World War I liberal theology's view of human nature. Public opinion did give force to scraps of paper; reason did prevail over passion if appealed to with sufficient firmness; governments would be peaceable toward their neighbors if only given sufficient opportunity, through the removal, by mutual disarmament, of the capitalistic pressure to war.

For the latter reason, church liberals considered FDR's diplomatic recognition of noncapitalist Russia particularly admirable. "The recognition of Russia is a move for world peace," the *Christian Advocate* declared:

We recognize other powers without our asking what they believe or how they worship. . . . Lenin the Terrible was not more bloody than Ivan the Terrible, with whose successors we exchanged diplomatic relations for a century and a half. . . . Happily, one result of the partial collapse of our own economic system has been a welcome spread of tolerance of the ideas of nations which are painfully engaged in breaking new routes to the goal which all profess to seek. Americans need not be communists in order to be willing to live neighborly with those who are hazarding that experiment.[4]

As long as the Roosevelt foreign policy was confined to verbal grandeur (i.e., the coining of phrases like "the Good Neighbor"), the politically liberal pacifist could follow the President wholeheartedly. But the course of the Roosevelt administration very early raised grave doubts for men with convictions of this sort, on account of the President's propensities to boatbuilding.

"Navies are for wars," a Methodist wrote bluntly in August, 1933; "is that what the United States is doing—preparing for another war?" And he went on, as pacifists in that period often did, to tie in a Social Gospel consideration: "This writer has visited school districts where, in deskless, windowless school buildings, the children were wearing overcoats during school hours and the term of instruction was less than six months of the year. Yet we build warships to kill the world's youth while we thus neglect to build schools!" [5]

For a variety of reasons the isolationist line, in this new era, was to be exploited in secular politics no longer by the liberals but by the conservatives. And the churches, by espousing part of that line, were to get themselves into a great deal of trouble. The Social Gospel, which had begun to disentangle itself from the toils of Prohibition and had shaken off the illiberal compromises of 1929, once again became politically confused.

The churches, for example, in general approved of the work of the Senate Munitions Investigating Committee, which got under way on April 12, 1934, under the chairmanship of Gerald P. Nye; the Federal Council, for example, formally supported the investigations. There was, to be sure, a "liberal" angle to this approval, since in the eyes of so many the "merchants of death" were simply a peculiarly soulless variation upon the intrinsic predatory nature of capitalism. But the Nye investigations, and the Neutrality Acts which in effect grew out of them, were to be seized upon as a *conservative* campaign issue. Running through 1935 and 1936—through, in other words, the launching of the "second" New Deal—these investigations consequently helped to blur the political witness of the Social Gospel.

This is not to say that men were lacking to interpret pacifism to the churches in terms of political liberalism or even radicalism. Pacifists who rejected the Marxist doctrine of socialism through violent revolution often could accept the Marxist-Leninist doctrine that "imperialist" wars are caused by factors inherent in capitalism's nature. They could therefore argue that the first step in their pacifist program of abolition of war had to be the abolition of capitalism. Moreover, men with views like these, "agitators" though they doubtless were in one sense, were heard in the churches and heard respectfully. The writer recalls for example a church conference in 1940 at which Kirby Page was a featured speaker. The man was presented as an outstanding church leader with a message which demanded a respectful hearing; and while there was much disagreement with Page's point of view, I do not recall the slightest public or private suggestion that he was "subversive" or "disloyal."

Of course this receptivity to pacifist preachment was connected with a mood of emotional rejection of war which remained from the trauma of the First World War. The preacher of the convention sermon at the Northern Baptist annual meeting of 1933 confessed that he personally had made war and had "helped to kill men"; and he swore "before enough witnesses so that it may be remembered . . . 'I will never do it again!' " [6]

Indeed, the 1930's were as marked by antiwar vows as any period in our history. The Oxford Union peace pledge had a vogue in American colleges; so did the more sardonic "Veterans of Future Wars," which Princeton undergraduates organized ostensibly to enable soldiers-to-be to collect their bonuses in advance. (Vassar girls, not to be outdone, organized "Gold Star Mothers of Veterans of Future Wars.") The Congregational Council for Social Action sponsored a "peace plebiscite," calling upon "the people of our churches to renounce war and all its works and ways and to refuse to support, sanction or bless it." Almost 20 per cent of the denomination's membership responded, and the majority compounded pacifism with isolationism by opposing war "except for defense." The Baptists followed up the Congregational ballot in 1936 with a poll of their own; this drew only 10,000 replies, but the results were even more striking: 42.5 per cent of those replying favored bearing arms in the event of attack, 27.6 per cent said they would refuse service in any and all wars, while only 2 per cent declared that they would willingly bear arms whenever the U.S. government chose to declare war. Deep and broad in American Protestantism lay the sentiment that "the Church is through with war!" [7]

But the essential pathos of the pacifist position was that it was both true and partial. "We must all love one another,"

Reinhold Niebuhr observed sadly, "but what are we to do since we are not good enough to love one another?" [8]

The pacifist position had become possible partly because the historians had overthrown the notion that any one power had been "responsible" for the First World War. Hence the pacifist was at a loss in coping with a power which was unmistakably an aggressor. The rise of what were to be the Axis nations posed a cruel dilemma to all men of good will: "The society of nations finds that it has an unruly member [which] breaks faith, robs a weak neighbor of his territory, destroys his cities and slaughters his people. . . . Is there anything to do but summon the police? And what is that but war?" [9]

The events within Germany after 1933 posed this problem to the American churches in a peculiarly acute form. The German Jews, for example, received quick sympathy from believers in the Social Gospel, who stood "with them, and for them, in protest against this barbarous tyranny." [10] But what was there, concretely, that a *pacifist* could do or say about governmental brutality in a foreign country?

Moreover, there was a deep immediacy for churchmen in the totalitarian challenge because of what was happening to the Christian Church in Germany. Christianity in its "purest" form, it now appeared, was distinctively a German phenomenon, and volumes of theology were written to demonstrate that Jesus had been a true Aryan. But the resistance to Hitler which had crumbled in university and trade union rallied in the parish, refusing to accept this Nazified version of Christianity.

The most vivid leader of the Christian Opposition in Germany was Martin Niemöller—the man of whom the German *Führer* is reported to have exclaimed, "It is Niemöller or Hitler!" The Oxford Conference had expected to hear Pastor Niemöller speak; he was unable to do so, having been arrested. The overt act for which he was jailed was to invite his Berlin congregation to contribute financially to the anti-Nazi Confessional Synod, within a week after Reichsminister Frick had declared this to be a crime. It was an act of conscious drama. As the forbidden offering was being taken, a gang of Hitler

Youth appeared at the church door and commenced to beat up the collection-takers. Niemöller "raised his hand and announced a hymn. Nobody who heard it will ever forget the impression created when high above the tumult at the entrances the majestic words rolled out." [11] It was *Ein' Feste Burg*— "A Mighty Fortress Is Our God."

The point of this story for our purposes is that this man was no pacifist. Niemöller had commanded a U-boat in the First World War; he had received the Iron Cross; and he still, in 1937, declared himself perfectly willing to fight France again. His quarrel with the Third Reich thus went deeper than its militarism. And after that heart-stirring performance in the Dahlem Church in Berlin, what had any American pacifist to say to Martin Niemöller?

Alongside the hostility of the Third Reich to the Church, as a dilemma for pacifists, lay the hostility of the Imperial cult promoted by the militarist group in power in Japan. Here, the leading Christian opponent of the regime, Toyohiko Kagawa, was a pacifist; nevertheless, the problem posed to American Christians was of the same nature as that posed by the persecution of Niemöller—complicated by the fact that Japan's external course of empire was carrying that country into China.

The American missionary investment in China was immense; Americans had dreamed of making China's millions Christian for more than a century. And the Chinese chief of state in the 1930's was himself a Christian (a fact which after the Second World War was to cause liberals in the churches no end of embarrassment). Contributors to Protestant foreign mission boards still thought of themselves, in the New Deal years, as having a special stake in China's destiny. Consequently, when the "China Incident" broke out and Christian hospitals and schools began to be bombed along with Chinese civilians, American pacifism was put to still further strain.

Yet in many areas of American Protestant opinion the pacifist lines held firm. When the gathering storm hit Europe, the *Christian Century* for example warned America to "Keep Out of Spain." The "ugly realities of the situation" it readily conceded; "a legitimate, republican government" was "being attacked by [a] revolt which seeks to turn the nation back to . . . feudalism." The direct military involvement of the Fascist powers was also conceded. The *Century's* "regard for law and order, for republican principles of government, and for the right of peoples to self-determination" made it "detest this Franco revolt"; its sympathies were "whole-heartedly with the government." Nevertheless, its pacifist principles forbade it to endorse any compromise with the neutral position of America. The duty of the United States was "to maintain a zone of sanity in a world going mad by keeping out of wars of any description in any place." [12]

The crescendo of unhappy events abroad—Ethiopia, the Rhineland, Spain, China—was paralleled by the crescendo in the national debate which surrounded the passing of the First, Second, Third, and Fourth Neutrality Acts. Then, at the height of it all, Franklin D. Roosevelt precipitated the political issue, as he so often did, through a well-timed bit of oratory. He called upon the nations of the world to "Quarantine the Aggressor."

The "Quarantine" speech not only precipitated the political issue in the nation; it also stirred a raging controversy in the Church. As voters divided between isolationism and interventionism, so churchmen divided between pacifism and resistance to aggression. It was the beginning of a great schism in the Social Gospel, the depth of which is nowhere better illustrated than in the political course taken by the Social Gospel's most renowned champion, the *Christian Century.*

Throughout all the international crises leading up to the "Quarantine" speech, the *Century* had maintained the disillusionment with armed force which it had inherited from the 20's. All wars were reducible to rival imperialisms; no war ever settled anything; the United States must safeguard the social gains of the New Deal by staying out of a war which would put the "merchants of death" back in the saddle. Also, the churches were on probation; they had been stampeded into compromising their principles in one war and must not do so again,

Hence the editor of the *Century,* Charles Clayton Morrison, greeted the "Quarantine" speech with mixed feelings. That Roosevelt had called "to life again the Wilsonian conception of American responsibility," he felt, was good; we had been too long without it. He also approved the explicit naming of Japan as the aggressor in China; it was high time that world public opinion was organized against the culprit. But the quarantine idea itself was "portentous." Did the President "propose to implement it with action? If so, what action?"

Morrison went on to invoke the old liberal fear of involvement in the fortunes of Britain and France, which were moved by "national and imperial ends with which America is not concerned." And if the World War had snuffed out the Progressive movement, he warned, the prospect of a second world war was infinitely more dangerous; it would "in all probability be followed by the downfall of democracy itself in all countries where it still survives, including the United States." Finally, he flatly declared the concept of "collective security, conceived in terms of military might," to be "a fallacy." [13]

Sadly for the Social Gospel, what happened next was that in their anxiety to remain true to the pacifist principle, many men in the churches were led to embrace one after another of the reactionary political formulas from which they had so painfully freed themselves. Left-wing pacifists, who kept their pacifism tied into a socialist critique, did not fall into this trap, but others, without such a frame of reference, quickly lost sight of what the Social Gospel was all about. Consider, for example, the implications of the Federal Council's statement on the Far Eastern conflict in 1938:

If Japan is deprived of some of her bombing planes by an American government embargo, she is being coerced and threatened, not by a disinterested party, but by a nation which has mobilized its weapons of violence in practice for making war upon her. . . . Government embargo is therefore limited both in its moral and its practical effectiveness. If on the other hand individual American citizens who profit by the sale of bombing planes forego their profit by refusing to be a part of Japanese war activities their action may be rendered comparatively disinterested and non-threatening. It is therefore more appropriate and surely as realistic for the churches to urge upon individual Christians such voluntary action rather than to support government embargo.[14]

These men were appalled at what government seemed increasingly to be committing citizens to do. The trouble with a formulation like this, however, was that not long since it had been urged by conservatives that, in matters economic, "it is more appropriate for the churches to urge upon individual Christians . . . voluntary action," rather than to support government action to overhaul the national economy. In divorcing themselves from the nation's drift to war, the pacifist churchmen thus tended to push themselves out of the field of collective social concern, to revert to an individualist approach to social evil, and, hence, to end by preaching the Social Gospel in theory but detaching themselves from it in practice. Such a view wiped out every advance of Rauschenbusch at a stroke.

A perfect instance of this quite unintended eclipse of the Social Gospel is what happened to the political orientation of the *Christian Century* toward Franklin D. Roosevelt. We have seen its dubious response to the "Quarantine" speech; his international activities thereafter made it no happier. He declined to invoke the Neutrality Act on the outbreak of the China Incident; he killed the Ludlow resolution which would have required a popular referendum before a declaration of war by the United States could take effect; he pushed the Naval Expansion Act which for the first time in our history looked forward to a two-ocean navy. And there was more to come.

The cessation of new domestic reforms in 1939 and the additional defense appropriations of that year, the *Century* saw as part and parcel of each other. As a typical sample of what liberals could expect in wartime, it quoted David Lawrence's opinion that if "national unity" were to be achieved it would first be necessary to scrap the Wages and Hours Act and the National Labor Relations Board. As with Progressivism, so with the New Deal; *plus ça change, plus c'est la même chose.*

This concern for the decline of liberalism in the gathering

war clouds was, of course, legitimate in terms of American experience. But the political solution hardly lay in going over to the conservative opposition. Yet that, increasingly, was what the *Christian Century*'s editor felt himself called upon to do. A journal which had enthusiastically supported the New Deal, criticizing it only on the ground that it did not do enough—a journal whose own domestic Social Gospel colors still flew as high as ever—felt driven by the overriding urgency of the peace issue to seek political refuge with the Republican Party.

Morrison did not do this happily. He had no particular fondness for Wendell Willkie, the man who had "fought the great social experiment of the TVA to a standstill" and who in any case agreed with the President on foreign policy. But his editorial steam against Roosevelt on pacifist grounds was rising higher; on June 17, 1940, he finally exploded. The harrowing events of the spring of that year had just roared to their climax with Mussolini's entrance into the war, and the way in which FDR spoke up on this matter led Morrison to demand editorially, "What comes next?":

When he [FDR] cried, "on this tenth day of June, 1940, the hand that held the dagger has struck it in the back of its neighbor," he was not using the sort of language which responsible heads of peaceful states customarily employ. The President at Charlottesville, pledging "the material resources of this nation" to the Allies, was an indignant, resentful, roused man in a fighting mood, determined to take his country just as close to the verge of war as his executive power could carry it.[15]

This was the turning point. A break with Roosevelt, when one could not approve the policies of his opponent as an alternative, seemed to require as rationalization that one adopt all the accusations of "dictatorship" in the Republican oratorical arsenal. If Willkie "conformed" to the administration's demand for "national unity," then it was that demand which must be impugned. The high-pressure, stage-managed manner in which the Democratic National Convention of 1940 chose Roosevelt for a third term—tactics which prompted H. L. Mencken to dub this "the *Ja*-convention"—lent plausibility to the line which the *Century* was now forced to take. Moving into the same camp with the Chicago *Tribune,* Morrison now declared Roosevelt's "An Ominous Nomination."

It was not simply that the New Deal had "exhausted its resources" for ending the depression, a judgment in which present-day historians would concur; it was not even only that "the party in power, unable to unify the national life at the level of its economic well-being, now turns to war as a unifying substitute," cruel as this charge was. The *Christian Century* in addition asserted that the nomination of Roosevelt for a third term was the decisive step toward Fascism:

This war policy of the present administration is not born of America's strength but of America's weakness. It is a compensatory shift from an unsolved economic problem . . . to a foreign issue by which a political unity may be achieved under the party now in power, with the almost certain prospect that this political unity, once it is accepted by the electorate, will establish the nation under a one-party system. This, of course, is fascism. There is no other explanation of the third term candidacy of Mr. Roosevelt.[16]

So it was that a journal which had supported FDR against Landon in 1936, and which even now said of the New Deal legislation that "most of it is of permanent value," came out in mid-October of 1940 with its front cover darkly blazoned: NO THIRD TERM. The campaign's heat was now such that even Morrison's pacifist motivation was pushed into the background. The third term, he now asserted, was "a domestic issue"—and the issue was that of Fascism.[17]

Although the declaration for Wendell Willkie may have served as a conscience-purge for an editor who sincerely believed that the repeal of the Neutrality Act, the destroyer deal, and the draft meant war and who believed that "all talk of defending civilization by war is irrational," at the same time the *Christian Century's* defection from the New Deal threw dismay into many believers in the Social Gospel.[18] Pointing out that the pro-German and pro-Italian groups in America were violently opposed to Roosevelt's re-election, a reader demanded to know why, if the third term spelled Fascism, the American Fascists were not for it. A Berea College coed exclaimed: "If *The Christian Century* can be persuaded to endorse Willkie, we are sunk!" [19] The split in the Social Gospel opened by FDR's "Quarantine" speech had yawned to the proportions of a chasm.

There had been rumblings on the left of the Social Gospel even before the "Quarantine" speech. At its fall conference in 1933 at Swarthmore College, the pacifist Fellowship of Reconciliation split, those who called themselves "Marxists" breaking with those who insisted upon nonviolence in all forms of social action. Ironically, since he was later to abandon Marxism also, Reinhold Niebuhr declared that he was willing to be a "pacifist" with respect to international (i.e., "imperialist") wars, but not with respect to the class war. "Recognizing, as liberal Christianity does not, that the world of politics is full of demonic forces," he wrote, "we have chosen on the whole to support the devil of vengeance against the devil of hypocrisy." [20]

The center of the Social Gospel felt the schism somewhat later. In the case of the Congregational Council for Social Action, which had had so auspicious a beginning, the division can be precisely dated. In 1936, the CSA's International Relations Committee released an Armistice Day message which rhetorically asked what the United States should do "if war cannot be prevented abroad"; and answered itself, "America can best serve the cause of peace by refusing to be drawn into the struggle." But the following year, on the same occasion, the same committee divided, 11 to 5, over the issue of quarantining the aggressor.[21] Two of the pacifist dissenters resigned from the CSA in September, 1938, just as the Munich crisis was building to its climax. Thereafter, the Council for Social Action let slip its ties with Quaker and pacifist groups and moved over into the collective-security camp.

The issue in the Church grew increasingly acute as more of the world burst into flame. President Roosevelt had his hand on the political pulse of the nation in this issue as in most others and was sufficiently aware of the pacifist appeal to Protestant voters that he appears, as late as the spring of 1938 and possibly as late as the spring of 1940, to have seriously considered appointing no less a pacifist leader than the Executive Director of the American Friends' Service Committee, Clarence Pickett, as the United States Ambassador to Germany. But this act was one gesture amid a flurry of preparations for the worst—a worst which events abroad seemed to be doing their utmost to confirm.[22]

September of 1939 came, and Neville Chamberlain's tragic broadcast to the world, "This is war." Then, anticlimactically, came the half-year of the "phony war," when an American reporter took a taxi ride from France via Luxemburg up to a German bridgehead and when soldiers came out from the Maginot and Siegfried Lines within full sight of each other to go fishing. During this period there was a breathing spell in the American church controversy, also, for it seemed that the *Christian Century*'s point of view was after all one of realism, that the United States, uninterested in "whether France can keep Mussolini from taking Tunis or Britain can escape from returning Kenya to Hitler," could use its good offices to negotiate a peace settlement that would be relatively just.[23]

This proposal was reminiscent of the Wilsonian neutralism of 1914–16. But, folklore to the contrary, history never quite repeats itself. The day before the Axis invasion of the Low Countries the *Century* had prepared for publication an editorial proposing that peace be negotiated by a conference of all the still-neutral powers. Niebuhr, in a mood of "I told you so," wrote at once to pour his wrath upon the proposal. The neutral capitals, Stockholm, Helsinki, Kaunas, Riga, Tallinn, Dublin, Berne—were these, with the aid of Washington, to bring peace to Europe? "Has it not occurred to you that most of them are shivering little mice waiting for the cat to pounce?" [24]

Then the Blitzkrieg rolled across France, and the Christian nonpacifists redoubled their effort to warn American Protestants of what a Hitler victory held in prospect for the United States. Henry P. Van Dusen accused the *Christian Century* of "irresponsible idealism," and contended that the only thing to do now was to "enlist the full national resources" of the United States "in assistance to Great Britain." Henry Sloane Coffin wrote on the pacifists' tendency to weigh Nazism against British and French imperialism as equal social evils: "How would a Gandhi fare under Hitler or Mussolini or Stalin or under Japan?" And a "Y" worker wrote from much-bombed Chungking: "War, to you, seems the supreme evil. Personally, I would rather go through a thousand air-raids than one occupation by Japanese troops." [25]

Men of the stamp of John A. Mackay, John Bennett, Douglas Horton, Francis McConnell, John R. Mott, and Henry Knox Sherrill were growing more and more impatient with the *Christian Century*'s version of the Social Gospel, particularly since, on account of the breach with Roosevelt, it appeared to be playing into the hands of the forces that were polarizing around Charles A. Lindbergh. In the winter of 1941, in the midst of the clamor over Lend-Lease, a group of these men formalized the schism in the Social Gospel by founding the periodical *Christianity and Crisis*—"in many ways . . . a direct protest against the stand of *The Christian Century*." [26] The new journal's introductory circular made its stand clear:

In the conflicts in Europe and Asia, ethical issues are at stake which claim the sympathy and support of American Christians. . . . When men or nations must choose between two great evils, the choice of the lesser evil becomes their duty. We hold that the halting of totalitarian aggression is prerequisite to world peace and order.

Pacifism, Reinhold Niebuhr declared, "is unable to distinguish between the peace of capitulation to tyranny and the peace of the Kingdom of God." [27] After December 7, 1941, this point of view carried the day in the churches; denominations formally endorsed the war effort, in many cases reversing standing antiwar legislation in order to do so. But the point was not carried without bitterness. Three years ago the writer was discussing Niebuhr's theology with a young Friend. The subject of pacifism had not come up in the conversation, but suddenly the Quaker burst out angrily: "More than anyone else Niebuhr got the American churches into the last war."

Still, 1941 was not quite a re-enactment of 1917. The war-making this time was more understanding and reluctant. For the essence of the Niebuhrian ethic was that it undercut any tendency to absolutize a social program into a dictate of God. It followed that an absolutized war crusade, of the First World War type, was as false to that ethic as an absolutized peace crusade. The demand of the older Social Gospel had been that men were obliged to pronounce religious judgment upon their society; the insight of the new Social Gospel, which the old had lacked, was that this religious act was both necessary and dangerous. What could happen when one stood by a particular concrete social program regardless of changes in its context had been dramatically shown in Prohibition and in Morrison's pathetic crusade against Roosevelt's "Fascism"; the cooler heads in the Church did not intend to make the same mistake with respect to the war effort in the Second World War.

There was endorsement of the war, to be sure—even the *Christian Century* broken-heartedly went along after Pearl Harbor—but it was an endorsement as much in sorrow as in anger. The new Christian nonpacifism saw, with Emil Brunner, that "we never . . . perceive the depth and universality of evil . . . until we are *obliged* to do something which, in itself, is evil." [28] Prominent churchmen who remained pacifist, such as Fosdick and Ernest F. Tittle, were not hounded as subversive or "pro-German"; there was too much on the consciences of those Christians who felt that they had to make war.

The quality of pacifism was changing also. In a significant article printed at the height of the Blitzkrieg, Georgia Harkness warned her fellow pacifists against their proneness to think of the conscientious nonpacifist as in some sense "un-Christian." "No one," she declared, "has a right to talk about force as if its meaning were unambiguous and its moral implications clear"; they must recognize the validity in the nonpacifist's insistence upon "the moral obligation not to condone evil." A chastened, less absolute pacifism was emerging, most notably from the pen of Elton Trueblood, editor of the *Friend,* a pacifism which would attempt "to maintain the sectarian protest against war while at the same time participating in the larger society," as the Society of Friends already was so admirably doing.[29]

"Vocational" pacifists such as Trueblood and "contrite" war-makers such as Niebuhr were both trying to preserve the Church from the schism which the pacifist controversy had opened in the Social Gospel, from "the strong tendency for the pacifist to be forced into the camp of the thoroughgoing isolationist, and for the religious interventionist to be forced into the camp of the militarist." Both, tacitly, accepted the pessimistic view of human nature which the Continental theologians had been urging upon American liberal Protestantism—or, to put it into their own terminology, both were agreed that "political controversies are not between righteous men and sinners, but between sinners." [30]

In part this mellowing of the pacifist and the Christian non-pacifist was forced upon both by their schism, if both were to play their role in the common fellowship of the Church. Here the crucial function of the ecumenical movement, particularly in its Faith and Order mode, becomes apparent. The Church, which had perforce to deal with secular social questions and pronounce and act on them, had perforce also to keep always in mind its own universality. The Oxford Conference had sensed the religious aspect of the schism in the world and had declared in its Message:

The universal Church, surveying the nations of the world, in every one of which it is now planted and rooted, must pronounce a condemnation of war unqualified and unrestricted. War can occur only as a fruit and manifestation of sin. This truth is unaffected by any question of what may be the duty of a nation which has to choose between entry upon war and a course which it believes to be a betrayal of right, or what may be the duty of a Christian citizen whose country is involved in war. The condemnation of war stands. . . .

If war breaks out, then pre-eminently the Church must manifestly be the Church, still united in the one body of Christ, though the nations wherein it is planted fight one another. . . . [The] fellowship of prayer must at all costs remain unbroken. The Church must

217

also hold together in one spiritual fellowship those of its members who take differing views concerning their duty as citizens in time of war.

To a far greater extent than in the First World War, this was actually done. This time, America's conscientious objectors were not left to shift for themselves; they received the full support of a National Service Board for Religious Objectors, with affiliated denominational boards—even while the same denominations were giving full support to the army chaplaincy program. The government, also, sensed this difference in the religious atmosphere, and created Civilian Public Service, in which more than eight thousand young men had been enrolled by March 1, 1945.[31]

Still more impressive from an ecumenical point of view was the promptness with which the churches ministered to the Japanese-Americans who were evacuated from the West Coast to what amounted to concentration camps beyond the Rocky Mountains. It was this writer's privilege to attend a Protestant church gathering during the summer of 1942 to which one of the largest delegations came from one of those Nisei relocation centers. It was the first, touch-and-go year of the war with Japan; the setting was a western state with an anti-Japanese tradition long antedating the war. But I do not believe that anyone who attended that conference will ever forget the poignancy of the religious fellowship there established, across what was virtually a battle line.

More subtly, the ecumenical impulse, in conjunction with the sense of guilt on the part of those who recanted from pacifism "for the duration," promoted the very considerable wartime labors by the churches in behalf of a "just and durable peace" when the war should be over. How much the ease with which the United Nations breezed through the United States Senate in 1945 was the product of this educational work of the churches, and how much it was due to the example of events themselves, can of course hardly be assessed; it is worth noting however that the churches during the past decade have sturdily backed the United Nations, both in the good years and in the years when the international body has met with disfavor on the part of American senators. The wartime and postwar championing of the United Nations by the churches was in a very real sense the cry of their pacifist conscience, transmuted.

Postscript: 1971. History may not exactly repeat itself, but it has a way of playing variations on the same themes. In the foregoing interpretation the United Nations became a vindication for the Second World War, as the League of Nations briefly had seemed to be for the First—with an implicit partisan moral that set Wilson's (and the old-style, "unrealistic" liberal's) failure against Roosevelt's (and the neo-orthodox "realist's") success.

A quarter-century after the writing of the United Nations Charter, it was not possible to see the events of the Forties with so much satisfaction. Two more wars had supervened. In the first, the United Nations—or temporary voting majorities thereof—had conceived of the Korean peninsula in collective-security terms, such as FDR had seemed to point toward in his "quarantine" speech of 1937; in the second, which took place flagrantly outside the United Nations framework altogether, Southeast Asia was conceived of in terms of Munich in 1938. Significantly, the champions of neo-orthodox "realism"—including Niebuhr himself—recoiled from making such an interpretation, and (along with Walter Lippmann) reverted to a position strikingly similar to what they had denounced in the late Thirties as isolationism.

As for pacifism, it reappeared, but in a far more particularist form. The war currently being waged was judged, not as a test of whether *any* war can be justified, but on its own terms, with attendant legal and moral complications for the person who had to decide personally whether or not to fight. But with the exception of the impressive ceremonies at the 1969 Washington, D.C., Moratorium, most of the organized religious responses to Vietnam—worship services climaxed by ritual burning of draft cards, or attempts to offer asylum to draft resisters in the sanctuary of a church—were, in general, pale echoes of a *secular* antiwar movement, more strenuous than anything of the kind seen in this country at least since the Mexican War. In the 1960's, the most vivid examples of religious political action against a government's war policies were to be found not in western Christendom but in South Asian Buddhism.

CHAPTER XV

The Social Gospel

and the Christian Faith

THE history of the Social Gospel between 1920 and 1940, as I have set it forth in these pages, is a history of decline and revival. The decline is associated, roughly, with the decade of the 20's; the revival, with that of the 30's. Still, "revival" is not quite accurate as a term to describe the quickened social conscience of the Protestant churches during the years of the New Deal. "One does not step into the same river twice." The Christian social consciousness of the followers of Reinhold Niebuhr would hardly have been recognizable to the followers of Walter Rauschenbusch, either in its social or in its Christian characteristics.

Other chapters have set forth, explicitly and implicitly, some of the transformations of the Social Gospel: the relativizing of the Social Gospel's ethic through the experiences of Prohibition and of pacifism, the supernaturalizing of its religious sanction through the experience of the European theological critique, the broadening of its social horizon through the experience of the ecumenical movement. On three issues—Prohibition, pacifism, and the social integration of the American Negro—I have shown how, in a complex pluralistic civilization, opposing sides could appeal to what had been a common body of social doctrine in 1920 and come out with diametrically opposed social positions. At the same time, I have shown the rise of a form and degree of Christian social awareness unknown to the American Protestantism of the years before the First World War through the growth of a deeper social and religious unity in Faith and Order.

So various and so fundamental were all these transformations that many churchmen now use the term "Social Gospel" only in the past tense; as a synonym for Christian social concern in recent times, these men say, it is obsolescent. Yet there were and are continuities between the "old" and "new" social creeds.

Both, for example, were in some sense the Church's response to the severe challenge of secularism. Most of the forces I have described as being adverse to the fortunes of the Social Gospel in the 20's had been to some degree overcome or eliminated by the 30's—except this one. Prohibition came and did untold damage to the churches, but it passed, and they began to live it down. Fundamentalism stirred great bitterness inside the Church and derision outside, but the Church shortly outgrew it. Conservatism in the laity bade fair to snuff out the Social Gospel, but the depression and the New Deal changed the atmosphere. The morale of the clergy slid perilously in the 20's, but by 1940 their sense of participation in an ecumenical Church Universal was drawing them up again. The experiences of the churches in the First World War seriously hurt the Social Gospel, but an atoning period of pacifism, followed by their taking a chastened middle-ground position, put them in better shape to face the Second World War. The European theologians unleashed an intellectual and polemical attack which seemed to cut the Social Gospel to shreds, but the American churches absorbed this "new" theology into their own viewpoint and then proceeded subtly to convert the Europeans to the Social Gospel. Yet the churches did not, to any appreciable degree in this period, alter or diminish the effectiveness of American secularism. There is, on the contrary, evidence that secularism continued to make headway in society at the expense of the churches.

When one compares, for example, the Federal Government's *Census of Religious Bodies* for 1936 with that of 1926, one discovers that over-all church membership in the United States increased during that decade by only 2.3 per cent—a sharp falling off from the decade 1916–26.[1] Furthermore, much of the increase that did take place was among such denominations as Christian Scientists (33.1 per cent) and Mormons (25.1 per cent). Several of the groups which have figured most prominently in this study, including the Methodists (North and South), the Presbyterians (North), the Episcopalians, and the Congregationalists, actually showed a net decrease. The Federal Council of Churches promoted an evangelistic National Christian Mission in the fall and winter of 1940–1941 with the declared purpose of reaching the unchurched half of the American population, but the results, according to the news weekly *Time,* were disappointing:

Protestantism's most ambitious venture in mass evangelism was found wanting . . . in most of the 22 cities visited by this winter's National Christian Mission. It had given the already faithful a notable stirring-up, but as a program for "reaching the unreached" it had barely scratched the surface. With 70,000,000 Americans still outside any church the best figure the Mission could claim was 50,000 new members added to the 40,000,000 already within the Protestant fold—a gain of about one-eighth of 1%, or about 1% of the Protestant church membership of the cities visited. . . . Few realistic churchmen could argue that such evangelism was an adequate answer to their problem of reaching America's 70,000,000 unreached.[2]

To be sure, since the Second World War the trend has shifted; currently the churches are gaining new members at a rate faster than that of population growth. But a trend is not reversed in a day, a fact sometimes forgotten by those who see the nation's religious life in 1956 as taking its tone from the personal commitment of Dwight Eisenhower. As of 1940, the churches were bound to accept the fact that statistically at least they were getting the worst of the competition with explicit or implicit secularism, and when one surveys Hollywood's incredibly materialistic interpretation of the Bible one wonders if this is not still the case even though statistics are now more favorable to the Church.

If the Church's standing in secular society was lower in 1940 than in 1920, it follows that the same was true to some extent for its Social Gospel, even though the political climate of America had once again turned liberal. A striking illustration of this fact is the difference in the role played by the Church in the steel strikes of 1919 and 1937 respectively. The steelworkers' violent struggle with the United States Steel Corporation in the former year had called forth the famous Interchurch Report on the Steel Strike of 1919 (discussed in Chapter II above). Men had listened to its signers because of their standing in the Church; the press had broken a long silence on the issues of the strike to publicize these findings. It had, in short, been social action of the most directly relevant kind. But by 1937, so much further had secularism and indifferentism progressed in America that a comparable action by churchmen was no longer capable of arousing excitement.

When Tom Girdler's Republic Steel forces and John L. Lewis's Steel Workers' Organizing Committee fought their bitter and bloody war over union recognition, one hundred American clergymen made a public appeal to the company to negotiate with the union "to the end that . . . our American principle of democracy [be] incorporated in the industrial relations . . . of this great industry." The standing of the signers of this appeal was as high in the Church as had been that of the signers of the 1919 Report; the list read, said the *Christian Century* at the time, "like the roster of the Protestant and Jewish leadership of the United States." By including Jews and one highly placed Catholic (Msgr. John Ryan), it was indeed a more broadly based statement than the 1919 Interchurch Report had been. The crucial difference lay in its reception. The Report on the 1919 steel strike had "created an unprecedented sensation"; the statement on the 1937 steel strike was "an incident . . . to which the press gave little attention." [3]

The CIO, for the first time in American labor annals, was finding it possible to organize American workers successfully on a large scale without the benefit of some middle-class moral support, while the press, which leaned to the management side in 1937 as it had in 1920, no longer felt as constrained to defer to the opinions of highly placed clergymen. The battles of the 30's were being fought and won in secular terms. The same had been true of the battles of the Progressive Era, but the battlers had then acknowledged some ideological debt to religion. With the exception of Henry Wallace, Frances Perkins, and a very few others, the New Dealers did not similarly acknowledge their ideological debt to journals like the *Churchman,* organizations like the Council of Social Action, and statements of principle like the revised Social Creed of the Churches.

This is not surprising; in a generation which took the Church less seriously than its fathers had, the role in society of the Church's Social Gospel was likewise bound to be more modest. But the responsibility of the Social Gospel bearers toward the Church itself thereby became all the greater. Both the Church's adjustment to a reactionary *status quo* and its adoption of a liberal but essentially secular social program had been attacked; it then became the problem of liberal churchmen to reformulate their doctrine in terms which would meet both of these shortcomings. The Social Gospel had to be so firmly based that it would neither yield to pressure from the secular political right nor abandon its Christian commitment in accommodating to the secular political left. Churchmen of the 30's and 40's increasingly believed that this firm basis would be found in the institutional church itself. So there arose what might well be called a "high-church" Social Gospel.

The threat from the right, as far as the American churches were concerned, was for the moment greatly diminished. But this would, of course, not always be the case. In due course a

Methodist prelate was to be haled before the House Committee on Un-American Activities and faced with charges quite as flimsy as those which had moved the Red Scare of the early 20's. The New Deal breathing space for liberals was a short one. If the Social Gospel were not to go beyond the New Deal in its formulation, it would be foredoomed to expand and contract passively with the lightening and darkening of the skies of politics, adjusting successively to a *status quo* of the left and then to one of the right until it petered out as the Church fully adjusted itself to its secular milieu and became simply a sum of social club plus benevolent society plus, perhaps, psychological counseling service.

To save both itself and the Church from this prospect, the Social Gospel perforce had to fall back upon the Oxford Conference slogan, "Let the Church be the Church!" The nineteenth-century doctrine of the continuity between the social order and the Kingdom of God was replaced by the Augustinian doctrine of the World and the Church as distinct entities in order to disentangle any and all purely secular social programs from the teaching function of the Church. In the long run, the men of the Social Gospel hoped, this strategy would keep that teaching function distinctively Christian, and thereby the Christian witness would be manifested in the World even though the World rejected or paid little attention to the Church.

At the same time, this accorded programmatically with the general drift of political liberalism, to the extent that the latter had begun to turn internationalist. For as soon as men of the Social Gospel took cognizance of the Church in their own country, they were thereby confronted with the Church universal. The most serious external problem of the world church was and is maintaining its integrity and its inclusiveness in a divided world. So, by turning somewhat away from secular agencies of reform, the Social Gospel was paradoxically turning toward the central social problem of the twentieth century— international anarchy. In 1955, four heads of government met "at the summit" in Geneva; two weeks later the Central Committee of the World Council of Churches scheduled its 1956 meeting to be held in Communist Hungary. The one act is the complement of the other.

This international and institutional emphasis in the new Social Gospel has been reinforced by the Church's confrontation of the totalitarian state. Not inappropriately, churches which on theological grounds had resisted the American-type Social Gospel were among the first to invoke their very conservatism to justify their independent existence against a New Order whose watchword was co-ordination from the top downward (*Gleichschaltung*). Secularists had based part of their appeal against the Church upon its absolutist pretensions, but in the Europe of Hitler on the one hand and Niemöller, Eivind Berggrav, and Otto Dibelius on the other, the shoe was on the other foot; it had become frighteningly true that "in large measure the secular powers refuse to accept the label of relative," and so it had become the Church's duty and privilege to remind the secular powers of the eternal limitations set upon the things which are Caesar's.[4]

Intransigence on the wrong ground, as in the case of Fundamentalism, had been positively harmful to the Church; but the intransigence of Karl Barth—"I say No, without reservation or qualification, to the letter and to the spirit of this doctrine" (of "Aryan" supremacy)—arouses admiration.[5] To "let the Church be the Church" in situations of this kind was to carry on and vindicate the tradition of the Social Gospel, even in a land where it had been a stranger; the record of East German Christian leadership today continues this great tradition.

Nor was the experience of German Christianity without certain practical lessons for Americans. It forced the Social Gospel's critique to extend over an issue which secular New Dealers understandably shied away from—bureaucratic centralism. "The more extensive the work of the state becomes, the more important it is to encourage associations within the larger community which are independent of the state," writes John Bennett. "The Church is the one association which has proved over and over again to be so tough that the state cannot absorb it."[6] This is as true for America as for Germany; as this nation's population and economy continue to expand and its internal relationships to be routinized, the state as an independent entity will increasingly be a problem, regardless of who happen to be the political "ins" and "outs" and regardless of what theoretical label is pinned to the American economic system. The Church's function as independent critic in American society will become more important, not less, in the future.

It is true however that this "high-church" Social Gospel contains social dangers. There were, and are, those in the separate denominations who view the ecumenical movement as no more than a field for the activities of church board secretaries on an unprecedentedly vast scale; my description on the injustice done to the American Negro Christian in the 30's in the name of ecumenicity illustrates the fact that the Church as well as the state has a problem of bureaucratic centralism to contend with.

A confirmed ecumenicalist would reply that a *fully* ecumenical Christianity would so thoroughly take cognizance of the Negro's rights as a brother in Christ that it would move for the abolition of the segregated churches, and he could quote the Oxford Conference report to prove his point. But the issue of church centralism would remain, as the recent litigation over the Congregational–Evangelical and Reformed merger so dramatically demonstrated. Fortunately for the ecumenical church —and for the secular world which has to reckon with that church —a basis exists for self-criticism through the new theological perspectives which have entered into and changed the Social Gospel in other areas besides its doctrine of the Church.

If the danger from the political right to the Social Gospel was that of attenuating it to the point where it would be harmless to the *status quo,* the danger from the left was one of applying the absolute sanction of the Christian ethic to the partial perspective of a specific and temporary social program. To abstain from the social struggle was perilous; it had lost, or very nearly lost, the workingman to the Protestant churches. But to participate in the struggle in a way which compromised their transcendental ethic out of existence was even more fatal. A prohibitionist, boasting of having lied in his cause in a way "to make Ananias ashamed of himself"; a pacifist, reasoning that because Franklin D. Roosevelt was not an isolationist he must be a Fascist; a bishop, rationalizing a surrender to Southern churchmen on the segregation issue as "the will of God"— all of these illustrated the perennial danger of confusing "Thy will be done" with "*this* will be done."

The old Social Gospel, in addition to accepting a theology which had made its social critique possible in the first place, had accepted also the perfectionistic outlook of the evangelical revivals. While it rejected the revivalist insistence upon a single, definitive religious experience for the individual, it carried over and translated into social terms the idea that the Christian community was a fellowship of "the saved." Implicit in the slogan "Christianizing the Social Order" was the assumption that the social order could, once-for-all, be Christianized. Thus the political and economic program of the old Social Gospel, being the instrument of salvation, had tended to become absolutized. The danger of thus hitching one's star to a wagon here below was shown in the churches' "crusade" in the First World War and in the several subsequent controversies which I have described.

The beginning, in the United States, of a definitive break with this tendency to absolutize the particular was the publication of Reinhold Niebuhr's *Moral Man and Immoral Society* in 1932. There were vestiges of the old absolutism even here, in the new guise of Marxism, but Niebuhr's writings through the rest of the New Deal years carried him away from this and left bare his relativistic critique of all social creeds. Marxism remained for him the definitive critique of bourgeois society only because it made manifest the relativities and ambiguities of that society's moral pretensions. But Marxism's own moral claims, particularly in their Soviet form, he now attacked just as savagely.

As all social absolutes melted in Niebuhr's dialectical acid, the transcendental absolutes of the neo-orthodox Continental theology flowed in to take their place. At the end of the period,

in the Gifford lectures which he delivered in 1939, Niebuhr
abandoned even the claim of the individual to more than a
relative perspective on the Christian ethic. The ground under
his feet had shifted; the perspective from which in 1927 one
could ask *Does Civilization Need Religion?* was dwarfed by the
inquiry into *The Nature and Destiny of Man.*

Here was a danger, as Barth and others made manifest, that
in thus escaping from the absolutization of any given social
perspective, one ran the risk of withdrawing above the social
struggle and accepting a condition of social impotence as the
price of a religiously relevant ideal. Niebuhr and his fellows
avoided this by their ethical paradox of an activist relativism.
That is to say, the same religious scruples which enjoined one
from equating the Kingdom of God with any given social order
nevertheless required one to become involved in the social
struggle. The ethical dicta "Be ye therefore perfect" and "There
is none good save God" were understood as being fully and
equally true. (That this was metaphysically unsatisfying bothered
Niebuhr not one whit; he and his friends rejected both the
Thomistic and the Platonic resolutions of religion into meta-
physics and let its logical contradictions stand.)

The resulting paradox is neatly expressed by Niebuhr in
Reflections on the End of an Era: "Upon the historical level,
where all things are relative, . . . distinctions between the
relatively good and the relatively evil are very important." [7]
The Kingdom of God was neither within the social purview of
man, so that it was to be achieved by party manifesto or Act
of Congress, nor yet so far beyond history that the social-
gospelers were committing any religious "heresy" in struggling
toward it. "History moves toward the realization of the Kingdom
but yet the judgment of God is upon every new realization." [8]

Some American Fundamentalists, hearing Niebuhr and Barth
and Brunner thus speak seriously of "judgment," "sin," "redemption," "the Word of God," at first hailed neo-orthodoxy as
confirmation of their own beliefs. They were appalled to discover
how fully these men accepted the drastic Biblical criticism of
the German universities. For the "new theology" was neither

Fundamentalist nor Modernist; it accepted both the evidences arrived at through secular science and scholarship, and the traditional Trinitarian Christian theology. Abandoning Biblical literalism but retaining Biblical relevance, it built its faith upon myth and paradox, asserting, together with a few secular thinkers, that myth and paradox were at the very heart of existence.

But this "dialectical theology" was not foolproof. Perhaps its greatest practical drawback was its rather narrow appeal, being primarily congenial to religious intellectuals. To reason "Either/Or" is to risk being quoted out of context; readers are baffled by the evident relish with which Niebuhr lives among contradictions. The average devout Christian in particular is likely to be irritated by a feeling that the neo-orthodox clergy are substituting the dialectic for belief.

The Union Theological Seminary student who argued that the dogma of the Incarnation would be unaffected one way or the other if it should be proved that the historical Jesus never existed may have been able to assent, "dialectically," to every article in the Nicene Creed; but he was speaking in an unknown tongue as far as pre-Barth Christian orthodoxy, or even Christian liberalism, was concerned. Admittedly the "new theology" does not usually go this far; but the reasoning of neo-orthodoxy is so far from being "orthodox" that a person in search of the "old-time religion" would find it outrageously sophisticated. The result is that a Social Gospel founded upon it, while hampered in its expression in the world by the secularist belief that religion is not intellectually respectable, is further circumscribed in its appeal to Christians by its very intellectual preciousness.

It is, nevertheless, a tremendous achievement to have created a means of expressing the whole of the traditional creed, from the Fall of Man to the Last Judgment, in a form which could not be dismissed as intellectually outdated. For the Social Gospel, it is an achievement to have been able, without destroying the *élan* of its program, to shift from an optimistic to a provisionally pessimistic basis. Whether this "new theology" and Social

Gospel can be translated into a form which can be assimilated by the casual churchgoer without simplifying it into Fundamentalism is, of course, an open question.

These ideas burst upon the European horizon with Karl Barth's *Römerbrief* in 1918; they enjoyed their first great vogue there in the 20's; they passed into the thinking of the more prominent American churchmen in the 30's; they became a part of the natural climate in some of the theological seminaries of the United States in the 40's. The ministerial generation of the 50's and 60's, the product of this Niebuhrian atmosphere, will answer the question of whether these ideas can be made to take root in American cultural soil—and whether the Church has succeeded in changing *with* the times without adapting itself *to* the times. In an age which makes a fetish of adjustment to a norm and powerfully facilitates that adjustment through the pressure of the mass media of communication, such a success would be a contribution of incalculable importance to American society, in addition to saving the soul of the American Church.

Notes

Chapter I. The Rise of American Social Christianity

1. The causal connection between this neglect and the appearance of an individualistic economic ideology has been a matter for voluminous discussion from the time of Max Weber onward, and an extensive treatment of that discussion would take us far afield from the present topic. It will be touched upon, by inference only, in Chapters V and VI, below.

2. R. T. Stevenson, in the Introduction to W. W. Sweet, *The Methodist Episcopal Church and the Civil War* (Cincinnati: Methodist Book Concern, n.d.), p. 9.

3. Ralph Gabriel, *The Course of American Democratic Thought* (New York: Ronald Press, 1940), p. 14.

4. I say "peak" because the post-Civil War "awakenings" were prompted as much by nostalgia as by fervor. Men often responded to evangelists of the Dwight L. Moody type with a regretful backward glance at Moody's genuine and simple faith, which for them had ceased to be possible. See W. E. Garrison, *The March of Faith* (New York: Harper, 1933), chap. v.

5. See Gilbert H. Barnes, *The Anti-Slavery Impulse, 1830–1844* (New York: Appleton-Century, 1933), chap. ii.

6. I make this point because a recent major study of Protestant social thought in the United States describes the Social Gospel as having arisen

more or less *de novo* out of a "Conservative Mold" of laissez-faire individualism. Cf. Henry F. May, *Protestant Churches and Industrial America* (New York: Harper, 1949), pt. 1. My quarrel with this judgment is that it contrasts the churches' social views with those of Jacksonian Democratic thinkers, as though the Age of Jackson had been an age of solidarist, welfare-state, "New Deal" political thought, which it was not. Jackson's government did not intervene in behalf of the "forgotten man" in quite the same fashion as would Roosevelt's; rather, its philosophy was dedicated to clearing away obstacles to competition, so that the "forgotten man" could scramble to the top on equal terms with, and at the expense of, other "forgotten men." See Richard Hofstadter, *The American Political Tradition* (New York: Knopf, 1948), chap. iii; R. B. Morris, "Andrew Jackson: Strikebreaker," *American Historical Review*, LV (Oct., 1949), 54f.

7. May, *op. cit.*, p. 91. For statements of this thesis, cf. *ibid.*, pt. 3, "Sources of Change"; A. M. Schlesinger, "A Critical Period in American Religion, 1875–1900," in Mass. Hist. Society, *Proceedings*, LXIV (1932), 523–547; A. I. Abell, *The Urban Impact on American Protestantism, 1865–1900* (Cambridge: Harvard University Press, 1943).

8. For a statement of this thesis, see Robert T. Handy, "The Protestant Quest for a Christian America," *Church History*, XXII (March, 1953), 8ff.

9. On this Social Gospel base for American ecumenicity, see below, Chapter VIII. Catholic thought lies outside the scope of this study; it should be noted, however, that the development of the Federal Council was paralleled by a contemporaneous development of a National Catholic Welfare Council.

10. Robert T. Handy, "Christianity and Socialism in America," *Church History*, XXI (March, 1952), 39ff.

11. May, *op. cit.*, p. 233.

12. These Rauschenbusch quotations are from C. H. Hopkins, *The Rise of the Social Gospel in American Protestantism, 1865–1915* (New Haven: Yale University Press, 1940), chap. xiii.

Chapter II. The Social Gospel and the Spirit of the Times—1920

1. For this controlled experiment in public opinion to be successful, it was essential that the same denominations—Methodist, Baptist, Presbyterian, Congregationalist, and Episcopalian—be used as subjects in the later as in the earlier sample. For the period of Dr. May's study, these well typified American Protestantism; "in them converge the principal early currents of American religious history" (May, *op. cit.*, p. x). By 1920 other bodies, such as the Disciples and the Lutherans, were moving into the main stream of American religious life; nevertheless it appeared to me that the original five continued to make a tenable basis for judgment. It was pos-

sible to use four of the journals that May had employed in his study—the *Christian Advocate* (Methodist), the *Watchman-Examiner* (Baptist—formerly *Christian Watchman*), the *Churchman* (Episcopalian), and the *Congregationalist*. To these were added the *Baptist*, because it was the official organ of that denomination, and the *Continent* (Presbyterian).

2. On the Non-Partisan League, see the *Congregationalist*, CV (Aug. 5, 1920), 178f. On the urban Negro, see the *Baptist*, I (Feb. 28, 1920), 154ff. On immigration, see the *Continent*, LI (Oct. 21, 1920), 1284ff.

3. *Churchman*, CXXII (Sept. 11, 1920), 12ff.; *ibid.*, CXXIII (Jan. 29, 1921), 28.

4. Quoted in the *Christian Advocate*, XCV (May 13, 1920), 654.

5. Quoted in the *Churchman*, CXXII (Aug. 29, 1920), 11f.

6. Quoted by Graham Taylor in the *Congregationalist*, CV (Oct. 14, 1920), 467.

7. *Christian Advocate*, XCV (Aug. 5, 1920), 1042.

8. Charles S. MacFarland, General Secretary of the Federal Council of Churches, on returning to the United States from supervising postwar relief work in Europe, quoted in the *Churchman*, CXXII (Oct. 16, 1920), 18.

9. *Presbyterian*, XC (Jan. 15, 1920), 7.

10. *Christian Advocate*, XCV (Jan. 29, 1920), 141; *ibid.* (May 20, 1920), p. 692. Presbyterian action was reported in the *Continent*, LI (June 3, 1920), 802. Baptist action was reported in the *Watchman-Examiner*, VIII (July 8, 1920), 871.

11. *Continent*, LI (April 8, 1920), 461.

12. *Congregationalist*, CV (June 24, 1920), 831, 841.

13. *Churchman*, CXXII (Oct. 23, 1920), 7; *ibid.* (Nov. 13, 1920), p. 8; *Continent*, LI (Oct. 28, 1920), 1309; *Baptist*, I (Oct. 2, 1920), 1221.

14. Full list reprinted in the *Churchman*, CXXI (Jan. 17, 1920), 19.

15. Quoted in the *Baptist*, I (July 10, 1920), 846.

16. *Churchman*, CXXI (May 1, 1920), 9.

17. *Congregationalist*, CV (May 27, 1920), 703f.; *ibid.* (May 13, 1920), p. 630.

18. *Churchman*, CXXII (Oct. 30, 1920), 7; *Congregationalist*, CV (April 16, 1920), 502; *Baptist*, I (May 1, 1920), 476.

19. *Churchman*, CXXII (Nov. 13, 1920), 7.

Chapter III. Prohibition, Left and Right

1. Episcopal Address to the Methodist General Conference of 1932, in the *Daily Christian Advocate*, XXII (Chicago, 1932), 57.

2. Texts of platforms down to 1924 in D. Leigh Colvin, *Prohibition in the United States* (New York: George H. Doran, 1926), a semiofficial history of the party.

3. *Continent*, LI (April 15, 1920), 493.

4. Documentary evidence for this statement is immense. Consult the indexes of the Methodist General Conference *Journal,* the Presbyterian General Assembly *Minutes,* the Northern Baptist Convention *Annual,* the National Council of the Congregational Churches *Minutes,* for any year from the turn of the century through repeal; reports, resolutions, and speeches on Prohibition abound, endorse it in unmistakable terms, and by about 1913 have so nearly approached unanimity as to make wearisome reading.

5. Virginius Dabney, *Dry Messiah* (New York: Knopf, 1948), p. 43. Even the unappealing Southern Methodist bishop who is the hero-villain of this study worked for the improvement of Southern factory conditions.

6. Federal Council of the Churches of Christ in America, *Annual Report,* 1912, p. 182.

7. Further proof that political liberalism and prohibitionism are not necessarily incompatible may be found in a "cross-cultural check" of the experience of other countries. Many of the early British Fabians were dry. The government of Mr. Nehru in India is dry (and enjoys bad relations with the Portuguese colony at Goa, which among other things is a focal point for bootlegging into India). Cannadian C.C.F. (Co-operative Commonwealth Federation), which at the time of writing was operating the only socialist government in North America, resolved to "commend the Saskatchewan Legislature for its financial appropriations for temperance legislation" and urged "all citizens to refrain from social and other drinking" *(sic)* in order to "strengthen the character of the youth of today" *(Commonwealth,* July 30, 1952. I am indebted to Mr. Jürgen Kraft of Göttingen for furnishing me with a copy of this party newspaper).

8. Dabney, *op. cit.,* p. 128.

9. *Daily Christian Advocate,* XXII (Chicago, 1932), 59.

10. E. H. Cherrington, ed., *Anti-Saloon League Yearbook,* 1931 (Westerville, O., 1932), p. 9. It is significant that this same power-struggle was reflected in the structure of the Anti-Saloon League itself, on whose board of directors no single state might have more than five representatives—"to prevent the populous urban states from gaining control" (Peter Odegard, *Pressure Politics: The Story of the Anti-Saloon League* [New York: Columbia, 1928], p. 10).

11. Proceedings of the 18th Convention of the Anti-Saloon League, 1917, p. 75, quoted in Odegard, *op. cit.,* p. 173. The wet-dry controversy was an issue in the holding-up of Congressional reapportionment throughout the 20's.

12. *Anti-Saloon League Yearbook,* 1931, p. 8.

13. Harding's speech was delivered at Denver on June 25, 1923, with the usual masterful Hardingesque sentence structure. Coolidge's was given at Washington on October 20, 1923. Hoover's was in New York on April 22,

1929; he also devoted a considerable portion of his inaugural to this theme.

14. Lippmann's article appeared in *Harper's* for December, 1926. Is it cricket to inquire how such a view can be squared with the profounder constitutionalism of Mr. Lippmann's more recent *Public Philosophy?*

15. *Daily Christian Advocate,* XXI (Kansas City, 1928), 412; *ibid.,* p. 322.

16. Dabney, *op. cit.,* p. 184.

17. William Allen White to Walter Lippmann, October 15, 1928, in Walter Johnson, ed., *Selected Letters of William Allen White, 1899–1943* (New York: Holt, 1947), p. 285.

18. Cf., e.g., Bishop James Cannon, "Al Smith: Catholic, Tammany, Wet," *Nation,* CXXVII (July 4, 1928), 9.

19. *Baptist,* I (Oct. 28, 1920), 1295; *ibid.* (Nov. 11, 1920), p. 1391.

20. And labor remembers. See for example the article apropos of the tenth anniversary of the repeal of the Eighteenth Amendment, "How Labor Helped Win Repeal," *Catering Industry Employee,* official journal of the Hotel and Restaurant Employees' and Bartenders' International Union, A. F. of L., LXII (Nov., 1953), 26ff.

21. *Churchman,* CXXII (Nov. 13, 1920), 12.

22. *Daily Christian Advocate,* XIX (Des Moines, 1920), 654.

23. *Ibid.,* XXII (Chicago, 1932), 57; *ibid.,* XX (Springfield, Mass., 1924), 593; *ibid.,* XXIII (Columbus, Ohio, 1936), 369.

24. Bishop Edwin D. Mouzon, before the Virginia Conference, quoted in Dabney, *op. cit.,* p. 322.

25. Quoted in *ibid.,* p. 136.

26. Quoted in Odegard, *op. cit.,* p. 393.

27. *Churchman,* CXXII (Nov. 13, 1920), 12.

28. *Daily Christian Advocate,* XXIII (Columbus, O., 1936), 468.

29. Edwin Holt Hughes, "Our Mistaken Legislation on Amusements," *Methodist Review* (bimonthly), CVI (5th ser., vol. XXXIX; 1923), 721.

Chapter IV. The Social Meaning of Fundamentalism

1. So one would judge from Paxton Hibben's account of the trial in *The Peerless Leader: William Jennings Bryan* (New York: Farrar & Rinehart, 1929), p. 403.

2. On this point see Richard Hofstadter, *Social Darwinism in American Thought 1860–1915* (Philadelphia: University of Pennsylvania, 1944), p. 173. Anyone acquainted with such tracts for the times as *The Passing of the Great Race* and Galton's *Hereditary Genius* knows that the doctrine of the survival of the fittest, translated into sociological terms, has indeed been often put to antidemocratic uses. Hofstadter comments: "In these, as in other matters, the soundness of Bryan's intuition . . . outstripped the powers of his intellect."

3. One thinks in particular of the Stewart brothers of California, Lyman and Milton, who founded Fundamentalist schools, financed Fundamentalist missionaries, and placed a copy of one Fundamentalist handbook in the hands of every ordained minister in the United States and Canada. Their social philosophy is known to have been pretty crudely reactionary.

4. Double-spread in the *Watchman-Examiner,* VIII (July 15, 1920), 904–905.

5. Stewart G. Cole has done a remarkably lucid job of mapping the intra- and interdenominational complexities of Fundamentalist organization in *The History of Fundamentalism* (New York: R. R. Smith, 1931). This work should be used with considerable caution beyond its descriptive level, however, since it was written prior to the penetration of neo-orthodox thinking and so does not posit a possible valid alternative between Fundamentalist and Modernist theologies.

6. *Watchman-Examiner,* VIII (July 1, 1920), 834.

7. Text in the *Baptist,* I (July 23, 1920). "Our" meant the ,denomination's, not the public schools.

8. *Watchman-Examiner,* VIII (July 1, 1920), 834.

9. *Baptist,* I (July 3, 1920), 807.

10. *Annual* of the Northern Baptist Convention, 1921, p. 92, quoted in Cole, *op. cit.,* p. 77.

11. Text of Fosdick's sermon in the *Christian Century,* XXXIX (June 8, 1922). The sermon itself was actually rather conciliatory; the "fighting" title was appended by the committee in Fosdick's church that was responsible for having sermons printed as pamphlets. The Straton counterblast is in the *Religious Searchlight,* later titled the *Fundamentalist,* I (Oct. 1, 1922).

12. *Annual,* 1923, p. 133, quoted in Cole, *op. cit.,* p. 69.

13. Letter to the *Baptist,* I (July 31, 1920), 942.

14. A summary of these findings is printed as Exhibit XIV in Herbert W. Schneider, *Religion in Twentieth-Century America* (Cambridge: Harvard University Press, 1952), pp. 104ff.

15. I am indebted for this descriptive title, and for invaluable aid in organizing contemporary Fundamentalist thought for the purposes of this study, to Mr. Ralph L. Roy, whose unpublished master's thesis "The Protestant Underworld" is on deposit in Columbia University (1952). Its conclusions are embodied in his *Apostles of Discord* (Boston: Beacon Press, 1953).

16. Ralph L. Roy, "A Ministry of Schism," *Pastor,* Oct., 1952, pp. 5f.

17. Johnson, *op. cit.,* pp. 383, 390. Correspondence with President Roosevelt *in re* the Winrod senatorial campaign is at pp. 386f.

18. *Fundamentalist,* II (Dec. 1, 1922), 4.

19. Adolf Harnack, *What Is Christianity?* (New York: G. P. Putnam, 1912), p. 229.

20. Reinhold Niebuhr, *Does Civilization Need Religion?* (New York: Macmillan, 1927), p. 2.

21. Schneider, *op. cit.*, p. 212, n. 6.

22. J. Gresham Machen, *Christianity and Liberalism* (New York: Macmillan, 1923), pp. 179f. Used by permission.

23. Schneider, *op. cit.*, pp. 14, 89.

Chapter V. The Churches' Business in a Business Society

1. Walter Rauschenbusch, *A Theology for the Social Gospel* (New York: Macmillan, 1917), pp. 96ff.

2. Federal Council of the Churches of Christ in America, *Annual Report,* 1928, p. 60.

3. Samuel Shoemaker, "A First-Century Christian Fellowship," *Churchman,* CXXXIX (Jan. 12, 19, 1929), 10f., 12ff.

4. George F. Baer, quoted in Frederick Lewis Allen, *The Big Change* (New York: Harper, 1952), p. 83.

5. Quoted in the *Congregationalist,* CV (Oct. 28, 1920), 530f.

6. Quoted in J. Milton Yinger, *Religion in the Struggle for Power* (Durham, N.C.: Duke University Press, 1946), p. 160.

7. See John C. Bennett, *Christian Ethics and Social Policy* (New York: Scribner's, 1946).

8. *Presbyterian,* XC (Feb. 26, 1920), 6; *ibid.* (Jan. 1, 1920), p. 9. This journal however saw no inconsistency in its own social editorializing, which was consistently right-wing.

9. *Christian Century,* XXXVII (Feb. 26, 1920), 8ff.

10. *Baptist,* I (June 26, 1920), 763f.; *Watchman-Examiner,* VIII (Nov. 28, 1920), 1453. It should be noted that the *Watchman-Examiner* spoke for the more moderate Fundamentalists, those who in the eventual showdown did not withdraw from their denomination's fellowship.

11. *Daily Christian Advocate,* XIX (Des Moines, 1920), 654.

12. Yinger, *op. cit.*, p. 160.

13. John R. Straton, "Let the Laymen Organize," *The Faith* (formerly the *Fundamentalist*), II (March 22, 1925), 9.

14. Cyrus R. Pangborn, "Free Churches and Social Change" (unpublished doctoral dissertation; Columbia University, 1951), p. 128.

15. Letter in the *Churchman,* CXXI (Feb. 21, 1920), 26; letter in the *Congregationalist,* CXIV (Sept. 12, 1929), 338. Editorial comment indicates that these were not isolated hardship cases.

16. *American Journal of Sociology,* LVIII (March, 1943), 579. Cf. Lynd and Lynd, *Middletown,* pp. 530–531; Hopkins, *op. cit.*, pp. 79–85; Norman L. Trott and Ross W. Sanderson, *What Church People Think about Social and Economic Issues* (New York: Association Press, 1938); Liston Pope,

"Religion and the Class Structure," in American Academy of Political and Social Science, *Annals,* 256 (March, 1948), 84–91. The list could be extended.

17. Jerome Davis, "A Study of Protestant Church Boards of Control," *American Journal of Sociology,* XXXVIII (Nov., 1932), 418.

18. Arthur L. Swift, *New Frontiers of Religion* (New York: Macmillan, 1938), pp. 113f.

19. Quotation by William Spofford of the Church League for Industrial Democracy, in the *Congregationalist,* CXIV (Nov. 21, 1929), 670. The story of these mill churches is told in full in Liston Pope, *Millhands and Preachers* (New Haven: Yale, 1942), esp. pp. 153, 158.

20. Quotation from John J. Chapman at a dinner under the auspices of the Harvard School of Business Administration, 1928, in H. E. Luccock, *Jesus and the American Mind* (New York: Abingdon, 1930), p. 123.

21. *Christian Advocate,* CIV (Jan. 10, 1929), 39.

22. I am here assuming Ernst Troeltsch's division of religious groups into "churches" and "sects," recognizing its limitations—the "church" as a body which seeks universality, generally at the expense of ideological compromise, and the "sect" as a body which seeks purity of life and doctrine, generally at the price of separation from the secular social order. Roman Catholicism and the Jehovah's Witnesses are respective examples of the types.

23. Story in May, *op. cit.,* p. 186.

24. Luccock, *op. cit.,* p. 194.

Chapter VI. The Changing Ministry: A Study in Clerical Self-Respect

1. Ellis J. Hough, "Terrors of the Protestant Ministry," *Presbyterian Advance,* XL (Jan. 30, 1930), 18.

2. *Christian Advocate,* CIV (Jan. 3, 1929), 7; *ibid.,* XCV (July 8, 1920), 917; *Presbyterian Advance,* XL (Sept. 26, 1929), 6, and *Homiletic Review,* LXXXVIII (Sept., 1924), 181; *ibid.,* LXXXVII (April, 1924), 290; *Baptist,* X (Aug. 3, 1929), 977; *Congregationalist,* CXIV (May 9, 1929), 636f.

3. *Ibid.,* CXIV (Feb. 14, 1929), 209f.

4. Diocesan newspaper *Pacific Churchman,* quoted in the *Churchman,* CXXXIX (May 4, 1929), 7.

5. Luccock, *op. cit.,* p. 121.

6. Reported in *Christian Advocate,* XCV (July 22, 1920), 985.

7. Quoted in *Homiletic Review,* LXXXVII (Jan., 1924), 8.

8. *Ibid.,* LXXXVI (Dec., 1923), 437ff.

9. *Churchman,* CXXI (Jan.–June, 1920), *passim;* CXXXIX (Jan. 19, 1929), 9; *Congregationalist,* CXIV (June 27, 1929), 860.

10. *Homiletic Review,* LXXXVII (Jan., 1924), 9.

11. *Congregationalist,* CXIV (June 27, 1929), 860.

12. *Homiletic Review,* LXXXVII (Feb., 1924), 125; *ibid.,* LXXXVI (Dec., 1923), 439.

13. Quoted in *Christian Advocate,* CIV (Feb. 21, 1929), 234.

14. *Ibid.,* CIV (July 4, 1929), 842.

15. *Homiletic Review,* LXXXVII (Jan., 1924), 12; *Christian Advocate,* XCV (July 8, 1920), 917; *Churchman,* CXXXIX (Jan. 19, 1929), 9.

16. Quoted in *Homiletic Review,* XCII (July, 1926), 11.

17. *Ibid.,* XCI (March, 1926), 207.

18. Quoted in *ibid.,* LXXXVII (May, 1924), 364.

19. Editorial, "Since Rauschenbusch—What?" *Christian Century,* XLIII (July 15, 1926), 887.

20. Quoted in the *Churchman,* CXL (July 15, 1929), 10f.

21. Gaius Glenn Atkins, quoted in the *Congregationalist,* CXIV (Oct. 24, 1929), 541.

22. The report summarized and reviewed in the *Homiletic Review,* LXXXVIII (Sept., 1924), 181ff. Questionnaire is in *ibid.,* LXXXVIII (Nov., 1924), 347.

23. *Ibid.,* LXXXIX (Jan., 1925), 5.

24. Report of the Special Commission of 1925, in General Assembly of the Presbyterian Church in the U.S.A., *Minutes* (Philadelphia, 1927).

25. Quoted in the *Churchman,* CXXXIX (Jan. 12, 1929), 25.

26. Quoted in the *Homiletic Review,* XCII (Oct., 1926), 277.

27. Henry Sloane Coffin, quoted in the *Churchman,* CXL (July 20, 1929), 25.

28. *Congregationalist,* CXIV (Feb. 14, 1929), 209.

29. E. C. Lindeman, "Is Preaching a Valid Method?" *Homiletic Review,* XCII (July, 1926), 29.

30. *Christian Advocate,* CIV (May 16, 1929), 615.

31. *Congregationalist,* CXIV (May 9, 1929), 637.

32. Halford E. Luccock, "Preaching in an Age of Disillusion," *Baptist,* X (March 2, 1929), 286f.

33. *Homiletic Review,* XCII (Nov., 1926), 359.

Chapter VII. The Impact of Secularism and War

1. Niebuhr, *op. cit.,* p. 1.

2. Quoted in the *Churchman,* CXXXIX (April 27, 1929), 23.

3. This happy incident is chronicled in H. L. Mencken, *Heathen Days* (New York: Knopf, 1947), pp. 225ff.

4. Schneider, *op. cit.,* p. 10.

5. Luccock, *Jesus and the American Mind,* p. 89.

6. Niebuhr, *op. cit.*, pp. 5f.

7. Committee on the War and the Religious Outlook, *Religion among American Men* (New York: Association Press, 1920), pp. vii, xv, 13, 22ff., 80.

8. Niebuhr, *op. cit.*, p. 189.

9. John A. Hutchison, *We Are Not Divided: A Critical and Historical Study of the Federal Council of the Churches of Christ in America* (New York: Round Table Press, 1941), p. 180.

10. Quoted in Yinger, *op. cit.*, p. 254, n. 10.

11. Hutchison, *op. cit.*, p. 178.

12. *Ibid.*, pp. 182, 184.

13. Reminiscence of clergy personally known to the author.

14. Niebuhr, *op. cit.*, p. 141.

15. Quoted in the *Churchman*, CXXXIX (Jan. 12, 1929), 25.

16. W. M. Horton, *Theism and the Modern Mood* (New York: Harper, 1930), pp. 7f. Used by permission.

17. *Churchman*, CXXII (Dec. 18, 1920), 9; *ibid.*, CXXXIX (Jan. 26, 1929), 10.

Chapter VIII. The Background of the Ecumenical Movement

1. Robert S. Bilheimer, *The Quest for Christian Unity* (New York: Association Press, 1952), p. 105.

2. For discussion of Reformation ecumenicalism, see John T. McNeill, *Unitive Protestantism* (New York: Abingdon, 1930).

3. Kenneth S. Latourette, *A History of the Expansion of Christianity*, VII (New York: Harper, 1945), 35.

4. *Ibid.*, p. 27.

5. See the recent history of the International Missionary Council by William Richey Hogg, *Ecumenical Foundations* (New York: Harper and Brothers, 1952). Hopkins, *op. cit.*, titles his chapter on the founding of the Federal Council "The Churches Federate for Social Action" and makes a convincing case for the thesis that in the minds of most of the founders social action was *the* purpose of the Council. But cf. below, Chapter IX.

Chapter IX. American Belief and the World Church

1. Henry Sloane Coffin, *The Practical Aims of a Liberal Evangelicalism* (New York, [1915]), p. 7.

2. Cf. W. A. Visser 't Hooft, *The Background of the Social Gospel in America* (Haarlem: H. D. Tjeenk Willink & Zoon, 1928); George Hammar, *Christian Realism in Contemporary American Theology* (Uppsala: A. B. Lundequistska Bokhandeln, 1940); W. M. Horton, *Contemporary Con-*

tinental Theology: An Interpretation for Anglo-Saxons (New York: Harper, 1938); "The German Church and the Social Gospel," *Christian Century,* XLII (Oct. 29, 1925), 1333f.

3. It will be noted that this conception of the Kingdom as *eschaton* resembles the premillennialist beliefs which had underlain the theology of Fundamentalism. Both were witnesses to the fact that an age of crisis was succeeding to an age of at least superficial national and personal security; and both were reactions against a naïvely optimistic ideology of progress which in the eyes of many had ceased to square with the observed facts of life. This is what I was pointing toward in discussing the "deeper appeal" of Fundamentalism in Chapter IV.

4. Walter Rauschenbusch, *Christianity and the Social Crisis* (New York: Macmillan, 1907), p. 7.

5. Visser 't Hooft, *op. cit.,* p. 173.

6. Edwin McNeill Poteat, quoted in *Christian Advocate,* CIV (March 28, 1929), 385.

7. Rauschenbusch, *A Theology for the Social Gospel,* pp. 48, 50.

8. Francis J. McConnell, *By the Way* (New York: Abingdon-Cokesbury, 1952), p. 189.

9. Karl Barth, *The Word of God and the Word of Man,* tr. by Douglas Horton (New York: Pilgrim Press, 1928), p. 18.

10. Hutchison, *op. cit.,* p. 35.

11. G. K. A. Bell, ed., *The Stockholm Conference, 1925* (London: Oxford, 1926), pp. 72, 641.

12. Hutchison, *op. cit.,* p. 242.

13. *Ibid.,* p. 42.

14. H. Richard Niebuhr, *The Social Sources of Denominationalism* (New York: Holt, 1929), p. 6.

15. *Ibid.,* pp. 25, 275, 266.

16. R. Niebuhr, *op. cit.,* p. 77.

Chapter X. Legacy: The Social Gospel in 1929

1. See discussion of all these men, as well as Reinhold Niebuhr, in J. Neal Hughley, *Trends in Protestant Social Idealism* (New York: King's Crown Press, 1948).

2. Visser 't Hooft, *op. cit.,* p. 30.

3. Don C. Seitz of the New York *World,* quoted in the *Churchman,* CXL (July 20, 1929), 15; *Congregationalist,* CXIV (Sept. 12, 1929), 337; *ibid.* (May 30, 1929), p. 729; *Baptist,* X (Aug. 24, 1929), 1047.

4. *Baptist,* X (Jan. 19, 1929), 67; *ibid.* (Nov. 16, 1929), p. 1394.

5. Villard, quoted in the *Churchman,* CXXXIX (March 2, 1929), 26.

6. The Presbyterian journal which I used in the 1920 sample, the *Conti-*

nent, had suspended by 1929. For consistency's sake I used the journal with which it merged. The other denominations are represented by the same papers as in the earlier sample.

7. *Christian Advocate,* CIV (May 23, 1929), 647.

8. Frank R. Shipman, "Some Labor Day Reflections," *Congregationalist,* CXIV (Sept. 12, 1929), 350.

9. *Christian Advocate,* CIV (Aug. 29, 1929), 1049.

10. H. R. Niebuhr, *op. cit.,* p. 253.

11. *Christian Advocate,* CIV (June 6, 1929), 711; *Presbyterian Advance,* XL (Sept. 5, 1929), 8; *Baptist,* X (Jan. 12, 1929), 42; *ibid.* (April 13, 1929), p. 474.

12. The quotation is an editorial in *ibid.* (May 4, 1929), p. 567.

13. *Presbyterian Advance,* XL (Nov. 28, 1929), 7.

14. *Baptist,* X (Nov. 16, 1929), 1402.

15. See, for example, the editorial "Quakers Face a New Day," *Congregationalist,* CXIV (Jan. 24, 1929), 100.

16. *Churchman,* CXXXIX (April 6, 1929), 7; *ibid.,* CXL (Aug. 3, 1929), 7.

17. Quoted (and denounced!) in the *Christian Advocate,* CIV (July 25, 1929), 915. *Wall Street Journal* editorial in question appeared on July 18; it was written apropos of the outbreak of hostilities between Russia and Japan along the Amur—the first large-scale violence since the signing of the Pact.

18. *Baptist,* X (July 20, 1929), 929; *ibid.* (Aug. 17, 1929), p. 1024.

19. *Ibid.* (Aug. 10, 1929), p. 999.

Chapter XI. Preparation: The Social Gospel in the Great Depression

1. Reminiscence of clergyman known to the author.

2. *Presbyterian Advance,* XLV (March 24, 1932), 4; *ibid.* (April 28, 1932), p. 4; *ibid.* (July 7, 1932), p. 3. On the international scene this journal's Social Gospel perspective was much better; it saw what Hitler meant to the world before any of the others did, and it followed every twist and turn of German politics in 1932 with fascinated horror.

3. General Assembly of the Presbyterian Church in the U.S.A., *Minutes,* 1932, pp. 124ff.

4. *Churchman,* CXLVI (July 9, 1932), 7; *ibid.,* CXLV (March 5, 1932), 9; *ibid.,* CXXXIX (April 27, 1929), 9; *ibid.,* CXLV (Jan. 9, 1932), 8.

5. *Baptist,* X (Nov. 9, 1929), 1367; *ibid.* (Dec. 28, 1929), p. 1591.

6. *Ibid.,* XIII (Jan. 30, 1932), 131 (a Christian with Marxist leanings would of course take umbrage at the use of the word "fair" in this connection).

7. *Congregationalist,* CXVII (Feb. 25, 1932), 253; *ibid.* (Sept. 15, 1932), p. 1191.

8. *Christian Advocate,* CVII (July 21, 1932), 769; *ibid.* (May 12, 1932),

p. 503; *ibid.* (June 2, 1932), p. 577. The reader should once again be cautioned that this study is not a quantitative study of the Social Gospel. The *Advocate's* reporter complained that this resolution contained "ideas to which only a small group of delegates had ever given a serious thought. Under the pressure of time no debate was possible." This particular criticism should be understood as applying in some measure to most legislative resolutions by denominations; it is the reason why I have refrained from attempting to use such resolutions statistically to establish formal "trends."

9. *Ibid.* (July 21, 1932), p. 771; H. C. Weber, ed., *Yearbook of American Churches, 1933* (New York: Round Table Press, 1933), p. 84.

10. *Christian Advocate,* CVII (Jan. 7, 1932), 9.

11. *Ibid.* (August 25, 1932), p. 885; *Congregationalist,* CXVII (July 21, 1932), 930; *ibid.* (June 30, 1932), p. 829; *ibid.* (July 21, 1932), p. 929.

12. *Baptist,* XIII (Feb. 13, 1932), 205; *ibid.* (April 25, 1932), p. 531.

13. *Christian Advocate,* CVII (May 19, 1932), 527.

14. Text of the new Social Creed in *Yearbook of the American Churches: 1937* (New York: Association Press, 1937), p. 319.

15. Text of this report (of the denomination's Social Service Commission) in the *Baptist,* XIII (Aug. 13, 1932), 842f.

16. Quoted in *Yearbook of the American Churches, 1933,* p. 33.

17. This intellectual debt to the depression is acknowledged in Reinhold Niebuhr, *Moral Man and Immoral Society* (New York: Scribner's, 1932), p. 189.

18. R. Niebuhr, *Does Civilization Need Religion?,* pp. 119, 209.

19. R. Niebuhr, *Moral Man and Immoral Society,* pp. xi, 63.

20. Barth, quoted in the *Baptist,* XIII (Feb. 13, 1932), 215.

21. It should not be necessary to say this, but the words "socialism" and "Marxism" are so emotionally loaded for Americans that it must be pointed out here that this viewpoint is transitional with Niebuhr. By 1939, in his famous Gifford Lectures on *The Nature and Destiny of Man,* he had definitely passed beyond and abandoned Marxism. The remainder of this chapter should be read with this fact in mind.

22. Text of this Manifesto in the *Churchman,* CXLV (Jan. 2, 1932), 22; *Baptist,* XIII (Jan. 2, 1932), 8.

23. R. Niebuhr, *Moral Man and Immoral Society,* pp. 49, xvi, xv, 163, 230, 22.

24. *Baptist,* XIII (Nov. 19, 1932), 1013; *ibid.* (March 12, 1932), p. 336.

25. *Congregationalist,* CXVII (Sept. 8, 1932), 1160; Stuart Chase, quoted in *ibid.* (Nov. 10, 1932), p. 1454.

26. R. Niebuhr, *Moral Man and Immoral Society,* pp. 192, 170.

27. *Christian Advocate,* CVII (Jan. 7, 1932), 13.

28. Quoted in the *Baptist,* XIII (March 5, 1932), 298.

29. *Congregationalist,* CXVII (Feb. 18, 1932), 203f.

30. *Moral Man and Immoral Society,* p. 222.

Chapter XII. Impact: The Hundred Days
and Afterward

1. *Christian Century*, XLIX (Oct. 5, 1932), 1192; *ibid.* (July 20, 1932), p. 903; *ibid.* (Oct. 17, 1932), p. 1229; *ibid.* (Nov. 9, 1932), pp. 1379ff.; *ibid.* (Nov. 23, 1932), p. 1430; *ibid.*, L (March 1, 1933), 277.

2. *Christian Advocate*, CVIII (March 16, 1933), 243.

3. *Christian Century*, L (May 17, 1933), 648; *Churchman*, CXLVII (June 1, 1933), 7.

4. Findings of President's [Hoover's] Research Committee on Social Trends, embodied in a paper read by C. Luther Fry before the Episcopal Social Work Conference, 1933, quoted in the *Churchman*, CXLVII (Sept. 1, 1933), 10f.

5. Personal communication to the author.

6. *Churchman*, CXLVII (Oct. 15, 1933), 8; *ibid.* (Aug. 15, 1933), p. 8.

7. Quoted in the *Christian Century*, L (June 7, 1933), 761.

8. *Christian Advocate*, CVIII (Aug. 3, 1933), 724.

9. *Churchman*, CXLVII (July 1, 1933), 15; *ibid.* (Nov. 1, 1933), p. 15.

10. Harry Ayres Relyea, "The Churches and the NRA," *Christian Advocate*, CVIII (Sept. 28, 1933), 923.

11. *Presbyterian Advance*, XLVII (Aug. 10, 1933), 4.

12. Walter Lippmann, "The Permanent New Deal," *Yale Review*, XXIV (June, 1935), 660.

13. Final report, National Recovery Review Board (unpublished), quoted in Eric Goldman, *Rendezvous with Destiny* (New York: Knopf, 1952), p. 347.

14. *World Tomorrow* article, quoted in the *Congregationalist*, CXVIII (Nov. 2, 1933), 1037.

15. Quoted in the *Christian Advocate*, CVIII (Dec. 7, 1933), 1165.

16. *Christian Century*, L (June 21, 1933), 807.

17. *Congregationalist*, CXVIII (Aug. 31, 1933), 875.

18. *Christian Advocate*, CVIII (Aug. 10, 1933), 747.

19. H. C. Weber, ed., *Yearbook of American Churches: 1935* (New York: Association Press, 1935), p. 31.

20. In this discussion I am heavily indebted to Cyrus R. Pangborn, "Free Churches and Social Change: The Council for Social Action" (unpublished dissertation; Union Theological Seminary, 1951).

21. *Advance*, CXXVI (May 10, 1934), 119f. The *Congregationalist* suspended publication early in 1934. For discussion of the physical decline of the denominational press, see below, Chapter XIII.

22. General Council, *Minutes*, pp. 90, 107f., quoted in Pangborn, *op. cit.*, pp. 48, 51.

23. Dwight J. Bradley in personal interview with Pangborn, quoted in Pangborn, *op. cit.*, p. 125.

24. Quoted in *ibid.*, p. 163.

25. *Ibid.*, p. 40.

26. Hutchison, *op. cit.*, p. 60.

Chapter XIII. The Ecumenical Movement in the 1930's

1. Henry S. Leiper, in Preface to J. H. Oldham, ed., *The Oxford Conference* (Official Report) (Chicago, New York: Willett, Clark, 1937), p. xiii.

2. Episcopal Address to the General Conference of the Methodist Church (South), 1938, quoted in P. Carter, "The Negro and Methodist Union," *Church History*, XXI (March, 1952), 59.

3. Address at the Methodist General Conference (North), 1936, quoted in *ibid.*, pp. 59f.

4. Douglas Horton, quoted in Pangborn, *op. cit.*, p. 199.

5. Oldham, *op. cit.*, p. 46.

6. Federal Council of Churches, *Annual Report*, 1940, p. 7.

7. Text in Oldham, *op. cit.*, pp. 259f.

8. Paraphrased from S. M. Cavert, in *ibid.*, p. 23.

9. *Ibid.*, pp. 45, 46.

10. Leonard Hodgson, ed., *The Second World Conference on Faith and Order* (New York: Macmillan, 1938), pp. 16f.

11. *Ibid.*, p. 48.

12. W. A. Visser 't Hooft, ed., *The First Assembly of the World Council of Churches* (New York: Harper, 1949), p. 9.

13. Reinhold Niebuhr, *Christianity and Power Politics* (New York: Scribner's, 1940), p. 218. The final chapter of this book contains the text of Niebuhr's Oxford address.

14. Edgar DeWitt Jones, President of the Federal Council, quoted in Henry S. Leiper, *World Chaos or World Christianity?* (Chicago, New York: Willett, Clark, 1937); Oldham, *op. cit.*, p. 108.

15. *Ibid.*, pp. 108f., 46.

16. *Baptist*, XIII (Feb. 13, 1932), 206.

17. *Christian Advocate*, CVII (May 19, 1932), 527.

18. Quoted in Carter, *op. cit.*, p. 56.

19. *Zion's Herald*, CXIV (March 4, 1936), 221, quoted in *ibid.*, p. 62. This independent Methodist paper opposed the Plan of Union on Social Gospel grounds. Its editor, Lewis Hartman, who died in the summer of 1955, was one of the great Methodist liberals of his day and well deserved a biographical study.

20. Quoted in Carter, *op. cit.*, p. 61.

21. Quoted in *ibid.*, p. 60. The essay cited contains fuller documentation of the opinions I have here expressed upon the Methodist merger.

Chapter XIV. The Social Gospel and the Coming of the War

1. Samuel Lubell, *The Future of American Politics* (New York: Harper, 1952), chap. i.

2. Hofstadter, *The American Political Tradition*, pp. 339f.

3. *Presbyterian Advance*, XLVII (June 1, 1933), 16; *Christian Century*, L (June 7, 1933), 761; *ibid.* (May 31, 1933), p. 709.

4. *Christian Advocate*, CVIII (Nov. 9, 1933), 1060.

5. *Ibid.* (Aug. 17, 1933), 770.

6. Quoted in the *Christian Century*, L (June 7, 1933), 761.

7. Pangborn, *op. cit.*, pp. 58f. Cf. Yinger, *op. cit.*, chap. vi for other examples of "no-war" pledges.

8. *Christian Century*, L (Jan. 4, 1933), 14.

9. *Christian Advocate*, CVII (Feb. 11, 1932), 140.

10. *Congregationalist*, CXVIII (March 30, 1933), 399.

11. Eyewitness account of the incident in Harold E. Fey, "The German Church Says No!" *Christian Century*, LIV (Sept. 1, 1937), 1067.

12. Editorial in the *Christian Century*, LIV (Jan. 27, 1937), 105f.

13. *Ibid.*, LIV (Oct. 20, 1937), 1285ff.

14. Federal Council of Churches, *Annual Report*, 1938, p. 177.

15. *Christian Century*, LVII (July 10, 1940), 871; *ibid.* (June 17, 1940), pp. 790f.

16. *Ibid.*, LVII (July 31, 1940), 942f.

17. *Ibid.*, LVII (Oct. 16, 1940), 1270, 1272.

18. Sermon in Rockefeller Chapel, University of Chicago, June 2, 1940; text in *ibid.*, LVII (July 3, 1940), 848ff.

19. *Ibid.*, LVII (Oct. 30, 1940), 1346f.

20. Reinhold Niebuhr, "Why I Leave the F.O.R.," *ibid.*, LI (Jan. 3, 1934), 19. Incidentally, the F.O.R.'s executive director, with whom Niebuhr sided as a Christian Marxist, was none other than J. B. Matthews.

21. Pangborn, *op. cit.*, pp. 61, 62.

22. The nominee's account of this decision by F.D.R. is in Clarence Pickett, *For More than Bread* (Boston: Little, Brown, 1953), pp. 166f.

23. *Christian Century*, LVI (Feb. 15, 1939), 207.

24. Letter in *ibid.*, LVII (May 29, 1940), 706.

25. *Ibid.* (July 24, 1940), p. 924; *ibid.* (Sept. 25, 1940), p. 1176; *ibid.* (July 17, 1940), p. 903.

26. Yinger, *op. cit.*, p. 205.

27. R. Niebuhr, *Christianity and Power Politics*, p. x.

28. Quoted in Bennett, *op. cit.*, p. 25.

29. *Christian Century*, LVII (May 29, 1940), 700; Elton Trueblood, "Vocational Christian Pacifism," *Christianity and Crisis* (Nov. 3, 1941), pp. 2ff.

30. Yinger, *op. cit.*, p. 216.

31. *Ibid.*, p. 209. "Figures differ" on the number of conscientious objectors who chose to serve as noncombatant medical corpsmen (Class 1A–O) in the army.

Chapter XV. The Social Gospel and the Christian Faith

1. U.S. Department of Commerce, Bureau of the Census, *Religious Bodies: 1936* (Washington: Government Printing Office, 1941), table 23, p. 315.

2. *Time* (April 14, 1941), pp. 68ff. (quoted in Hutchison, *op. cit.*, p. 285). Used by permission.

3. *Christian Century*, LIV (July 7, 1937), p. 860.

4. Yinger, *op. cit.*, p. 225.

5. Quoted in the *Congregationalist*, CXVIII (Nov. 23, 1933), 1088.

6. Bennett, *op. cit.*, p. 91.

7. Reinhold Niebuhr, *Reflections on the End of an Era* (New York: Scribner's, 1934), p. 170.

8. Reinhold Niebuhr, *The Nature and Destiny of Man* (New York: Scribner's, 1944), II, 286.

Bibliography

A. Bibliographies

The most fruitful bibliographical source was the denominational press. What Henry F. May discovered for earlier periods I found to be true for the 1920's and 30's, namely, that virtually every significant book bearing upon social religion was noted or reviewed in their pages at the time of publication.

After this, the most helpful bibliographies for my purpose were found in the studies by Virginius Dabney, George Hammar, J. Neal Hughley, John A. Hutchison, Henry F. May, Herbert W. Schneider, E. C. Vanderlaan, and J. Milton Yinger, all of which are enumerated below.

B. Official sources: denominational, ecumenical, and U.S. Government

Bell, G. K. A., ed. *The Stockholm Conference, 1925.* London: Oxford University Press, 1926.

Cherrington, E. H., ed. *Anti-Saloon League Yearbook.* Westerville, Ohio, 1920–1933.

Doctrines and Discipline of the Methodist Church. Nashville and elsewhere: Methodist Publishing House, 1940, 1944, 1948.

Federal Council of the Churches of Christ in America. *Annual Reports.* New York, 1920–1940.

General Assembly, Presbyterian Church in the U.S.A. *Minutes.* 1920–1940.

General Conference of the Methodist Episcopal Church. *Daily Christian Advocate.* 1920–1940.

General Convention of the Protestant Episcopal Church. *Minutes.* 1920–1940.

General (formerly National) Council of the Congregational and Christian Churches. *Minutes.* 1920–1940.

Hodgson, Leonard, ed. *The Second World Conference on Faith and Order, held at Edinburgh, August 3–18, 1937.* New York: The Macmillan Company, 1938.

Northern Baptist Convention. *Annual.* 1920–1940.

Oldham, J. H., ed. *The Oxford Conference: Official Report.* Chicago, New York: Willett, Clark & Co., 1937.

U.S. Department of Commerce, Bureau of the Census. *Religious Bodies: 1926.* Washington: Government Printing Office, 1929.

——. *Religious Bodies: 1936.* Washington: Government Printing Office, 1941.

Visser 't Hooft, W. A., ed. *The First Assembly of the World Council of Churches, held at Amsterdam, August 22nd to September 4th, 1948.* New York: Harper & Brothers, 1949.

Weber, H. C., and others, eds. *Yearbook of American Churches.* New York, 1920–1949.

C. Denominational press, 1920–1940

Weekly publication unless otherwise indicated.

The Baptist. Merged with *The Christian Century,* 1932.

The Christian Advocate. Methodist.

The Christian Century. Nondenominational.

Christianity and Crisis. Founded 1941.

The Churchman. Episcopalian.

The Congregationalist. Suspended publication 1934.

The Continent. Presbyterian. Merged with *Presbyterian Advance,* 1924.

Crusader's Champion. Fundamentalist, 1920's.

Homiletic Review. Monthly. Written and edited for clergy.

The Presbyterian. Read for 1920 only.

Presbyterian Advance. Suspended publication 1934.

Religious Searchlight, later *The Fundamentalist,* later *The Faith.*
Personal journal of Fundamentalist leader John R. Straton. Publication irregular, 1920's.

The Watchman-Examiner. Baptist.

D. Books and articles bearing on the Social Gospel

Barth, Karl. *The Word of God and the Word of Man.* Translated by Douglas Horton. New York: Pilgrim Press, 1928.

Barton, Bruce. *The Man Nobody Knows: A Discovery of the Real Jesus.* Indianapolis: Bobbs-Merrill Company, 1925.

Bennett, John C. *Christian Ethics and Social Policy.* New York: Charles Scribner's Sons, 1946.

——. *Social Salvation: A Religious Approach to the Problems of Social Change.* New York: Charles Scribner's Sons, 1935.

Bilheimer, Robert S. *The Quest for Christian Unity.* New York: Association Press, 1952.

Cannon, James. "Al Smith: Catholic, Tammany, Wet," *The Nation,* CXXVII (July 4, 1928), 9.

Chaffee, Edmund B. *The Protestant Churches and the Industrial Crisis.* New York: The Macmillan Company, 1933.

Coffin, Henry Sloane. *The Practical Aims of a Liberal Evangelicalism.* New York, [1915]. A pamphlet.

Darrow, Clarence, and Yarros, Victor. *The Prohibition Mania.* New York: Boni & Liveright, 1927.

Dixon, A. C., *et al. The Fundamentals.* Chicago, Los Angeles: [priv. printed], 1909.

Ferm, Vergilius, ed. *The American Church of the Protestant Heritage.* New York: Philosophical Library, 1953.

Fisher, Irving. *Prohibition at Its Worst.* New York: The Macmillan Company, 1926.

——, and Brougham, H. Bruce. *Prohibition Still at Its Worst.* New York: Alcohol Information Committee, 1928.

Fleming, Daniel J. *Ethical Issues Confronting World Christians.* New York: International Missionary Council, 1935.

Gladden, Washington. *Recollections.* Boston: Houghton Mifflin Company, 1909.

Hammar, George. *Christian Realism in Contemporary American Theology.* Uppsala: A. B. Lundequistska Bokhandeln, 1940.

Harnack, Adolf. *What Is Christianity?* New York: G. P. Putnam, 1912.

Horton, Walter Marshall. *Contemporary Continental Theology: An Interpretation for Anglo-Saxons.* New York: Harper & Brothers, 1938.

——. *Theism and the Modern Mood.* New York: Harper & Brothers, 1930.

Hughes, Edwin Holt. "Our Mistaken Legislation on Amusements," *Methodist Review* (bimonthly), CVI (Fifth Series, Vol. XXXIX), 1923, 719ff.

James, William. *The Varieties of Religious Experience.* New York [etc.]: Longmans, Green & Company, 1902.

Johnson, F. Ernest. *Economics and the Good Life.* New York: Association Press, 1934.

——. *The Social Gospel Re-examined.* New York: Harper & Brothers, 1940.

Landis, Benson Y. *The Third American Revolution.* New York: Association Press, 1933.

Leiper, Henry S. *World Chaos or World Christianity?: A Popular Interpretation of Oxford and Edinburgh, 1937.* Chicago, New York: Willett, Clark & Company, 1937.

Lewis, Sinclair. *Elmer Gantry.* New York: Harcourt, Brace & Company, 1927.

Loud, Grover C. *Evangelized America.* New York: Dial Press, 1928.

Luccock, Halford E. *Jesus and the American Mind.* New York: Abingdon Press, 1930.

McConnell, Francis J. *By the Way.* New York: Abingdon-Cokesbury Press, 1952.

Machen, J. Gresham. *Christianity and Liberalism.* New York: The Macmillan Company, 1923.

Mencken, H. L. *Heathen Days.* New York: Alfred A. Knopf, Inc., 1947.

Niebuhr, H. Richard. "The Attack Upon the Social Gospel," *Religion in Life,* V (Spring, 1936), 176ff.

——. *Christ and Culture.* New York: Charles Scribner's Sons, 1951.

——. *The Social Sources of Denominationalism.* New York: Henry Holt & Company, 1929.

Niebuhr, Reinhold. *Christianity and Power Politics.* New York: Charles Scribner's Sons, 1940.

——. *Does Civilization Need Religion? A Study in the Social Resources and Limitations of Religion in Modern Life.* New York: The Macmillan Company, 1927.

——. *Moral Man and Immoral Society.* New York: Charles Scribner's Sons, 1932.

——. *The Nature and Destiny of Man.* New York: Charles Scribner's Sons, 1944.

——. *Reflections on the End of an Era.* New York: Charles Scribner's Sons, 1934.

Pickett, Clarence. *For More Than Bread: An Autobiographical Account of Twenty-Two Years' Work with the American Friends Service Committee.* Boston: Little, Brown & Company, 1953.

Rall, Harris F. *Modern Millennialism and the Christian Hope.* New York: Abingdon Press, 1920.

Rauschenbusch, Walter. *Christianity and the Social Crisis.* New York: The Macmillan Company, 1907.

——. *Christianizing the Social Order.* New York: The Macmillan Company, 1909.

——. *A Theology for the Social Gospel.* New York: The Macmillan Company, 1917.

Ross, Edward A. *Sin and Society.* Boston: Houghton Mifflin Company, 1907.

Ryan, John A., and Husslein, Joseph. *The Church and Labor.* New York: The Macmillan Company, 1920.

Roy, Ralph L. "A Ministry of Schism," *Pastor,* Oct., 1952.

Schweitzer, Albert. *The Quest of the Historical Jesus.* Translated by W. Montgomery. New York: The Macmillan Company, 1948.

Stamm, Frederick J. *If This Be Religion—.* New York: John Day, 1950.

Stelzle, Charles. *Why Prohibition!* New York: George H. Doran, 1918.

Swift, Arthur L. *New Frontiers of Religion.* New York: The Macmillan Company, 1938.

Visser 't Hooft, W. A. *The Background of the Social Gospel in America.* Haarlem: H. D. Tjeenk Willink & Zoon, 1928.

Ward, Harry F. *In Place of Profit: Social Incentives in the Soviet Union.* New York: Charles Scribner's Sons, 1933.

Willebrandt, M. W. *The Inside of Prohibition.* New York: The Bobbs-Merrill Company, 1929.

E. Monographs and studies

Abell, A. I. *The Urban Impact on American Protestantism.* ("Harvard Historical Studies," LIV.) Cambridge, Mass.: Harvard University Press, 1943.

Abrams, Ray H. *Preachers Present Arms.* New York: Round Table Press, 1933.

Allinsmith, Wesley and Beverly. "Religious Affiliation and Politico-Economic Attitude," *Public Opinion Quarterly,* XII (Fall, 1948), 385ff.

Barnes, Gilbert H. *The Anti-Slavery Impulse, 1830–1844.* New York: Appleton-Century Company, 1933.

Brewster, Edward. "Patterns of Social Concern in Four Protestant Denominations." Unpublished doctoral dissertation, Boston University, 1952.

Cantril, Hadley. "Educational and Economic Composition of Religious Groups: An Analysis of Poll Data," *American Journal of Sociology,* XLVIII (March, 1943), 574–579.

Carter, Paul A. "The Negro and Methodist Union," *Church History,* XXI (March, 1952), 59–71.

Clark, Elmer T. *The Small Sects in America.* Rev. ed. New York: Abingdon-Cokesbury Press, 1949.

Cole, S. C. *The History of Fundamentalism.* New York: R. R. Smith, 1931.

Colvin, D. Leigh. *Prohibition in the United States.* New York: George H. Doran, 1926.

Commager, Henry Steele. *Theodore Parker: Yankee Crusader.* Boston: Beacon Press, 1947.

Commission of Inquiry, The Interchurch World Movement. *Report on the Steel Strike of 1919.* New York: Harcourt, Brace, and Howe, 1920.

Committee on the War and the Religious Outlook. *Religion Among American Men as Revealed by a Study of Conditions in the Army.* New York: Association Press, 1920.

Cross, Whitney R. *The Burned-Over District: The Social and Intellectual History of Enthusiastic Religion in Western New York, 1800–1850.* Ithaca, N.Y.: Cornell University Press, 1950.

Dabney, Virginius. *Dry Messiah: The Life of Bishop Cannon.* New York: Alfred A. Knopf, 1948.

Davis, Jerome. "A Study of Protestant Church Boards of Control,"

BIBLIOGRAPHY

American Journal of Sociology, XXXVIII (Nov., 1932), 418–431.

Douglass, H. Paul. *Church Unity Movements in the United States.* New York: Institute for Social and Religious Research, 1934.

——. *A Decade of Objective Progress in Church Unity, 1927–1936.* New York: Harper & Brothers, 1937.

——. *The Springfield Church Survey: A Study of Organized Religion with Its Social Background.* New York: George H. Doran, n.d. [*ca.* 1926].

Garrison, Winfred E. *The March of Faith: The Story of Religion in America Since 1865.* New York: Harper & Brothers, 1933.

Handy, Robert T. "Christianity and Socialism in America, 1900–1920," *Church History*, XXI (March, 1952), 39ff.

——. "The Protestant Quest for a Christian America," *Church History*, XXII (March, 1953), 8ff.

Hogg, William Richey. *Ecumenical Foundations: A History of the International Missionary Council and Its Nineteenth-Century Background.* New York: Harper & Brothers, 1952.

Hopkins, Charles H. *The Rise of the Social Gospel in American Protestantism, 1865–1915.* ("Yale Studies in Religious Education," XIV.) New Haven: Yale University Press, 1940.

Hughley, J. Neal. *Trends in Protestant Social Idealism.* New York: King's Crown Press, 1948.

Hutchison, John A. *We Are Not Divided: A Critical and Historical Study of the Federal Council of the Churches of Christ in America.* New York: Round Table Press, 1941.

Krout, John A. *The Origins of Prohibition.* New York: Alfred A. Knopf, 1925.

Latourette, Kenneth Scott. *A History of the Expansion of Christianity.* Vol. VII: "Advance through Storm." New York: Harper & Brothers, 1945.

McNeill, John T. *Unitive Protestantism: A Study in Our Religious Resources.* New York: Abingdon Press, 1930.

May, Henry F. *Protestant Churches and Industrial America.* New York: Harper & Brothers, 1949.

Miller, Orlando. "The Social Gospel, 1920–1940." Unpublished master's essay, Columbia University, 1948.

Odegard, Peter. *Pressure Politics: The Story of the Anti-Saloon League.* New York: Columbia University Press, 1928.

Pangborn, Cyrus R. "Free Churches and Social Change: A Critical Study of the Council for Social Action of the Congregational

Christian Churches of the United States." Unpublished doctoral dissertation, Joint Committee on Graduate Instruction, Columbia University and Union Theological Seminary, 1951.

Pope, Liston. *Millhands and Preachers: A Study of Gastonia.* New Haven: Yale University Press, 1942.

——. "Religion and the Class Structure," American Academy of Political and Social Science, *Annals,* CCLVI (March, 1948), 84–91.

Roy, Ralph L. *Apostles of Discord.* Boston: Beacon Press, 1953.

——. "The Protestant Underworld." Unpublished master's essay, Columbia University, 1952.

Schlesinger, A. M. "A Critical Period in American Religion, 1875–1900," Massachusetts Historical Society, *Proceedings,* LXIV (1932), 523–547.

Schneider, Herbert W. *Religion in Twentieth-Century America.* Cambridge, Mass.: Harvard University Press, 1952.

Sweet, William Warren. *The Methodist Episcopal Church and the Civil War.* Cincinnati: Methodist Book Concern, n.d.

——. *Religion in Colonial America.* New York: Charles Scribner's Sons, 1949.

——. *Religion in the Development of American Culture.* New York: Charles Scribner's Sons, 1952.

Tawney, R. H. *Religion and the Rise of Capitalism.* New York: Harcourt, Brace & Company, 1926.

Trott, Norman L., and Sanderson, Ross W. *What Church People Think About Social and Economic Issues.* New York: Association Press, 1938.

Vanderlaan, E. C. *Fundamentalism vs. Modernism.* New York: H. W. Wilson Company, 1925.

Weber, Max. *The Protestant Ethic and the Spirit of Capitalism.* Translated by Talcott Parsons. New York: Charles Scribner's Sons [1930].

Yinger, J. Milton. *Religion in the Struggle for Power.* Durham, N.C.: Duke University Press, 1946.

F. Other sources

Allen, Frederick Lewis. *The Big Change.* New York: Harper & Brothers, 1952.

Freidel, Frank. *Franklin D. Roosevelt: The Apprenticeship.* Boston: Little, Brown & Company, 1953.

——. *Franklin D. Roosevelt: The Ordeal*. Boston: Little, Brown & Company, 1954.

Gabriel, Ralph. *The Course of American Democratic Thought: An Intellectual History since 1815*. New York: The Ronald Press Company, 1940.

Goldman, Eric. *Rendezvous with Destiny: A History of Modern American Reform*. New York: Alfred A. Knopf, 1952.

Hansen, Marcus Lee. *The Immigrant in American History*. Cambridge, Mass.: Harvard University Press, 1940.

Hibben, Paxton. *The Peerless Leader: William Jennings Bryan*. New York: Farrar & Rinehart, 1929.

Hofstadter, Richard. *The American Political Tradition*. New York: Alfred A. Knopf, 1948.

——. *Social Darwinism in American Thought 1860–1915*. Philadelphia: University of Pennsylvania Press, 1944.

"How Labor Helped Win Repeal," *The Catering Industry Employee* (official journal of Hotel and Restaurant Employees' and Bartenders' International Union, A. F. of L.), LXII (Nov., 1953), 26ff.

Hunt, Gaillard, ed. *The Writings of James Madison*. New York: G. P. Putnam, 1908.

Johnson, Walter, ed. *Selected Letters of William Allen White, 1899–1943*. New York: Henry Holt & Company, 1947.

Josephson, Matthew. *Sidney Hillman: Statesman of American Labor*. New York: Doubleday & Company, Inc., 1952.

Lippmann, Walter. "The Permanent New Deal," *Yale Review*, XXIV (June, 1935), 649–667.

Lubell, Samuel. *The Future of American Politics*. New York: Harper & Brothers, 1952.

Lynd, Robert S. and Helen M. *Middletown: A Study in Contemporary American Culture*. New York: Harcourt, Brace & Company, [1929].

Neumann, Sigmund. *The Future in Perspective*. New York: G. P. Putnam's Sons, 1946.

Perkins, Frances. *The Roosevelt I Knew*. New York: Viking Press, 1946.

Rauch, Basil. *History of the New Deal, 1933–1938*. New York: Creative Age Press, Inc., 1944.

Riesman, David, and associates. *The Lonely Crowd*. New Haven: Yale University Press, 1951.

Slosson, Preston E. *The Great Crusade and After, 1914–1928*. ("History of American Life," XII.) New York: The Macmillan Company, 1930.

U.S. Department of Commerce, Bureau of the Census. *Historical Statistics of the United States, 1789–1943*. Washington: Government Printing Office, 1949.

Wecter, Dixon. *The Age of the Great Depression, 1929–1941*. ("History of American Life," XIII.) New York: The Macmillan Company, 1948.

White, William Allen. *Autobiography*. New York: The Macmillan Company, 1946.

Index

INDEX

Roosevelt, Franklin D. (*cont.*)
176f.; foreign policy, 164, 173, 201f., 203, 213f., 215, 228; "good neighbor" policy, 202, 203; inaugural, 3, 165; "quarantine" speech, 208f.; Supreme Court and, 172, 201, 222; third term, 211-213; *see also* New Deal

Roosevelt, Theodore, *see* Progressive movement

Rural *versus* urban folkways, 35-37, 41, 55, 73, 79, 88f., 236n.

Russia, 17, 26, 91, 138, 185, 202; recognition of, 203; social-gospelers' opinion of, 157-159; *see also* Iron Curtain, Marxism, Red Scare, Stalin

Russian Orthodox Church, 83; *see also* Eastern Orthodox churches

St. John, John P., 34, 35

Schneider, Herbert, 57, 88f.

Science, 46, 80, 87f.; *see also* Secularism

Second World War, 136, 193, 201, 207, 209, 214-219, 221, 222

Sectarianism, 102f., 118, 119f.

Secularism, 44, 54ff., 68f., 81f., 85-90, 93-95, 107, 185f., 190, 191, 221-224, 225, 226

Seminaries, *see* Theological seminaries

Seventh-Day Adventists, 47, 104

Sinclair, Upton, 34

Smith, Alfred E., 38-41, 147

Smith, Gerald L. K., 54

Smith, Gerrit, 32, 34

Smoot-Hawley Tariff, 132

Social Creed of the Churches (1912), 15, 34; 1928 revision of, 150, 224

Social Gospel: defined, 4f.; origins, 3, 5-8, 10f.; *see under related topics*

"Social" *versus* "individual" gospel, 55f., 59-63, 68f., 120, 210

Socialism, Christian, 13, 15, 53, 155f., 164, 204, 209; *see also* Marxism

Socialist Party (U.S.), 26, 127, 156

Society of Friends, *see* Quakers

Söderblom, Nathan, 106

Spain, civil war in, 188, 207f.

Stalin, Joseph, 138, 215

Steel strike: of 1919, 21f., 223f.; of 1937, 223f.

"Stimson Doctrine," 160, 164

Stock market crash, *see* Depression

Stockholm Conference on Life and Work (1925), 115, 117, 118, 188

Strong, Josiah, 104

Student Volunteer Movement, 23

"Summit conference" (1955), 137, 225

Temple, William F., 191

Tennessee Valley Authority, 164, 211

Theological seminaries, 52, 78f.

Theology: European objections to the Social Gospel, 61, 109-114, 139, 153, 221; Fundamentalist equivalent, 56, 243n.; *see also* Barth, Ecumenical movement, Neo-orthodoxy, Niebuhr, Visser 't Hooft

Thomas, Norman, 164

Tittle, Ernest F., 216

Toynbee, Arnold J., 10, 87, 93

Troeltsch, Ernst, 240n.

Trueblood, Elton, 216f.

Unitarians, 12, 100, 116

United Nations, 218f.

Van Dusen, Henry P., 153, 214

Visser 't Hooft, W. A., 126, 127

Volstead Act, *see* Prohibition

Wagner Act, 202

Wallace, Henry A., 168, 224; *see also* Agricultural Adjustment Act

Ward, Harry F., 126

Weber, Max, 64, 233n.

Weld, Theodore, 8

Wheeler, Wayne, 37, 44

White, William Allen, 39, 54

Willard, Frances E., 34, 35

Willkie, Wendell L., 168, 211, 212, 213

Wilson, Woodrow, 18, 23, 24, 35, 91

Winrod, Gerald B., 54

Woman's Christian Temperance Union, 34, 39

World Alliance for International Friendship Through the Churches, 106, 107

World Christian Fundamentals Association, 51

World Council of Churches, 108, 188, 192-194, 225f.; founding of (Amsterdam, 1948), 193

Young Men's Christian Association, 100, 105, 161

"Younger" churches, 105, 189